MW01070376

IDW Publishing
Robbie Robbins, Preside
Chris Ryall, Publisher/Editor-in-Ch
Ted Adams, Vice Preside
Kris Oprisko, Vice Preside
Neil Uyetake, Art Direc
Dan Taylor, Edi
Aaron Myers, Distribution Manag
Tom B. Long, Design
Chance Boren, Editorial Assista
Matthew Ruzicka, CPA, Control
Alex Garner, Creative Direc
Yumiko Miyano, Business Developme
Rick Privman, Business Developme

ISBN: 1-933239-84-0
5 4 3 2 1   06 07 08 09
www.idwpublishing.com

SHADOWPLAY TPB. March 2006. FIRST PRINTING. IDW Publishing, a division of Idea and Design Works, LLC. Editorial offices: 4411 Morena
Blvd., Suite 106, San Diego, CA 92117. Demon Father John's Pinwheel Blues © 2006 Amber Benson, Ben Templesmith, and Idea and Design
Works, LLC. Shunt © 2005 Christina Z, Ashley Wood and Idea and Design Works, LLC.The IDW logo is registered in the U.S. Patent and
Trademark Office. All Rights Reserved. Any similarities to persons living or dead are purely coincidental. With the exception of artwork used for review
purposes, none of the contents of this publication may be reprinted without the permission of Idea and Design Works, LLC. Printed in Korea.

SHADOWPLAY™

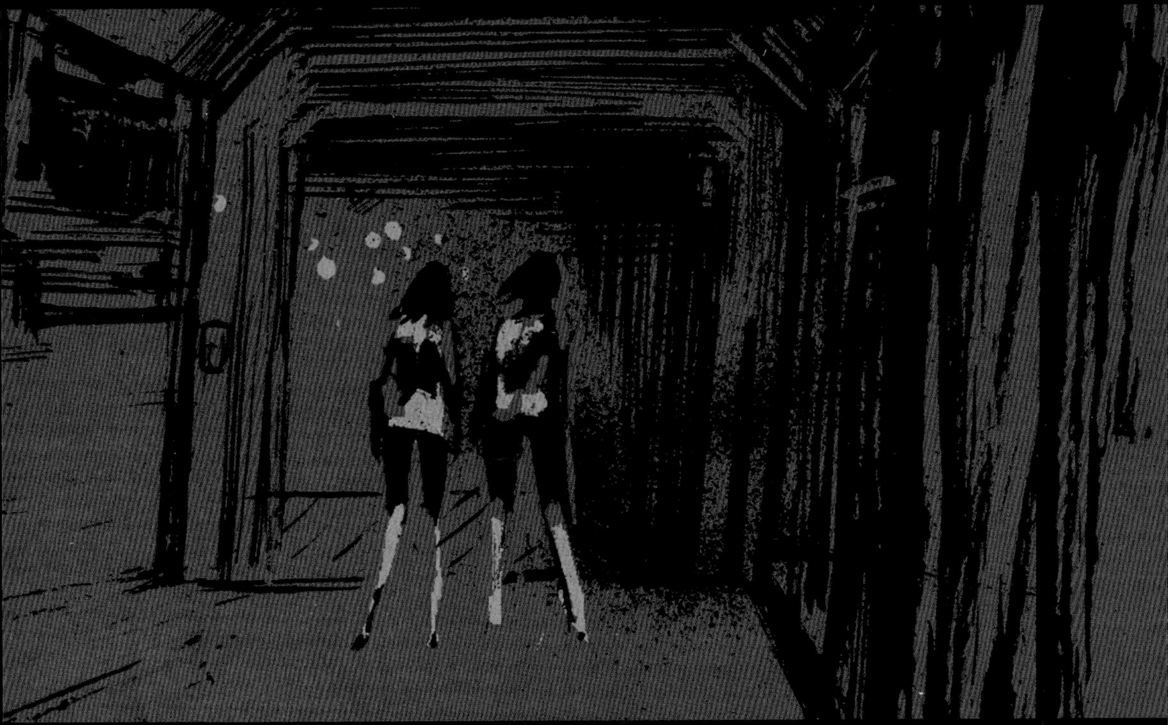

Shunt

story: Christina Z

art: Ashley Wood

letters: Tom B. Long

editor: Chris Ryall

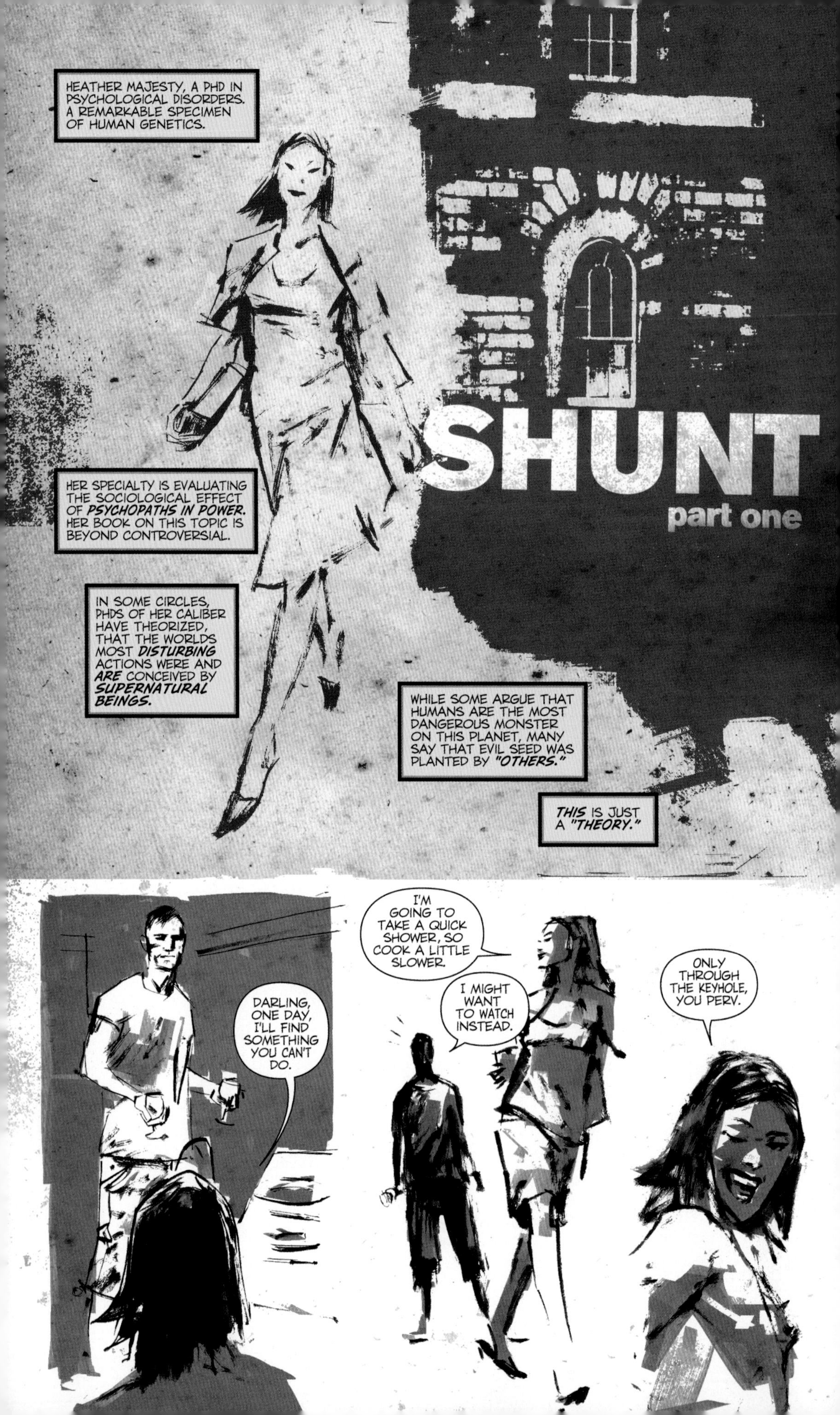
HEATHER MAJESTY, A PHD IN PSYCHOLOGICAL DISORDERS. A REMARKABLE SPECIMEN OF HUMAN GENETICS.
SHUNT
part one
HER SPECIALTY IS EVALUATING THE SOCIOLOGICAL EFFECT OF PSYCHOPATHS IN POWER. HER BOOK ON THIS TOPIC IS BEYOND CONTROVERSIAL.
IN SOME CIRCLES, PHDS OF HER CALIBER HAVE THEORIZED, THAT THE WORLDS MOST DISTURBING ACTIONS WERE AND ARE CONCEIVED BY SUPERNATURAL BEINGS.
WHILE SOME ARGUE THAT HUMANS ARE THE MOST DANGEROUS MONSTER ON THIS PLANET, MANY SAY THAT EVIL SEED WAS PLANTED BY "OTHERS."
THIS IS JUST A "THEORY."
DARLING, ONE DAY, I'LL FIND SOMETHING YOU CAN'T DO.
I'M GOING TO TAKE A QUICK SHOWER, SO COOK A LITTLE SLOWER.
I MIGHT WANT TO WATCH INSTEAD.
ONLY THROUGH THE KEYHOLE, YOU PERV.

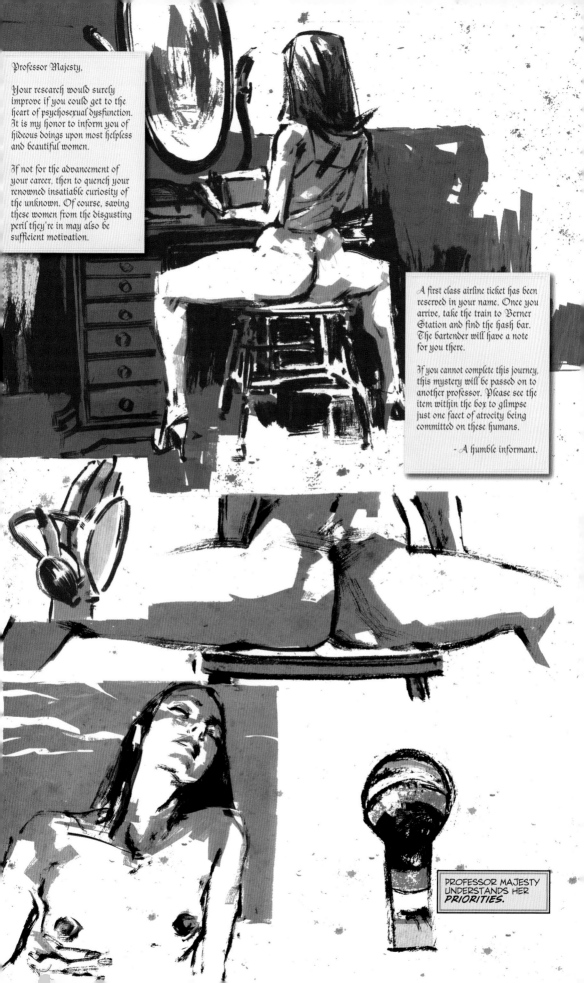

Professor Majesty,

Your research would surely improve if you could get to the heart of psychosexual dysfunction. It is my honor to inform you of hideous doings upon most helpless and beautiful women.

If not for the advancement of your career, then to quench your renowned insatiable curiosity of the unknown. Of course, saving these women from the disgusting peril they're in may also be sufficient motivation.

A first class airline ticket has been reserved in your name. Once you arrive, take the train to Berner Station and find the hash bar. The bartender will have a note for you there.

If you cannot complete this journey, this mystery will be passed on to another professor. Please see the item within the box to glimpse just one facet of atrocity being committed on these humans.

— A humble informant.

PROFESSOR MAJESTY UNDERSTANDS HER *PRIORITIES.*

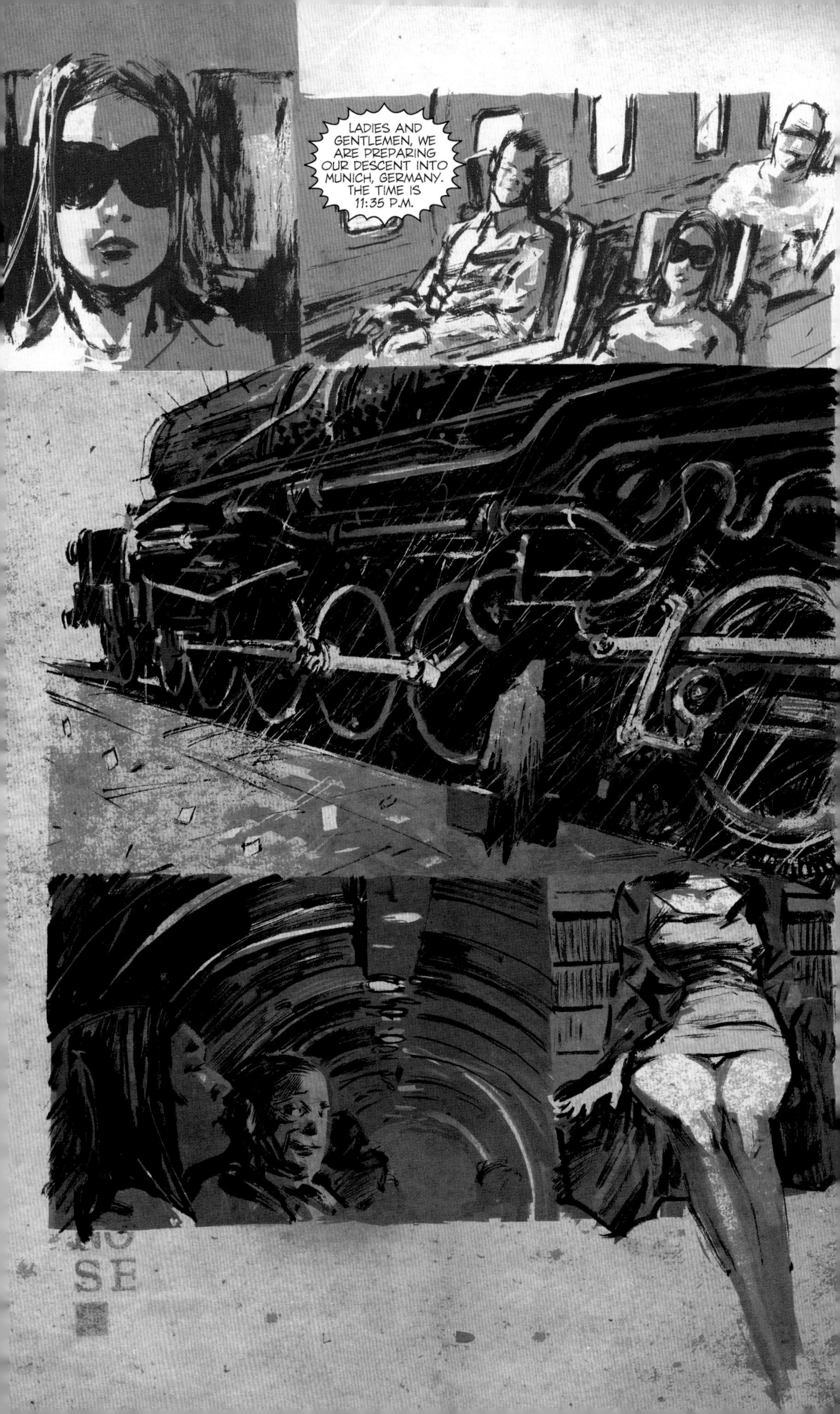
LADIES AND GENTLEMEN, WE ARE PREPARING OUR DESCENT INTO MUNICH, GERMANY. THE TIME IS 11:35 P.M.

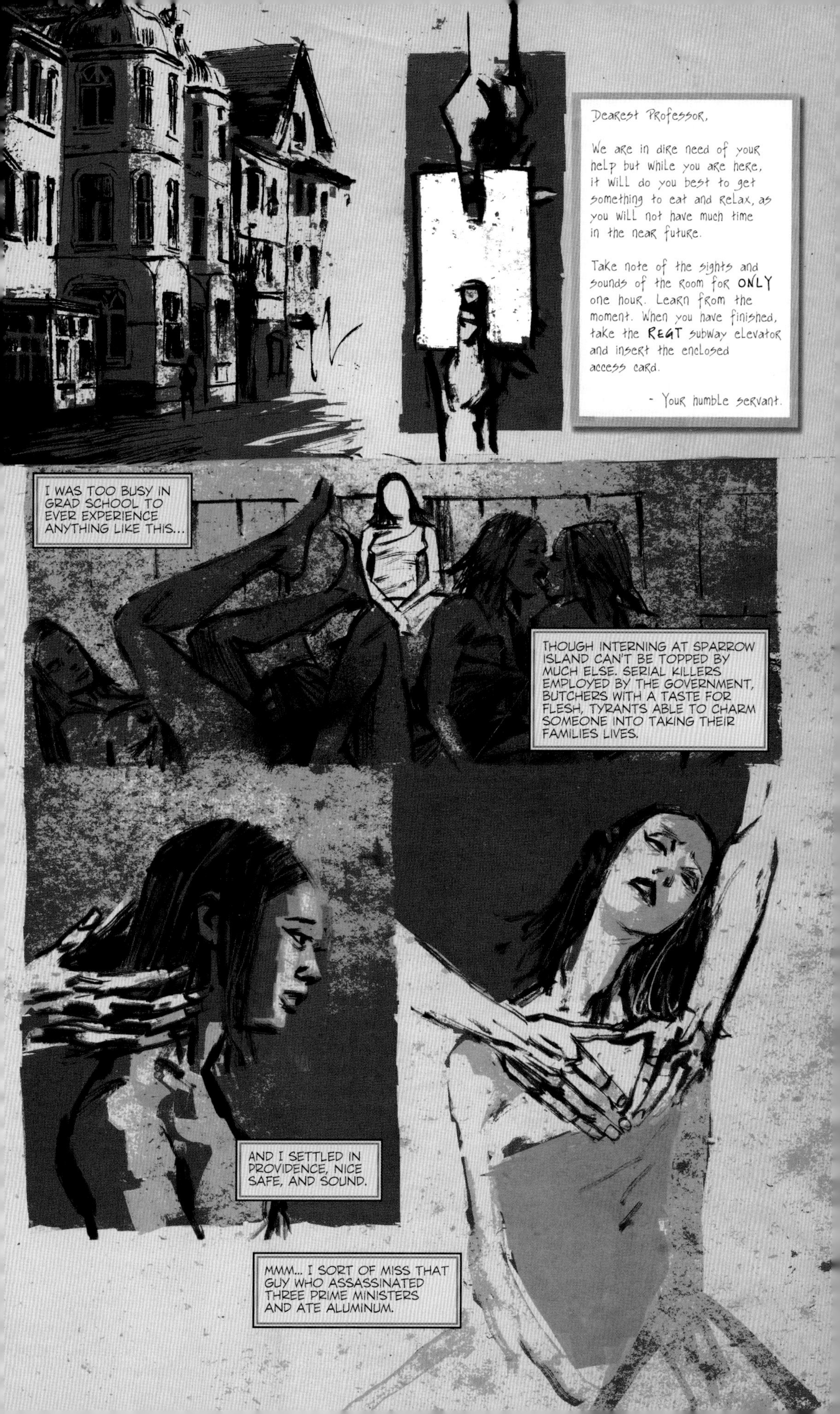
Dearest Professor,
We are in dire need of your help but while you are here, it will do you best to get something to eat and relax, as you will not have much time in the near future.
Take note of the sights and sounds of the room for ONLY one hour. Learn from the moment. When you have finished, take the REGT subway elevator and insert the enclosed access card.
- Your humble servant.
I WAS TOO BUSY IN GRAD SCHOOL TO EVER EXPERIENCE ANYTHING LIKE THIS...
THOUGH INTERNING AT SPARROW ISLAND CAN'T BE TOPPED BY MUCH ELSE. SERIAL KILLERS EMPLOYED BY THE GOVERNMENT, BUTCHERS WITH A TASTE FOR FLESH, TYRANTS ABLE TO CHARM SOMEONE INTO TAKING THEIR FAMILIES LIVES.
AND I SETTLED IN PROVIDENCE, NICE SAFE, AND SOUND.
MMM... I SORT OF MISS THAT GUY WHO ASSASSINATED THREE PRIME MINISTERS AND ATE ALUMINUM.

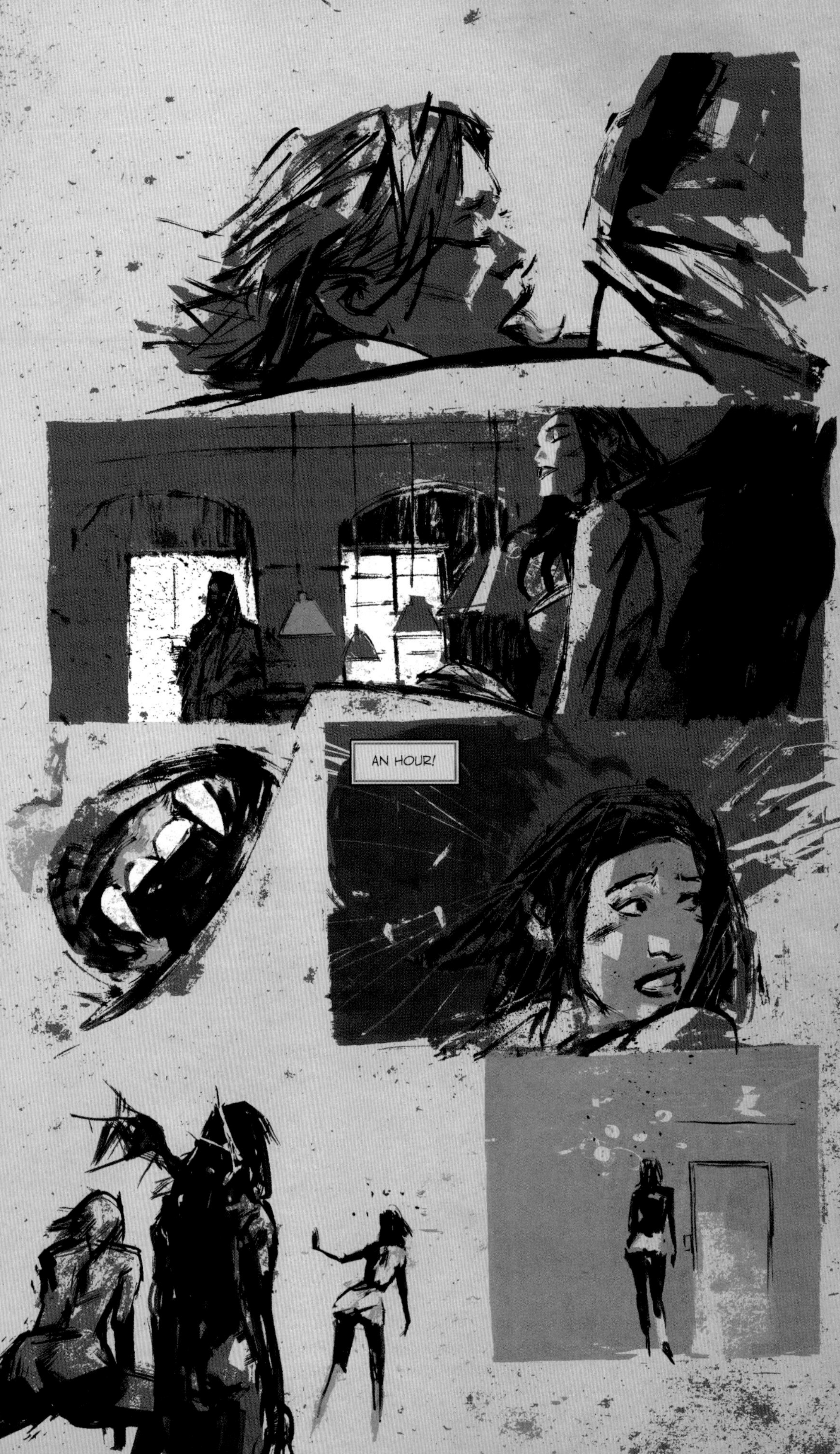
AN HOUR!

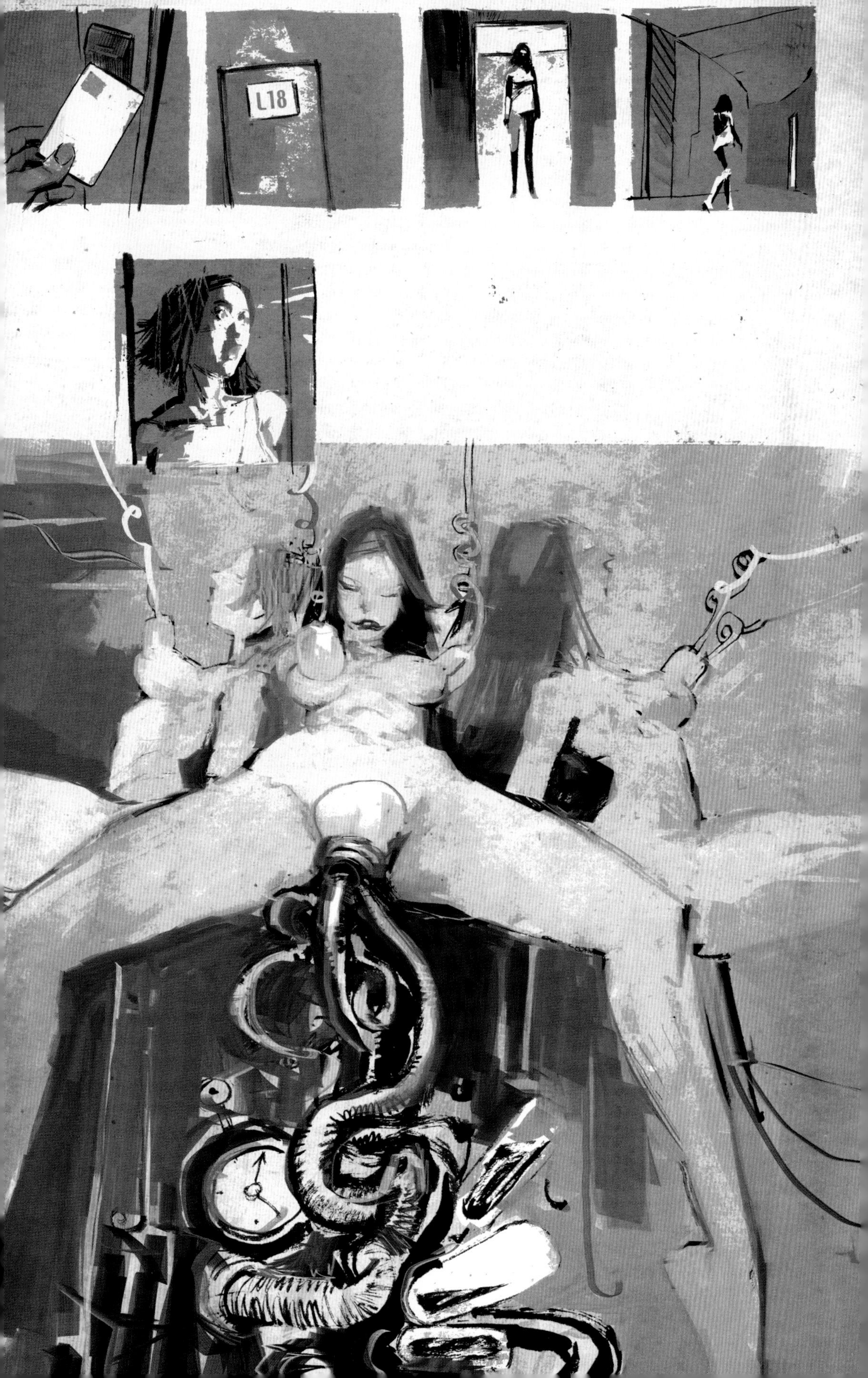
L18

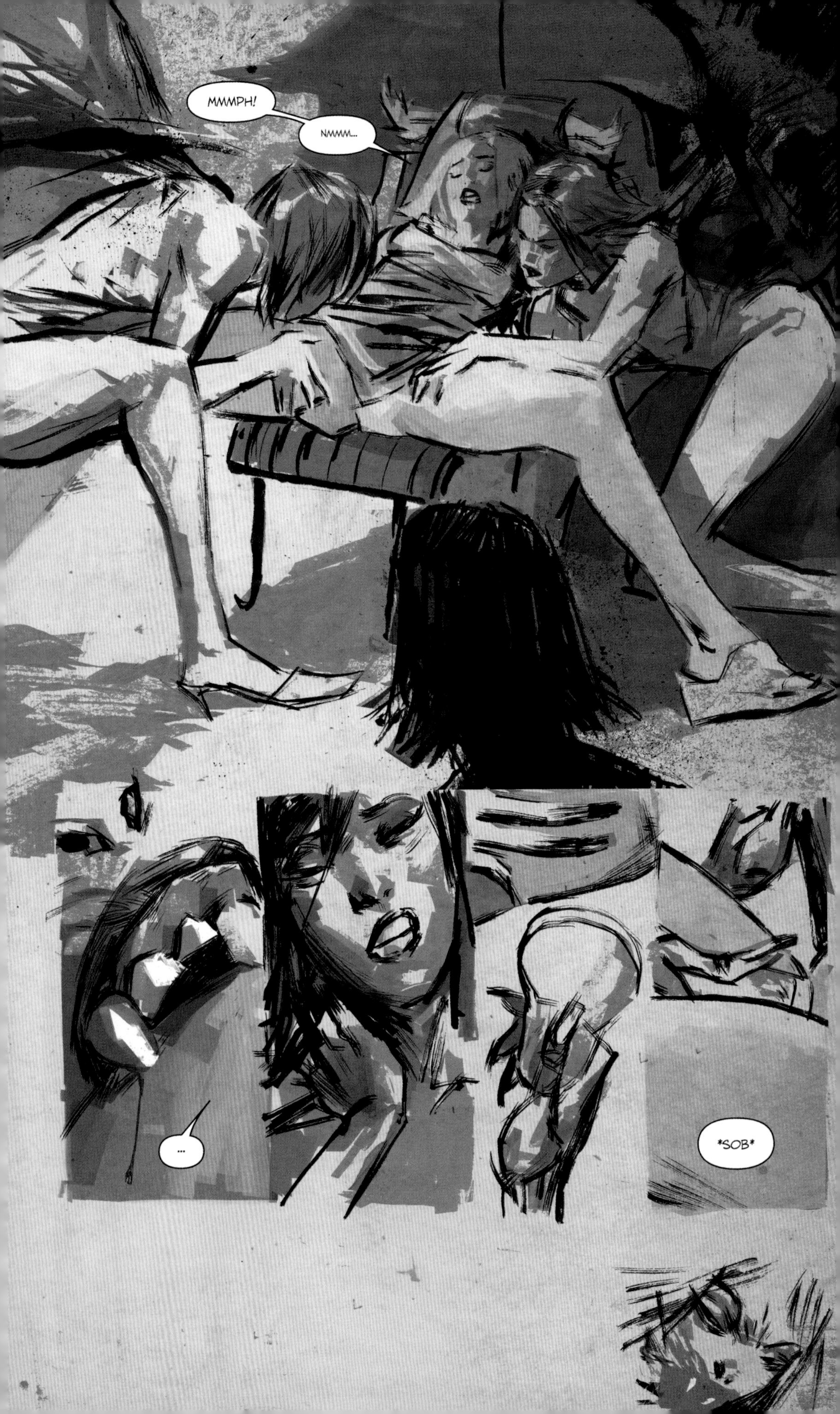
MMMPH!
NMMM...
...
SOB

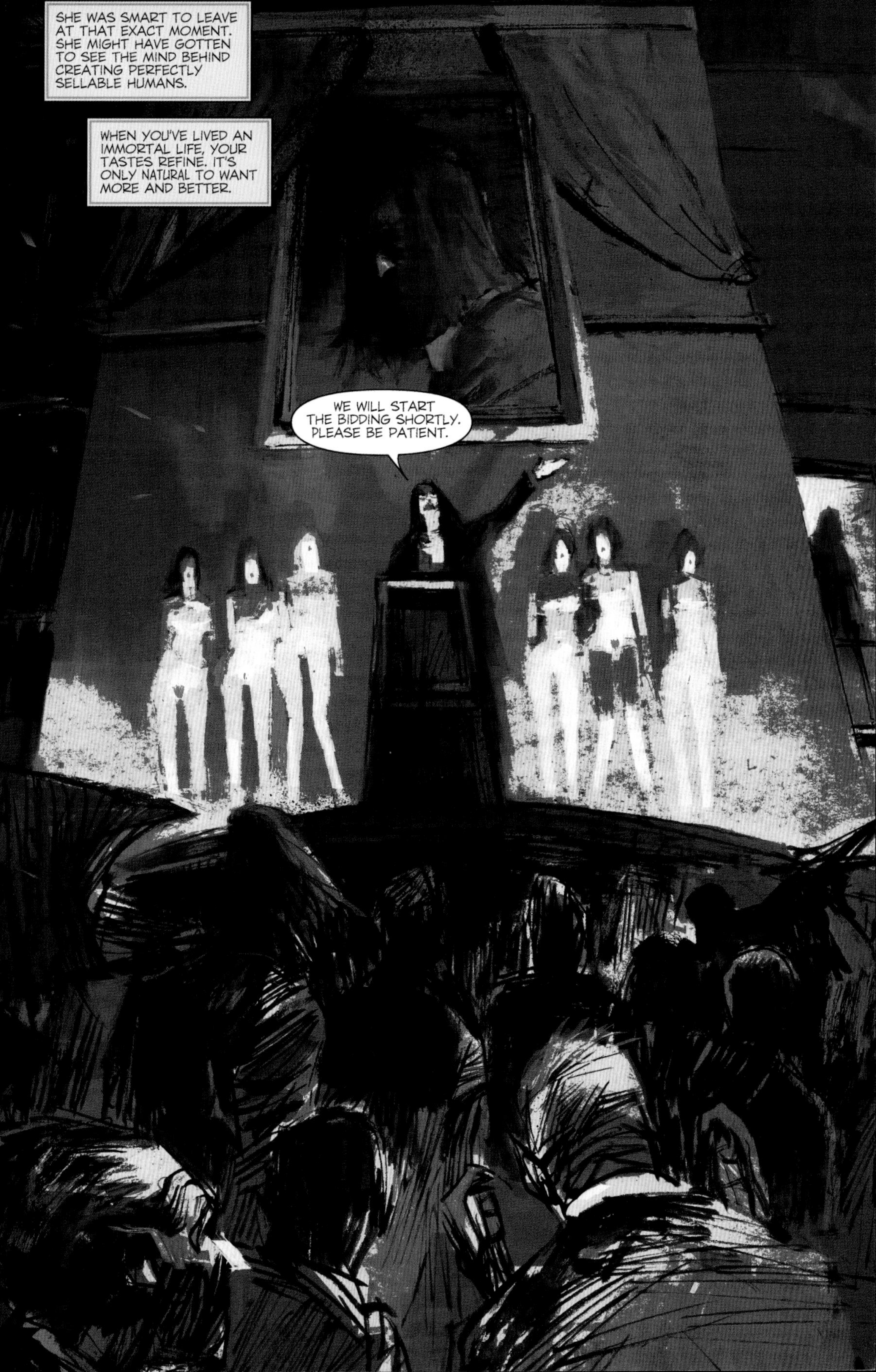
SHE WAS SMART TO LEAVE AT THAT EXACT MOMENT. SHE MIGHT HAVE GOTTEN TO SEE THE MIND BEHIND CREATING PERFECTLY SELLABLE HUMANS.
WHEN YOU'VE LIVED AN IMMORTAL LIFE, YOUR TASTES REFINE. IT'S ONLY NATURAL TO WANT MORE AND BETTER.
WE WILL START THE BIDDING SHORTLY. PLEASE BE PATIENT.

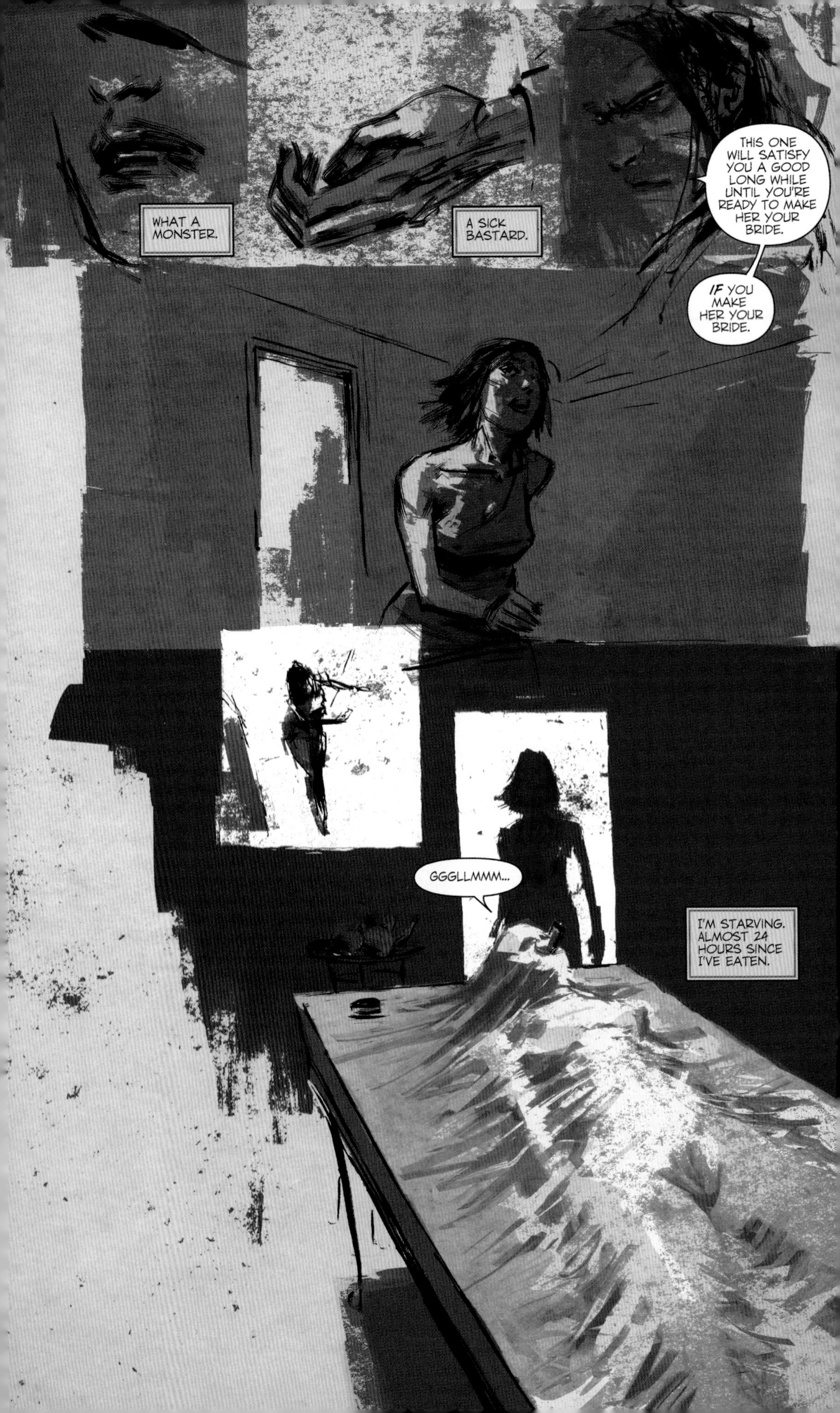
WHAT A MONSTER.
A SICK BASTARD.
THIS ONE WILL SATISFY YOU A GOOD LONG WHILE UNTIL YOU'RE READY TO MAKE HER YOUR BRIDE.
IF YOU MAKE HER YOUR BRIDE.
GGGLLMMM...
I'M STARVING. ALMOST 24 HOURS SINCE I'VE EATEN.

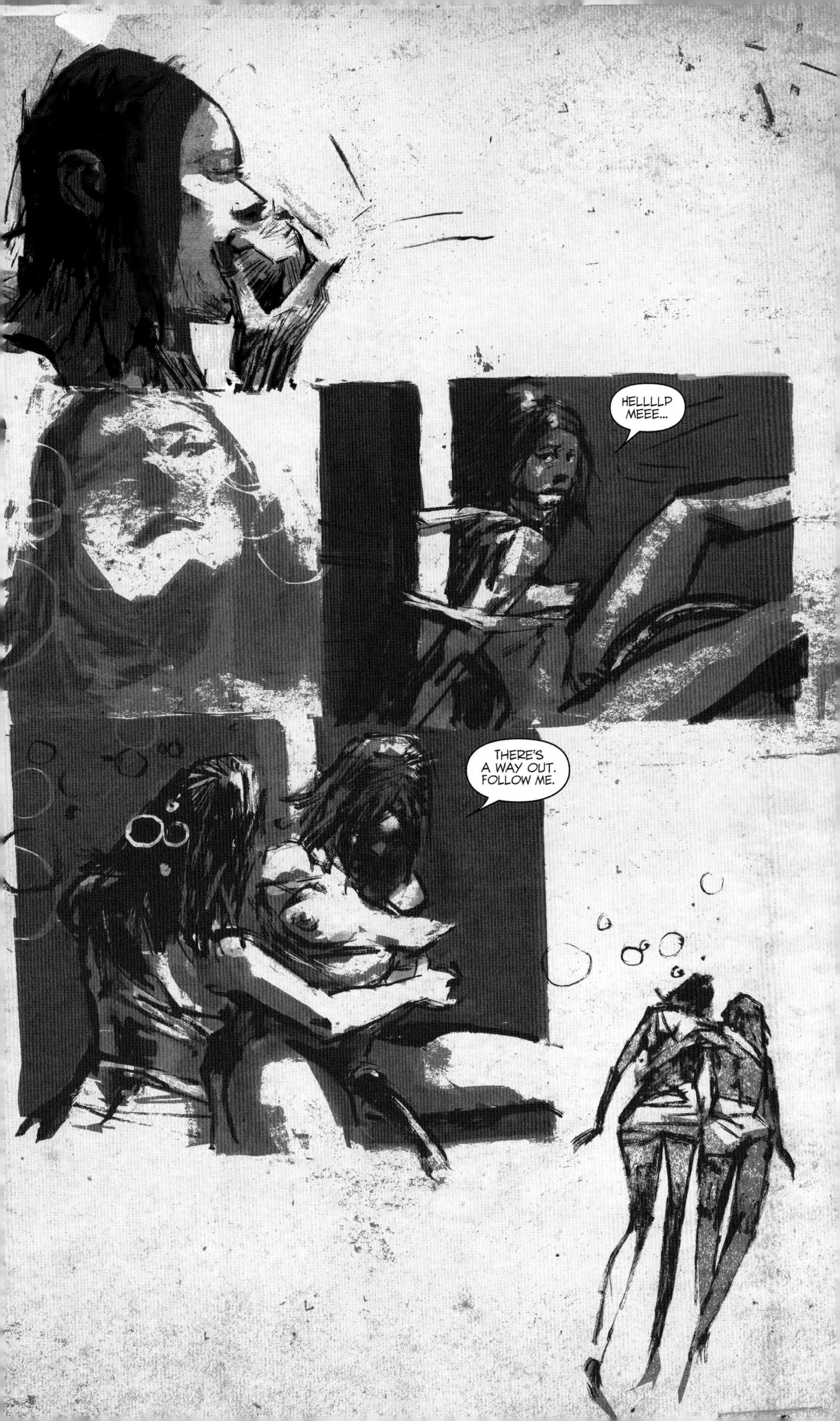
HELLLLP MEEE...
THERE'S A WAY OUT. FOLLOW ME.

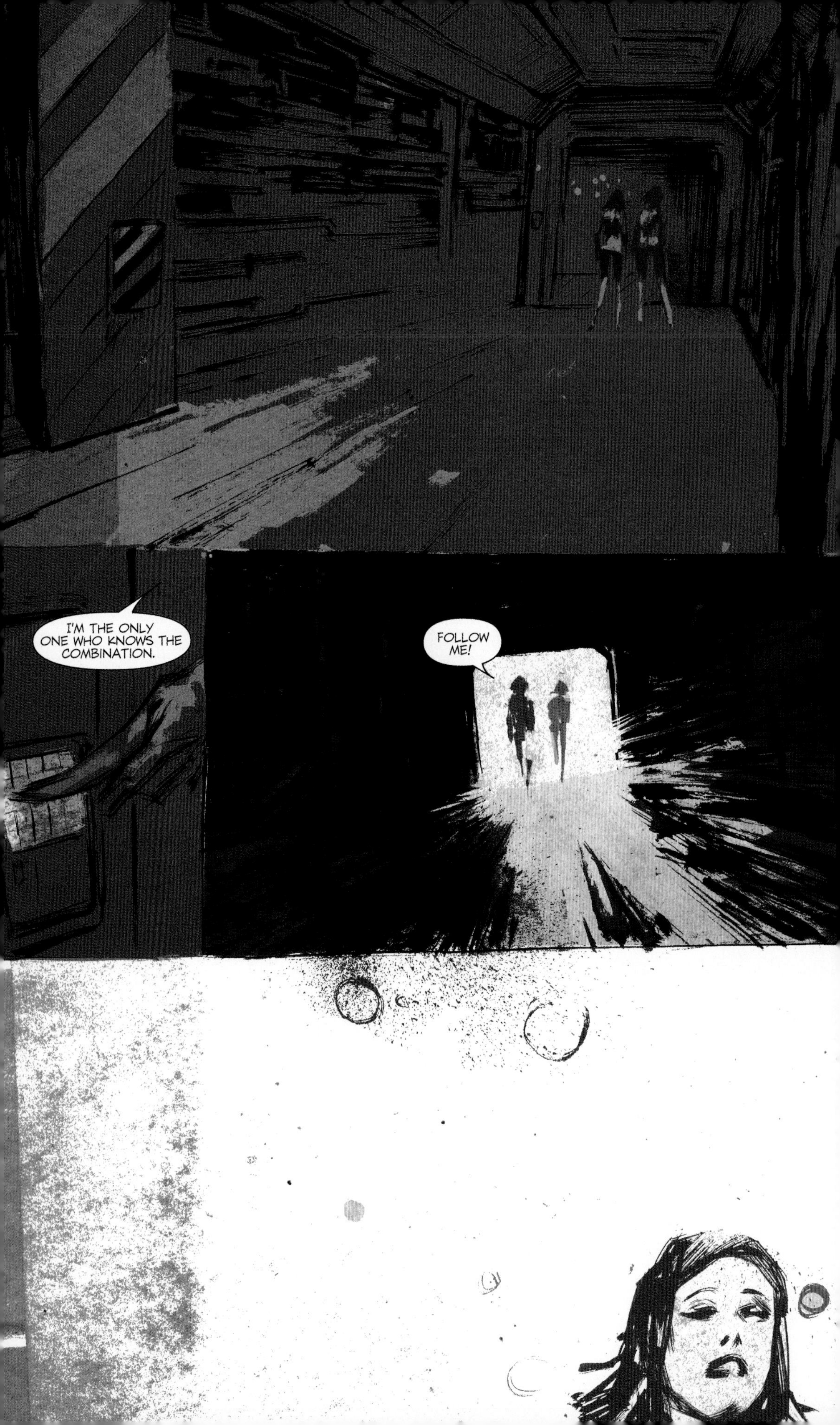

I'M THE ONLY ONE WHO KNOWS THE COMBINATION.
FOLLOW ME!

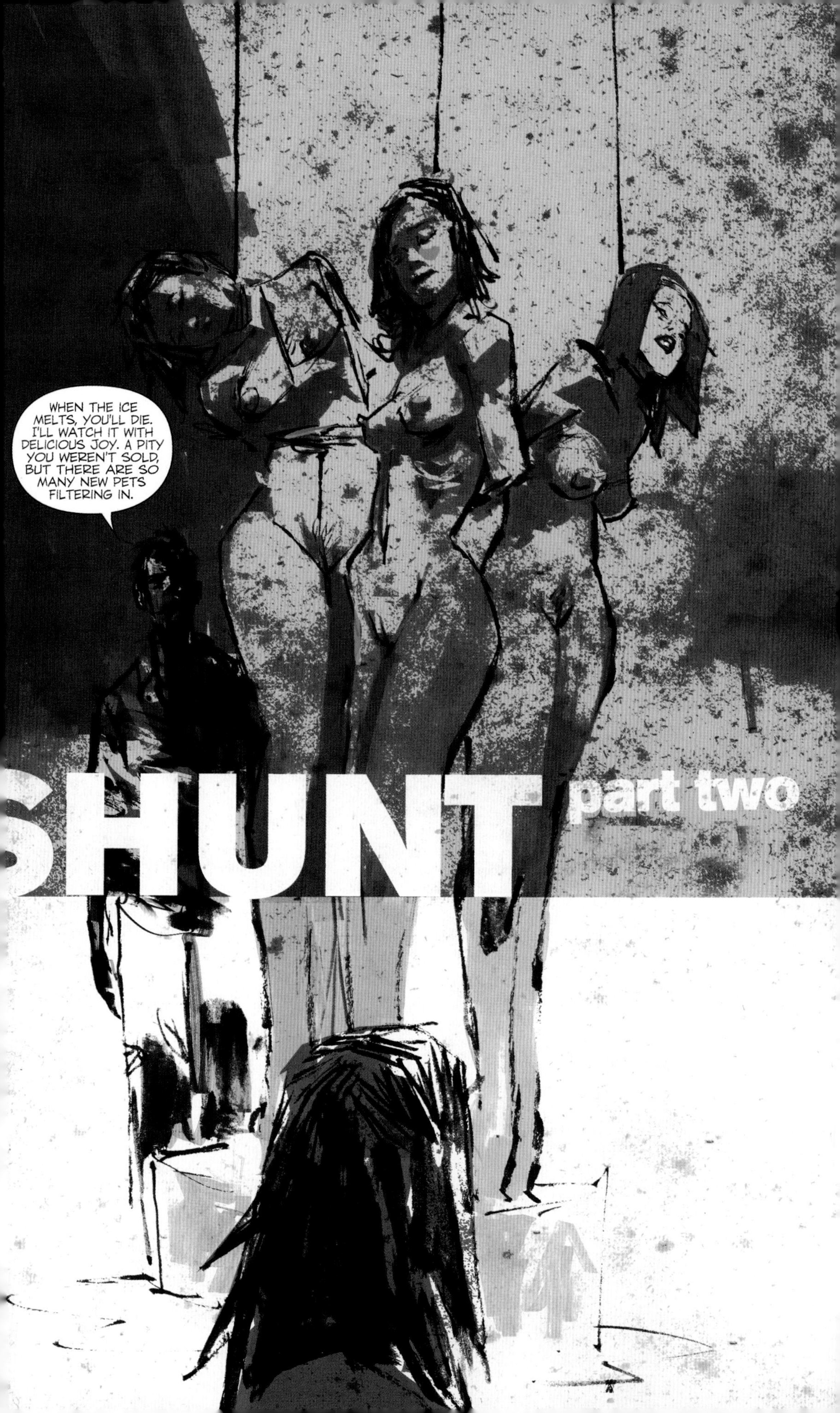
WHEN THE ICE MELTS, YOU'LL DIE. I'LL WATCH IT WITH DELICIOUS JOY. A PITY YOU WEREN'T SOLD, BUT THERE ARE SO MANY NEW PETS FILTERING IN.
SHUNT part two

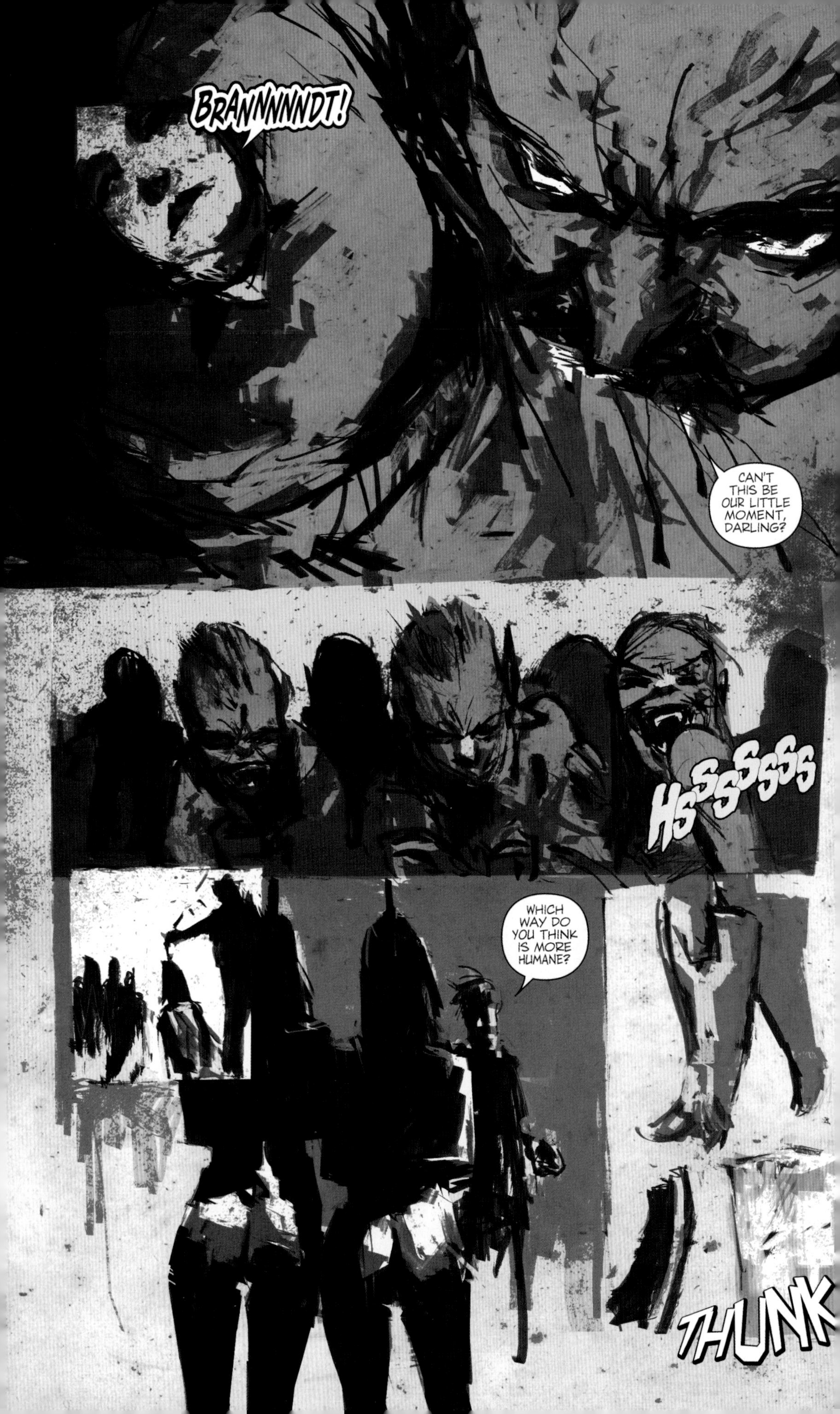
BRANNNNNDT!
CAN'T THIS BE OUR LITTLE MOMENT, DARLING?
HSSSSSSS
WHICH WAY DO YOU THINK IS MORE HUMANE?
THUNK

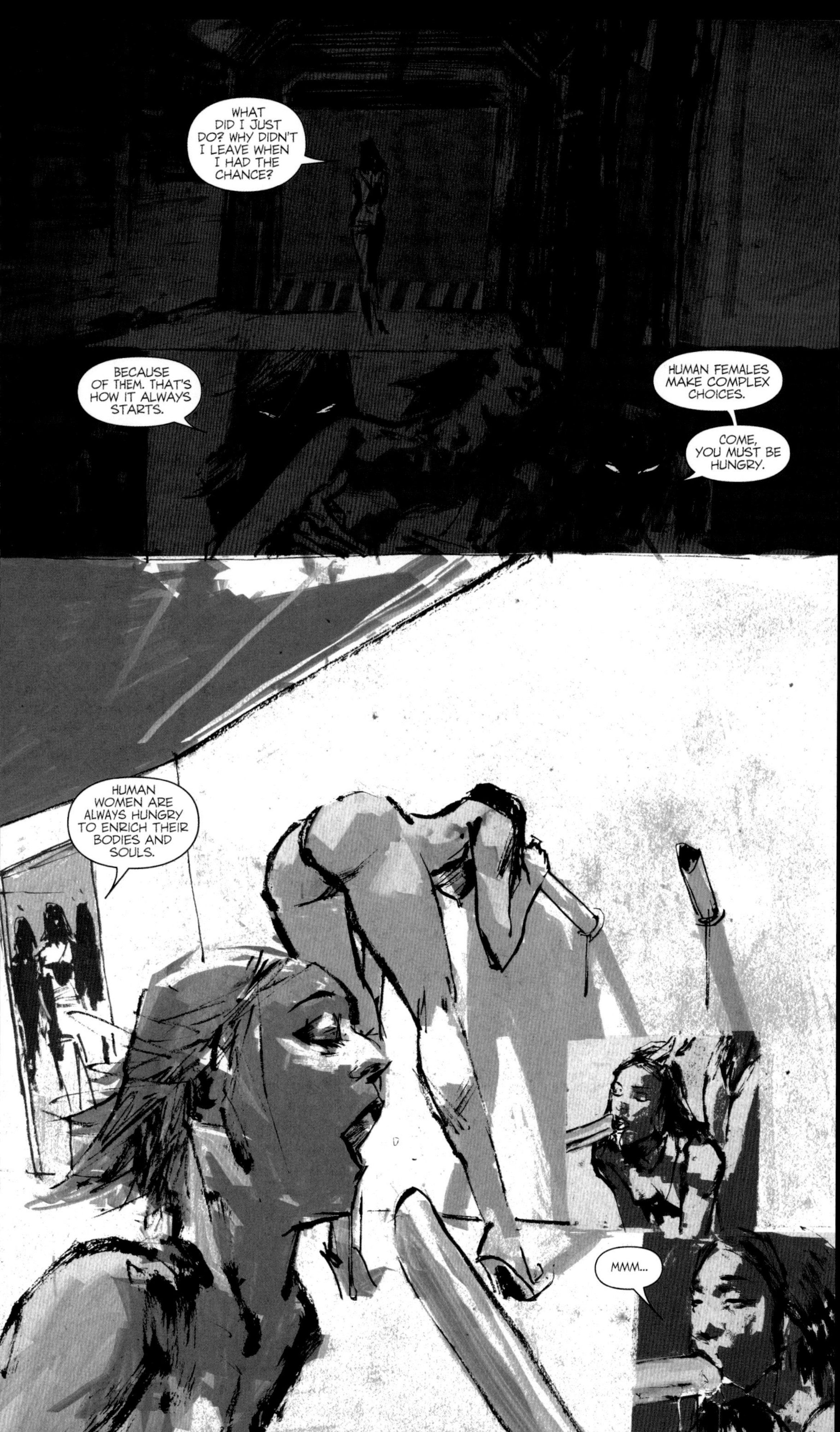
WHAT DID I JUST DO? WHY DIDN'T I LEAVE WHEN I HAD THE CHANCE?
BECAUSE OF THEM. THAT'S HOW IT ALWAYS STARTS.
HUMAN FEMALES MAKE COMPLEX CHOICES.
COME, YOU MUST BE HUNGRY.
HUMAN WOMEN ARE ALWAYS HUNGRY TO ENRICH THEIR BODIES AND SOULS.
MMM...

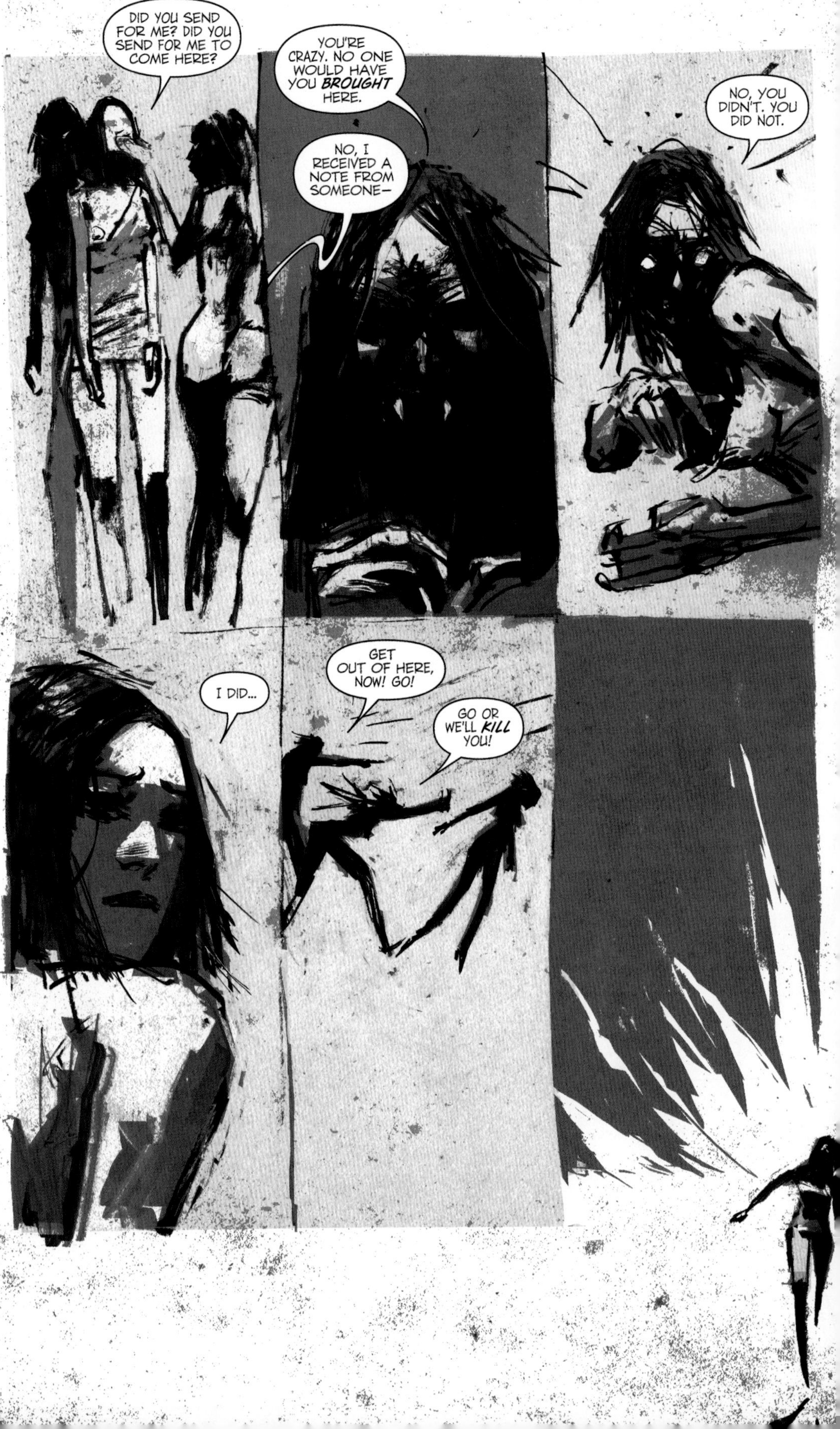
DID YOU SEND FOR ME? DID YOU SEND FOR ME TO COME HERE?
YOU'RE CRAZY. NO ONE WOULD HAVE YOU BROUGHT HERE.
NO, I RECEIVED A NOTE FROM SOMEONE–
NO, YOU DIDN'T. YOU DID NOT.
I DID...
GET OUT OF HERE, NOW! GO!
GO OR WE'LL KILL YOU!

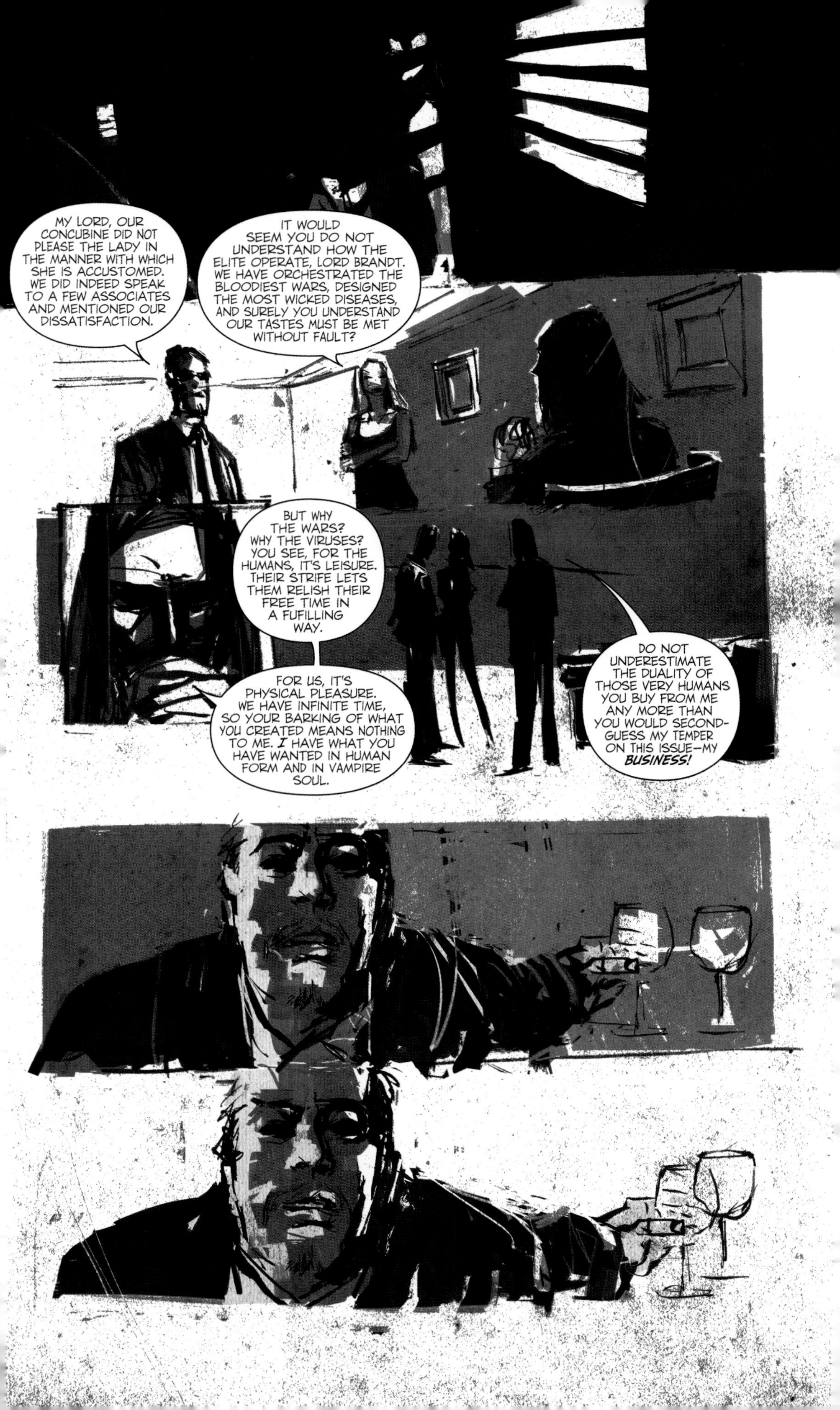
MY LORD, OUR CONCUBINE DID NOT PLEASE THE LADY IN THE MANNER WITH WHICH SHE IS ACCUSTOMED. WE DID INDEED SPEAK TO A FEW ASSOCIATES AND MENTIONED OUR DISSATISFACTION.
IT WOULD SEEM YOU DO NOT UNDERSTAND HOW THE ELITE OPERATE, LORD BRANDT. WE HAVE ORCHESTRATED THE BLOODIEST WARS, DESIGNED THE MOST WICKED DISEASES, AND SURELY YOU UNDERSTAND OUR TASTES MUST BE MET WITHOUT FAULT?
BUT WHY THE WARS? WHY THE VIRUSES? YOU SEE, FOR THE HUMANS, IT'S LEISURE. THEIR STRIFE LETS THEM RELISH THEIR FREE TIME IN A FUFILLING WAY.
FOR US, IT'S PHYSICAL PLEASURE. WE HAVE INFINITE TIME, SO YOUR BARKING OF WHAT YOU CREATED MEANS NOTHING TO ME. *I* HAVE WHAT YOU HAVE WANTED IN HUMAN FORM AND IN VAMPIRE SOUL.
DO NOT UNDERESTIMATE THE DUALITY OF THOSE VERY HUMANS YOU BUY FROM ME ANY MORE THAN YOU WOULD SECOND-GUESS MY TEMPER ON THIS ISSUE—MY ***BUSINESS!***

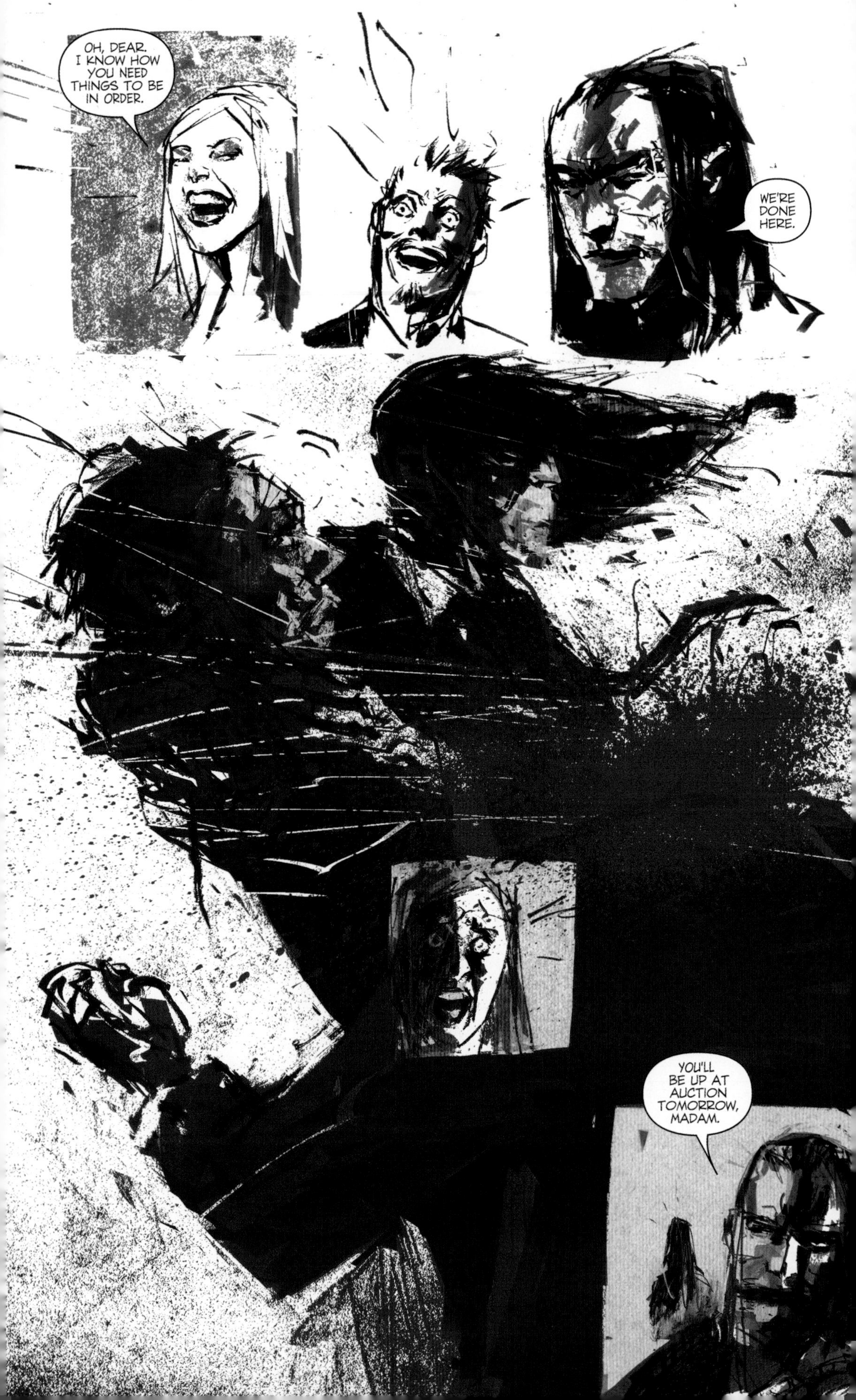
OH, DEAR. I KNOW HOW YOU NEED THINGS TO BE IN ORDER.
WE'RE DONE HERE.
YOU'LL BE UP AT AUCTION TOMORROW, MADAM.

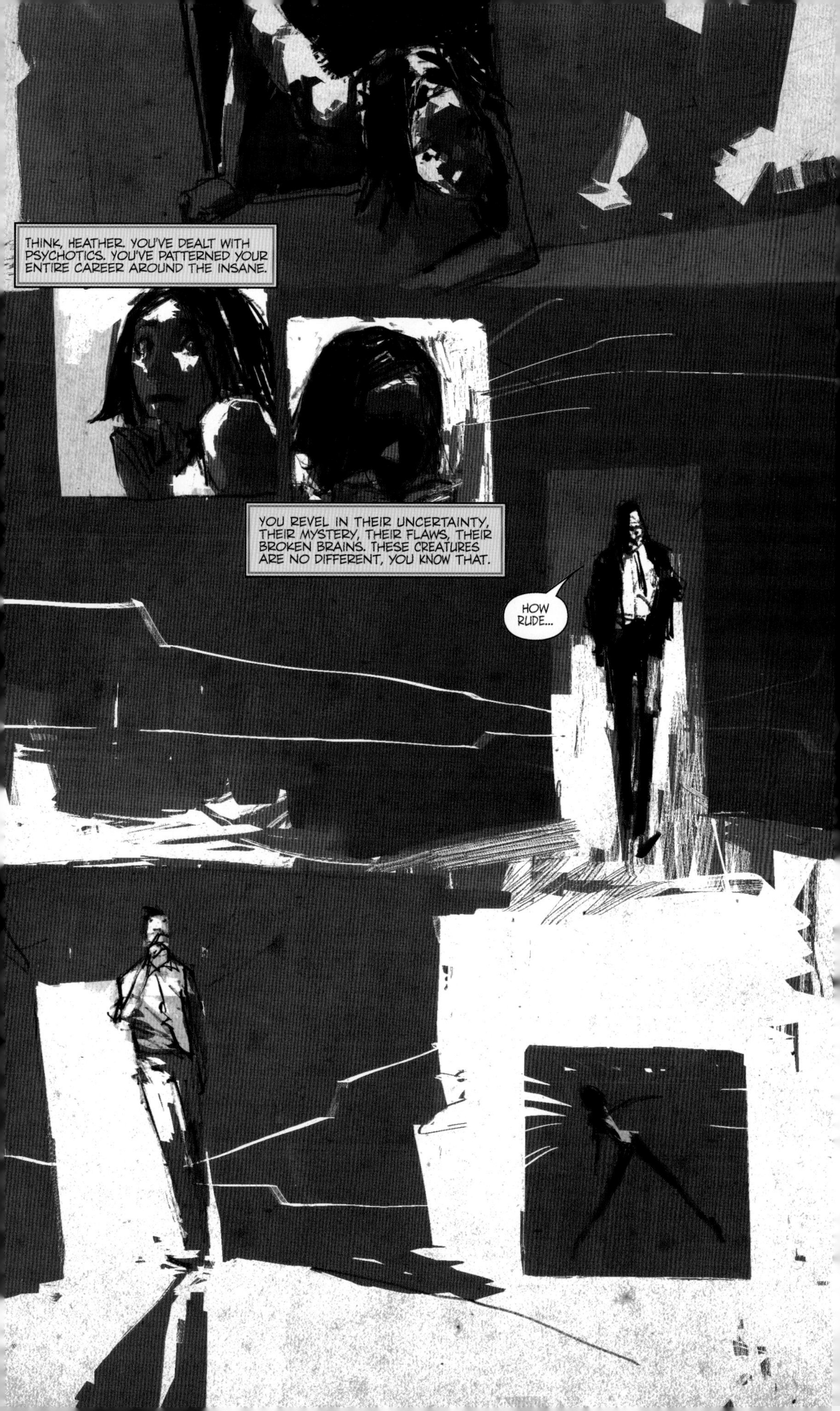
THINK, HEATHER. YOU'VE DEALT WITH PSYCHOTICS. YOU'VE PATTERNED YOUR ENTIRE CAREER AROUND THE INSANE.
YOU REVEL IN THEIR UNCERTAINTY, THEIR MYSTERY, THEIR FLAWS, THEIR BROKEN BRAINS. THESE CREATURES ARE NO DIFFERENT, YOU KNOW THAT.
HOW RUDE...

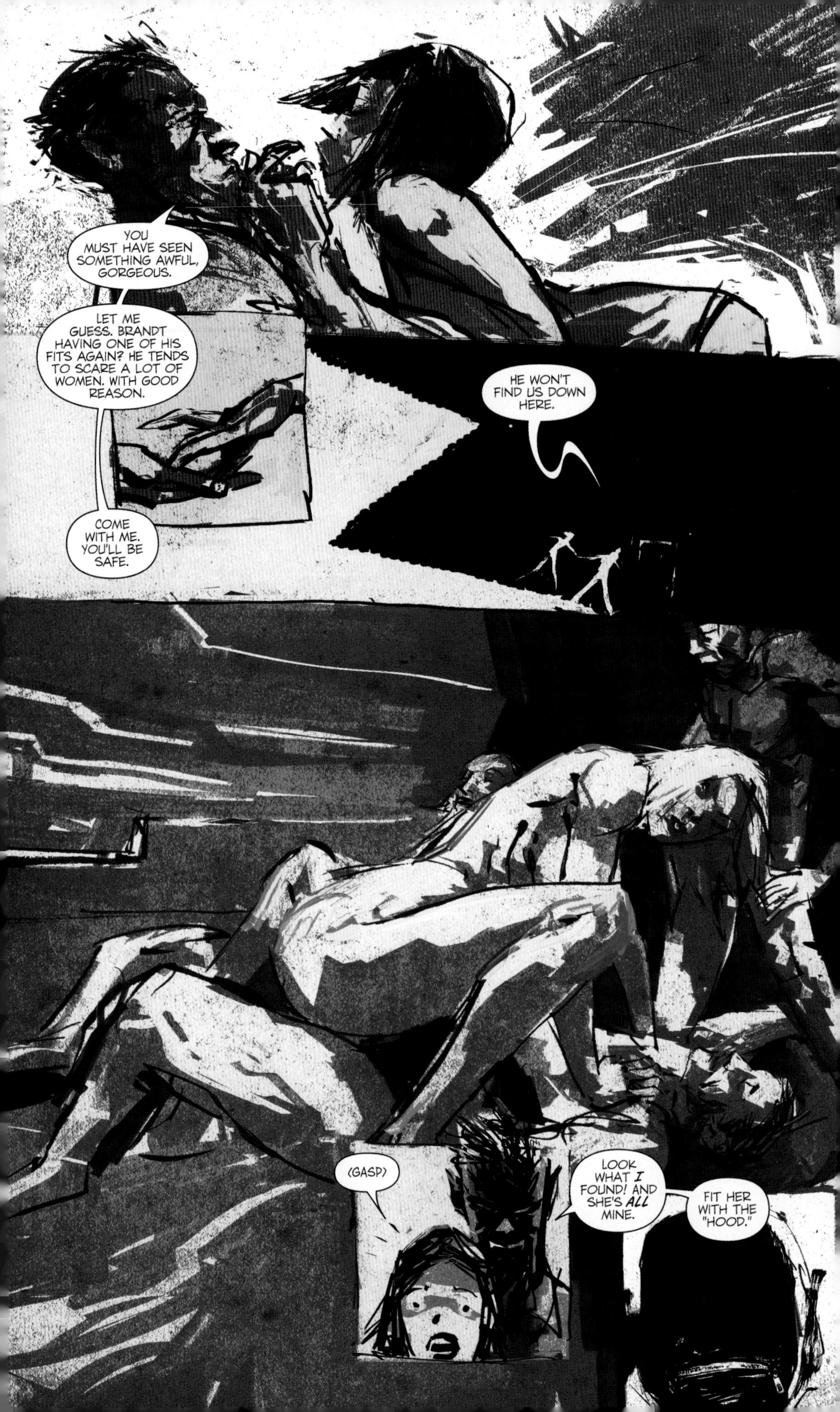
YOU MUST HAVE SEEN SOMETHING AWFUL, GORGEOUS.
LET ME GUESS. BRANDT HAVING ONE OF HIS FITS AGAIN? HE TENDS TO SCARE A LOT OF WOMEN. WITH GOOD REASON.
COME WITH ME. YOU'LL BE SAFE.
HE WON'T FIND US DOWN HERE.
(GASP)
LOOK WHAT *I* FOUND! AND SHE'S ***ALL*** MINE.
FIT HER WITH THE "HOOD."

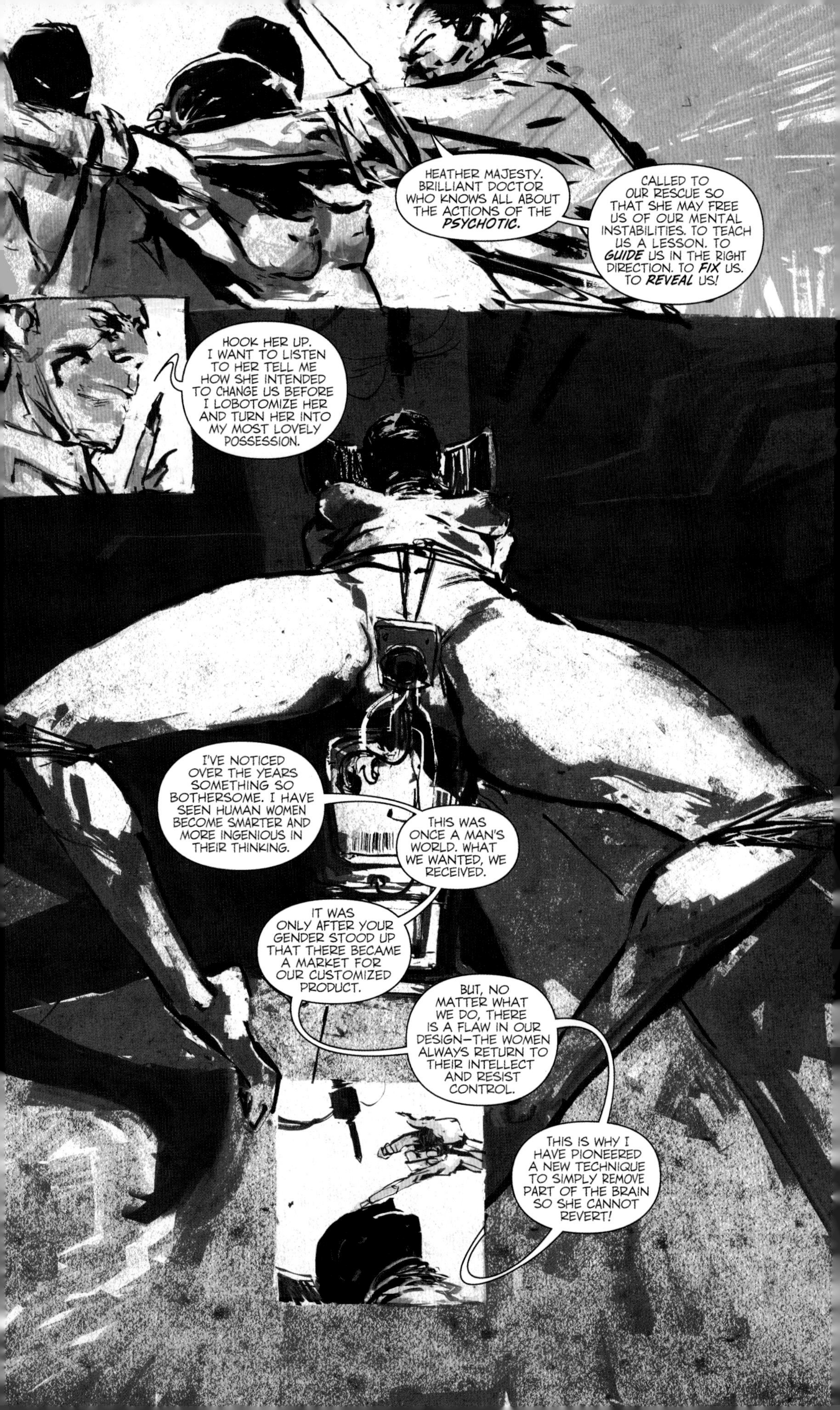

HEATHER MAJESTY. BRILLIANT DOCTOR WHO KNOWS ALL ABOUT THE ACTIONS OF THE ***PSYCHOTIC.***
CALLED TO OUR RESCUE SO THAT SHE MAY FREE US OF OUR MENTAL INSTABILITIES. TO TEACH US A LESSON. TO ***GUIDE*** US IN THE RIGHT DIRECTION. TO ***FIX*** US. TO ***REVEAL*** US!
HOOK HER UP. I WANT TO LISTEN TO HER TELL ME HOW SHE INTENDED TO CHANGE US BEFORE I LOBOTOMIZE HER AND TURN HER INTO MY MOST LOVELY POSSESSION.
I'VE NOTICED OVER THE YEARS SOMETHING SO BOTHERSOME. I HAVE SEEN HUMAN WOMEN BECOME SMARTER AND MORE INGENIOUS IN THEIR THINKING.
THIS WAS ONCE A MAN'S WORLD. WHAT WE WANTED, WE RECEIVED.
IT WAS ONLY AFTER YOUR GENDER STOOD UP THAT THERE BECAME A MARKET FOR OUR CUSTOMIZED PRODUCT.
BUT, NO MATTER WHAT WE DO, THERE IS A FLAW IN OUR DESIGN—THE WOMEN ALWAYS RETURN TO THEIR INTELLECT AND RESIST CONTROL.
THIS IS WHY I HAVE PIONEERED A NEW TECHNIQUE TO SIMPLY REMOVE PART OF THE BRAIN SO SHE CANNOT REVERT!

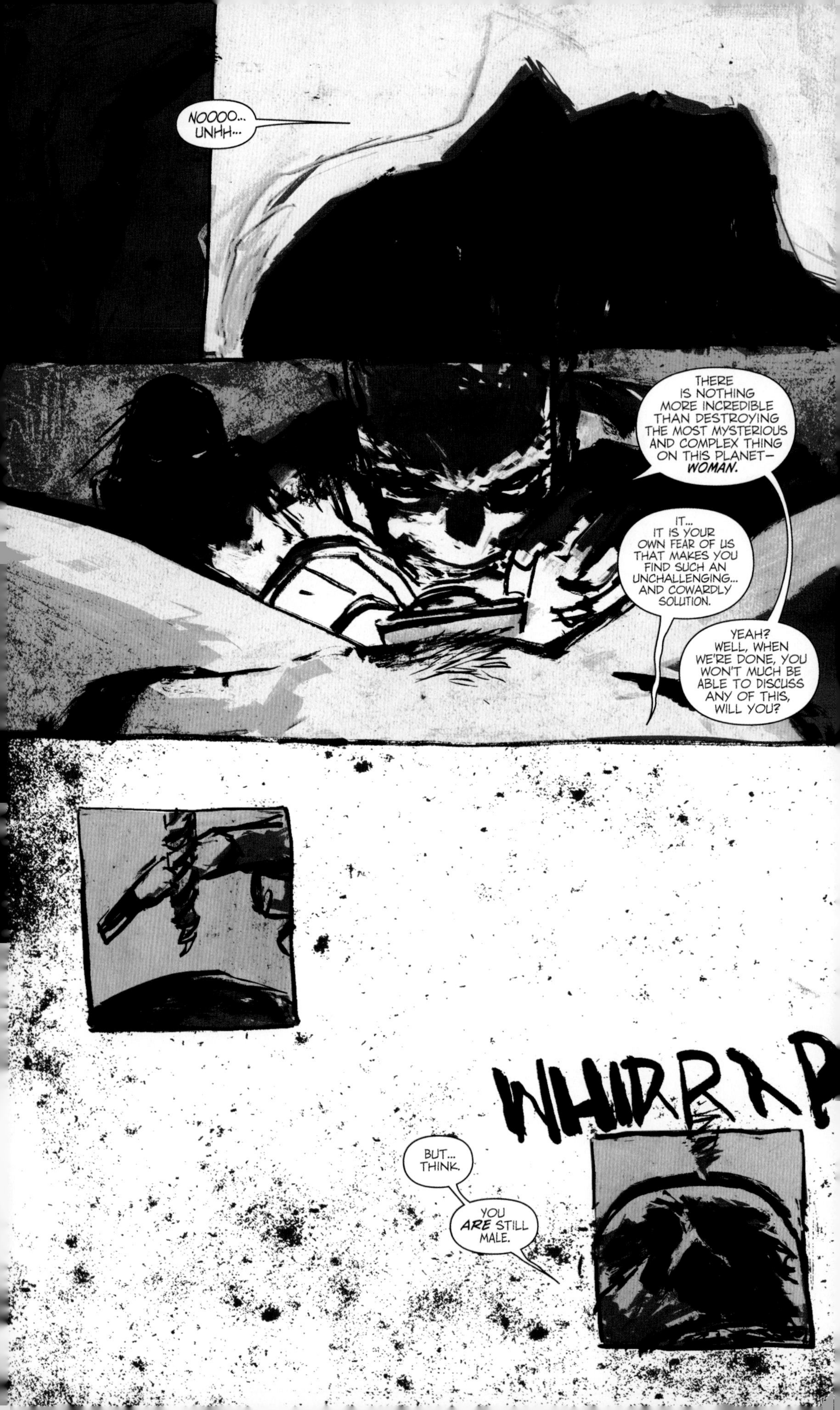
NOOOO... UNHH...
THERE IS NOTHING MORE INCREDIBLE THAN DESTROYING THE MOST MYSTERIOUS AND COMPLEX THING ON THIS PLANET— WOMAN.
IT... IT IS YOUR OWN FEAR OF US THAT MAKES YOU FIND SUCH AN UNCHALLENGING... AND COWARDLY SOLUTION.
YEAH? WELL, WHEN WE'RE DONE, YOU WON'T MUCH BE ABLE TO DISCUSS ANY OF THIS, WILL YOU?
WHIRRR
BUT... THINK.
YOU ARE STILL MALE.

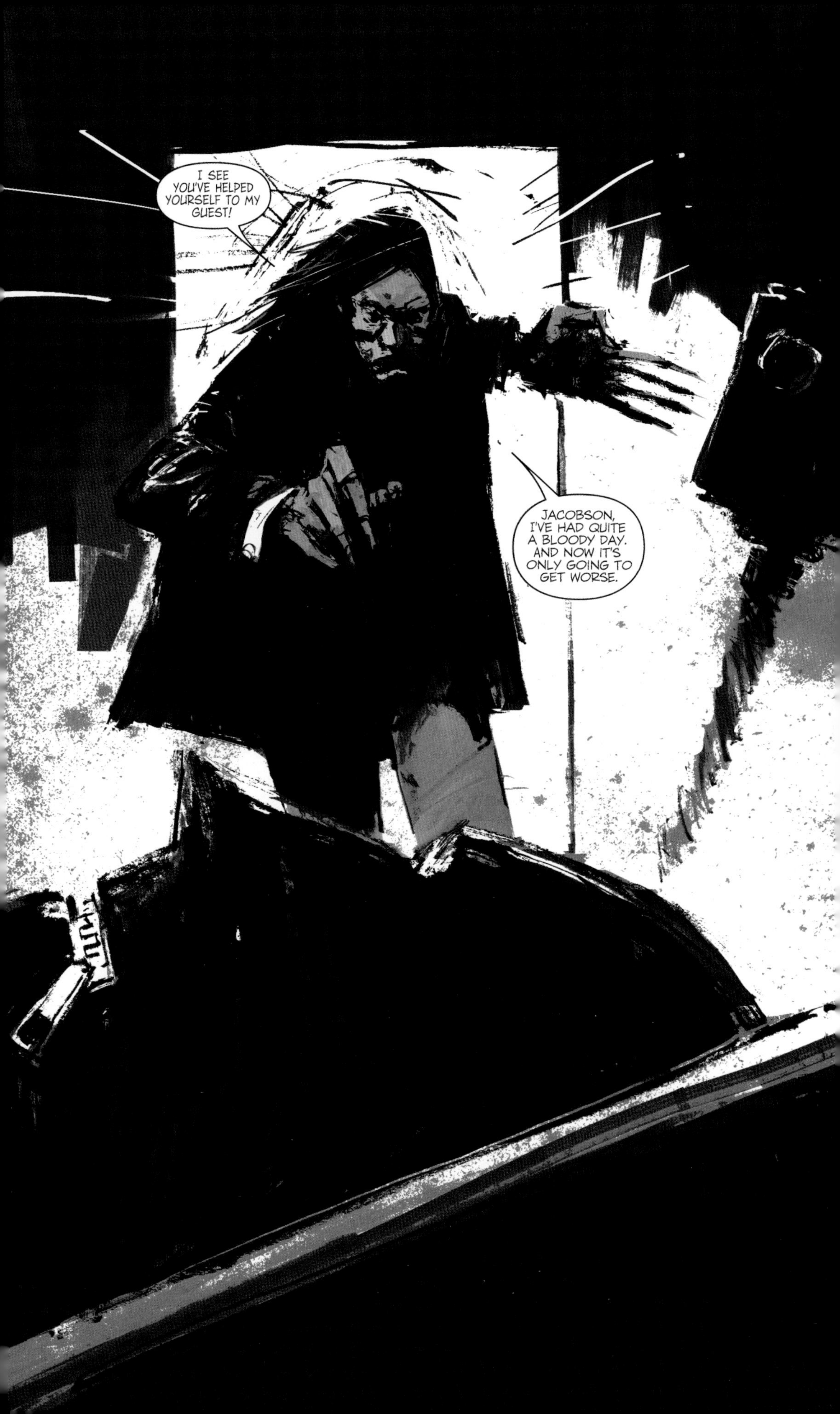
I SEE YOU'VE HELPED YOURSELF TO MY GUEST!
JACOBSON, I'VE HAD QUITE A BLOODY DAY. AND NOW IT'S ONLY GOING TO GET WORSE.

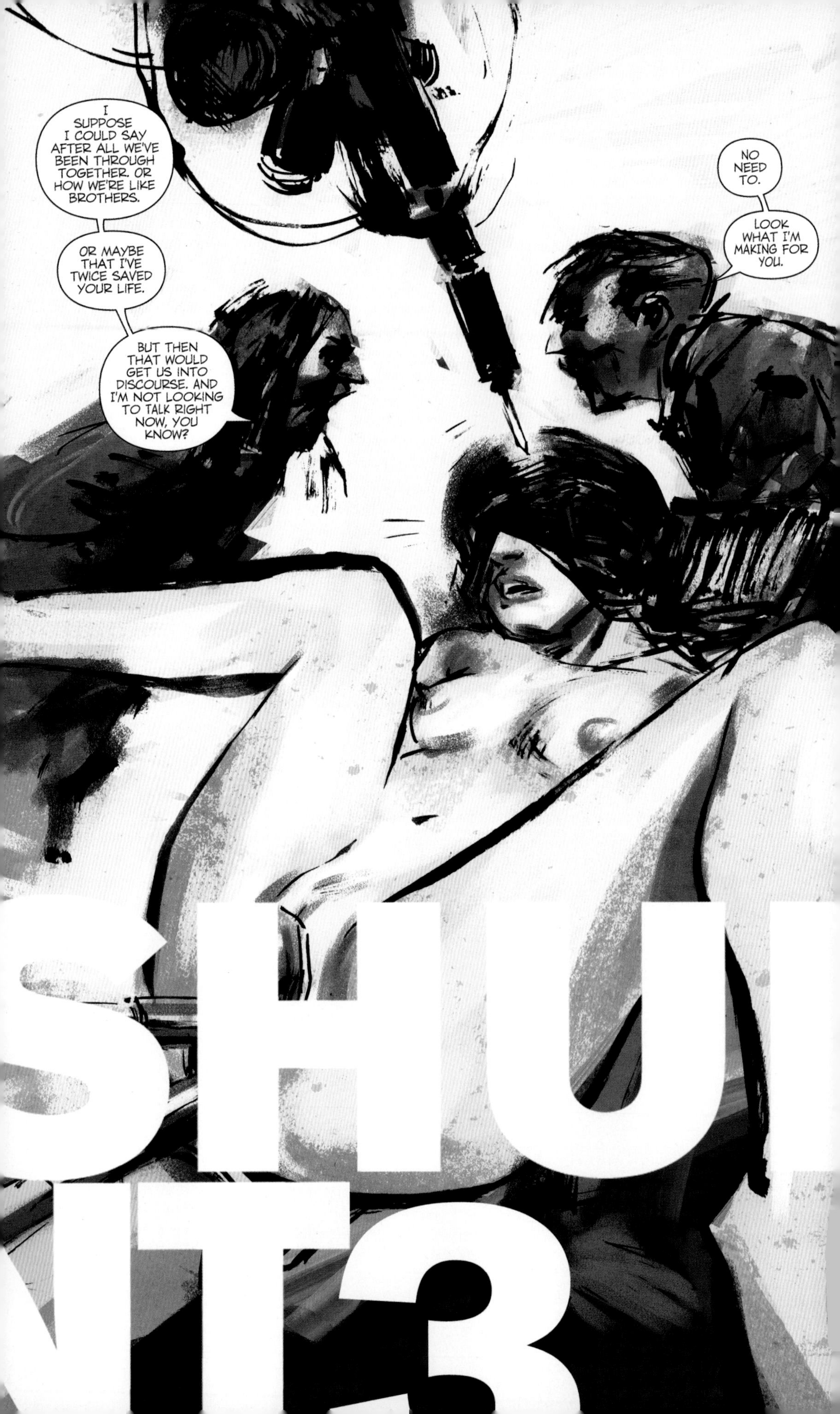
I SUPPOSE I COULD SAY AFTER ALL WE'VE BEEN THROUGH TOGETHER. OR HOW WE'RE LIKE BROTHERS.
OR MAYBE THAT I'VE TWICE SAVED YOUR LIFE.
BUT THEN THAT WOULD GET US INTO DISCOURSE. AND I'M NOT LOOKING TO TALK RIGHT NOW, YOU KNOW?
NO NEED TO.
LOOK WHAT I'M MAKING FOR YOU.

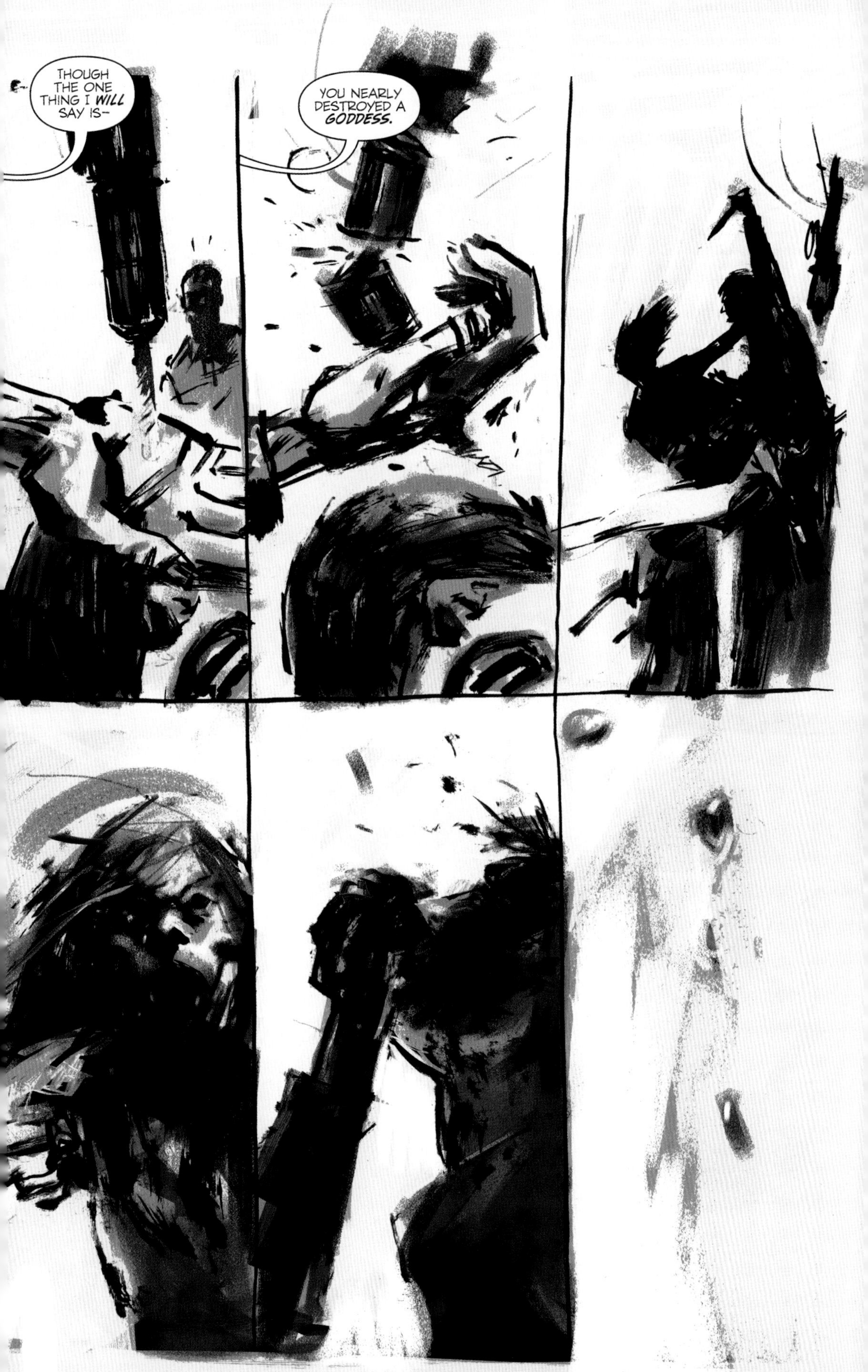
THOUGH THE ONE THING I **WILL** SAY IS–
YOU NEARLY DESTROYED A ***GODDESS.***

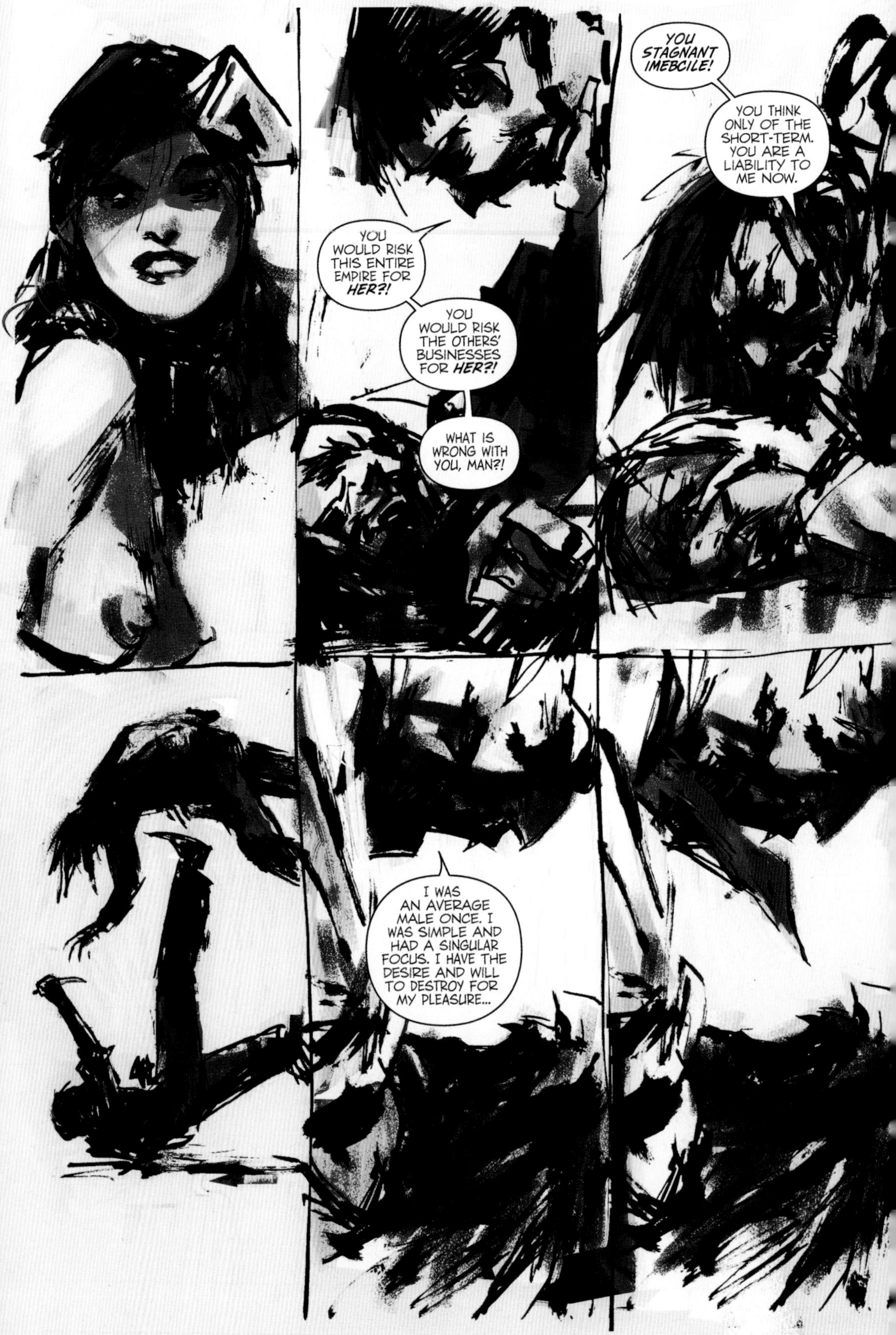

YOU WOULD RISK THIS ENTIRE EMPIRE FOR *HER?!*
YOU WOULD RISK THE OTHERS' BUSINESSES FOR *HER?!*
WHAT IS WRONG WITH YOU, MAN?!
YOU STAGNANT IMEBCILE!
YOU THINK ONLY OF THE SHORT-TERM. YOU ARE A LIABILITY TO ME NOW.
I WAS AN AVERAGE MALE ONCE. I WAS SIMPLE AND HAD A SINGULAR FOCUS. I HAVE THE DESIRE AND WILL TO DESTROY FOR MY PLEASURE...

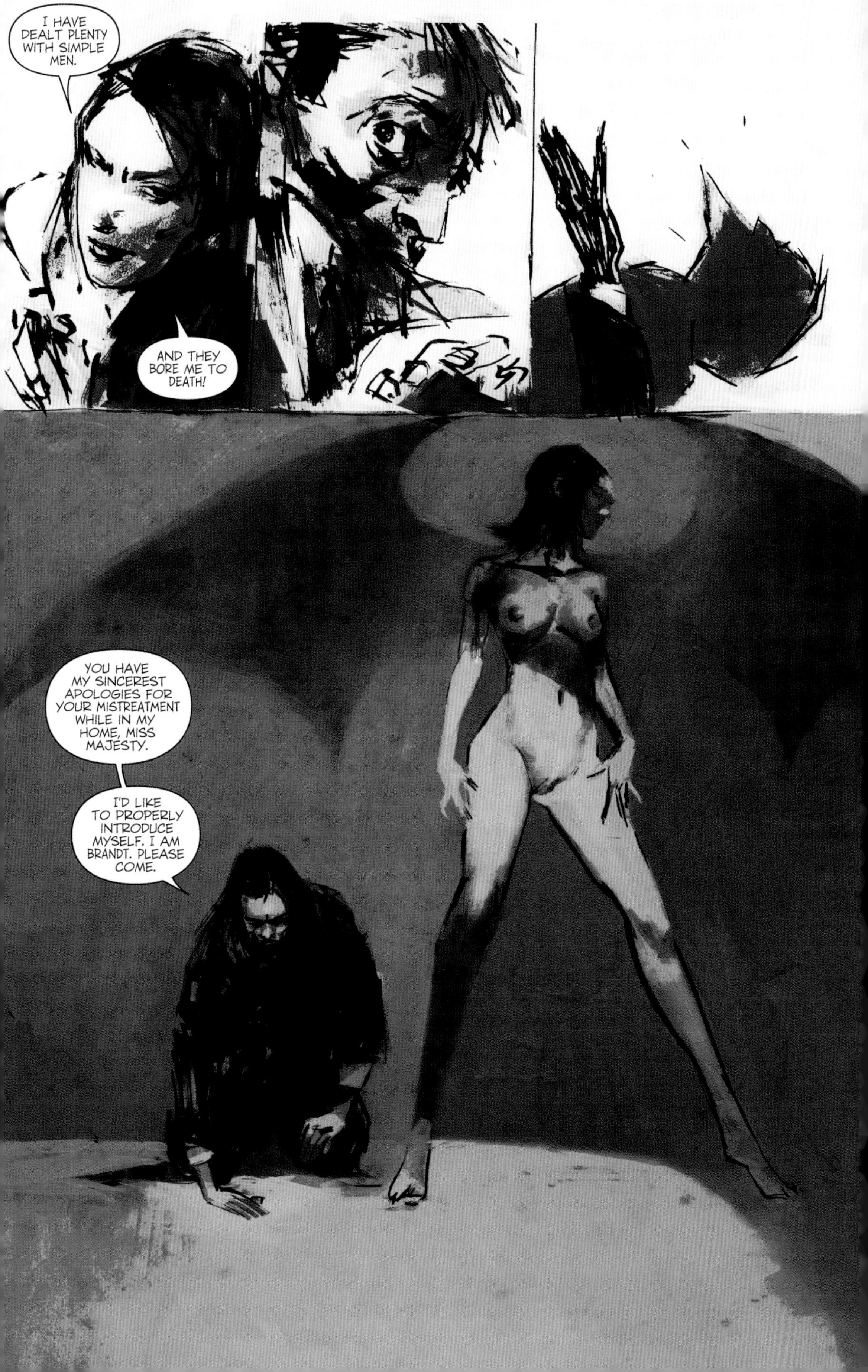
I HAVE DEALT PLENTY WITH SIMPLE MEN.
AND THEY BORE ME TO DEATH!
YOU HAVE MY SINCEREST APOLOGIES FOR YOUR MISTREATMENT WHILE IN MY HOME, MISS MAJESTY.
I'D LIKE TO PROPERLY INTRODUCE MYSELF. I AM BRANDT. PLEASE COME.

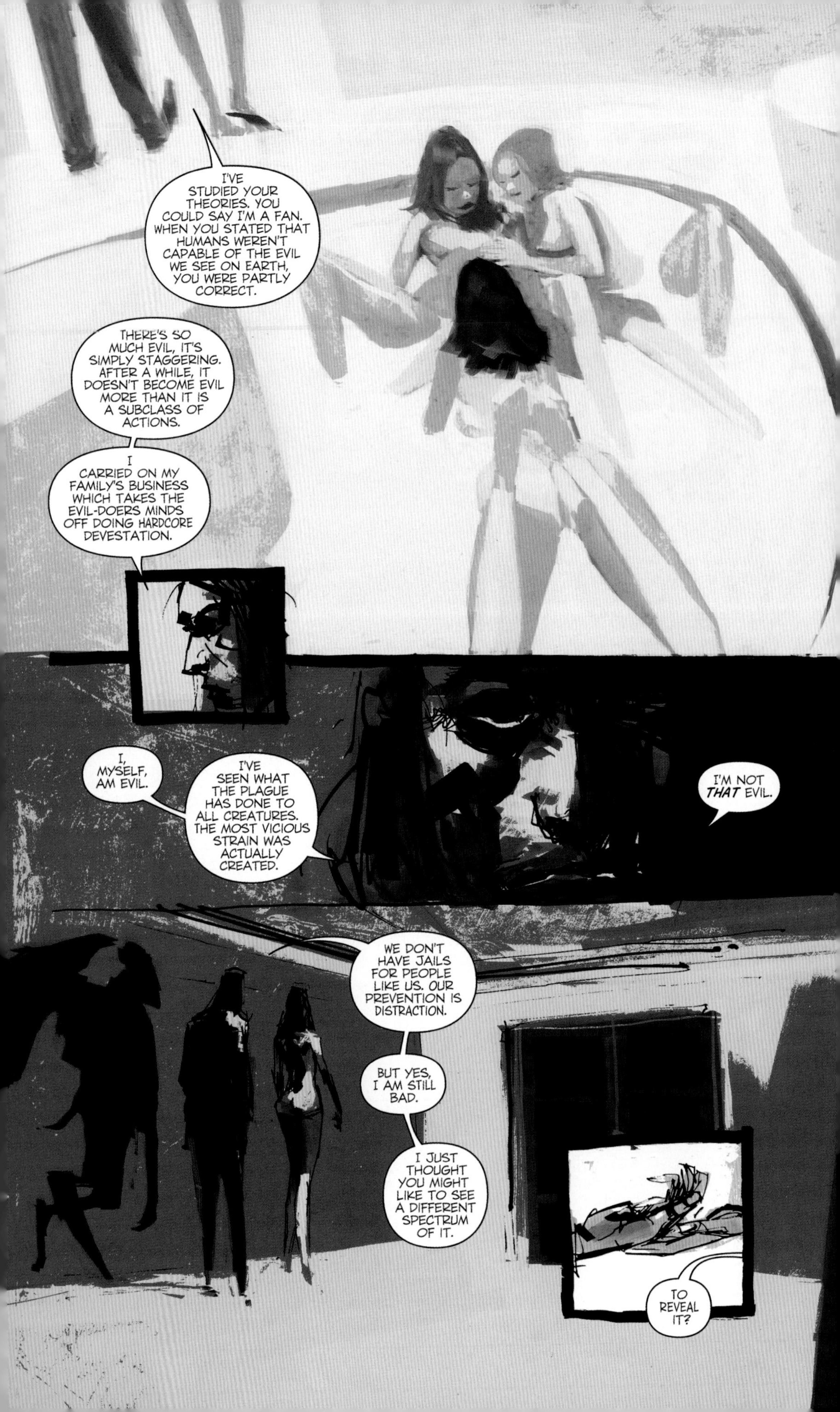
I'VE STUDIED YOUR THEORIES. YOU COULD SAY I'M A FAN. WHEN YOU STATED THAT HUMANS WEREN'T CAPABLE OF THE EVIL WE SEE ON EARTH, YOU WERE PARTLY CORRECT.
THERE'S SO MUCH EVIL, IT'S SIMPLY STAGGERING. AFTER A WHILE, IT DOESN'T BECOME EVIL MORE THAN IT IS A SUBCLASS OF ACTIONS.
I CARRIED ON MY FAMILY'S BUSINESS WHICH TAKES THE EVIL-DOERS MINDS OFF DOING HARDCORE DEVESTATION.
I, MYSELF, AM EVIL.
I'VE SEEN WHAT THE PLAGUE HAS DONE TO ALL CREATURES. THE MOST VICIOUS STRAIN WAS ACTUALLY CREATED.
I'M NOT *THAT* EVIL.
WE DON'T HAVE JAILS FOR PEOPLE LIKE US. OUR PREVENTION IS DISTRACTION.
BUT YES, I AM STILL BAD.
I JUST THOUGHT YOU MIGHT LIKE TO SEE A DIFFERENT SPECTRUM OF IT.
TO REVEAL IT?

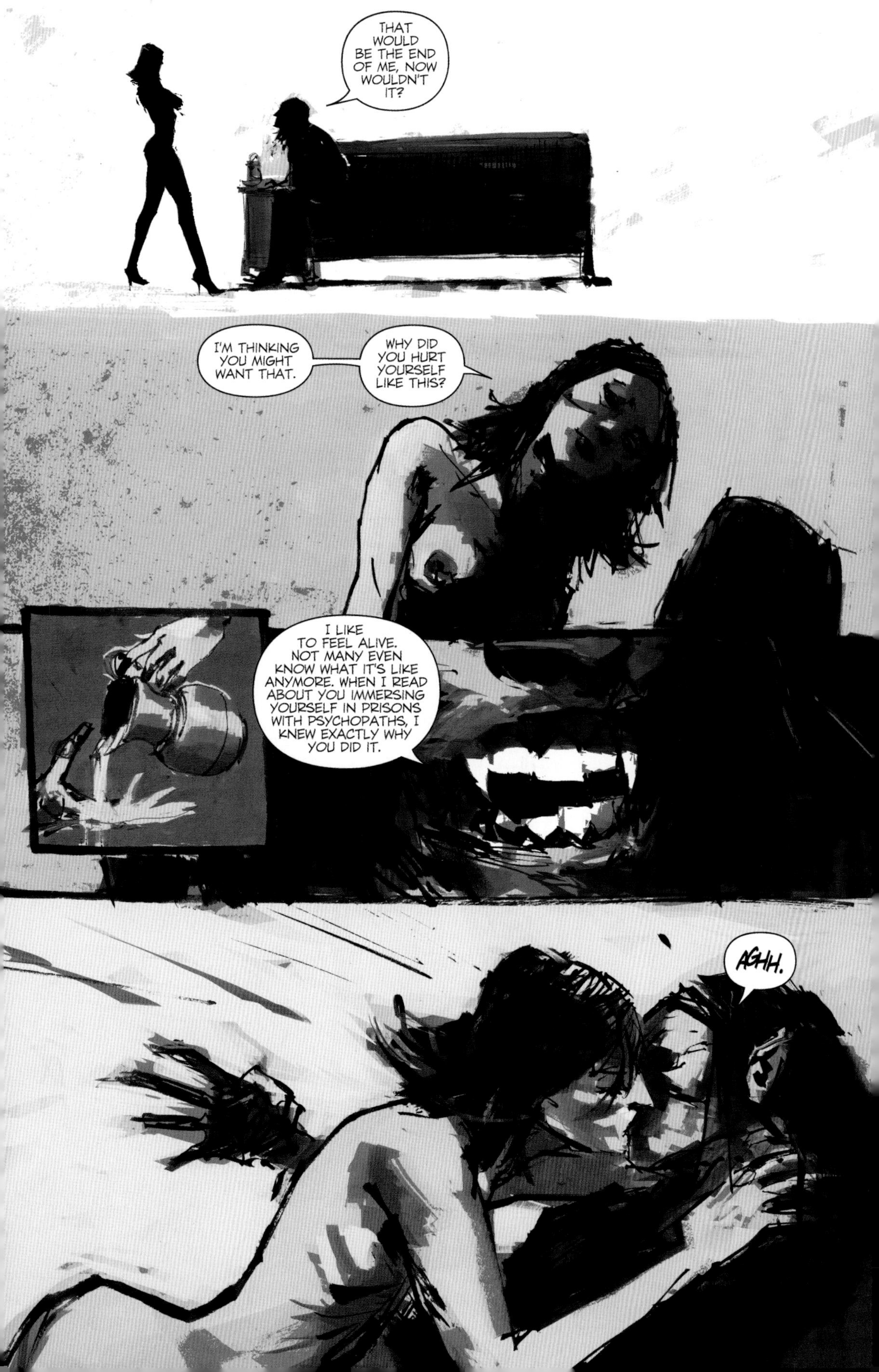
THAT WOULD BE THE END OF ME, NOW WOULDN'T IT?
I'M THINKING YOU MIGHT WANT THAT.
WHY DID YOU HURT YOURSELF LIKE THIS?
I LIKE TO FEEL ALIVE. NOT MANY EVEN KNOW WHAT IT'S LIKE ANYMORE. WHEN I READ ABOUT YOU IMMERSING YOURSELF IN PRISONS WITH PSYCHOPATHS, I KNEW EXACTLY WHY YOU DID IT.
AGHH.

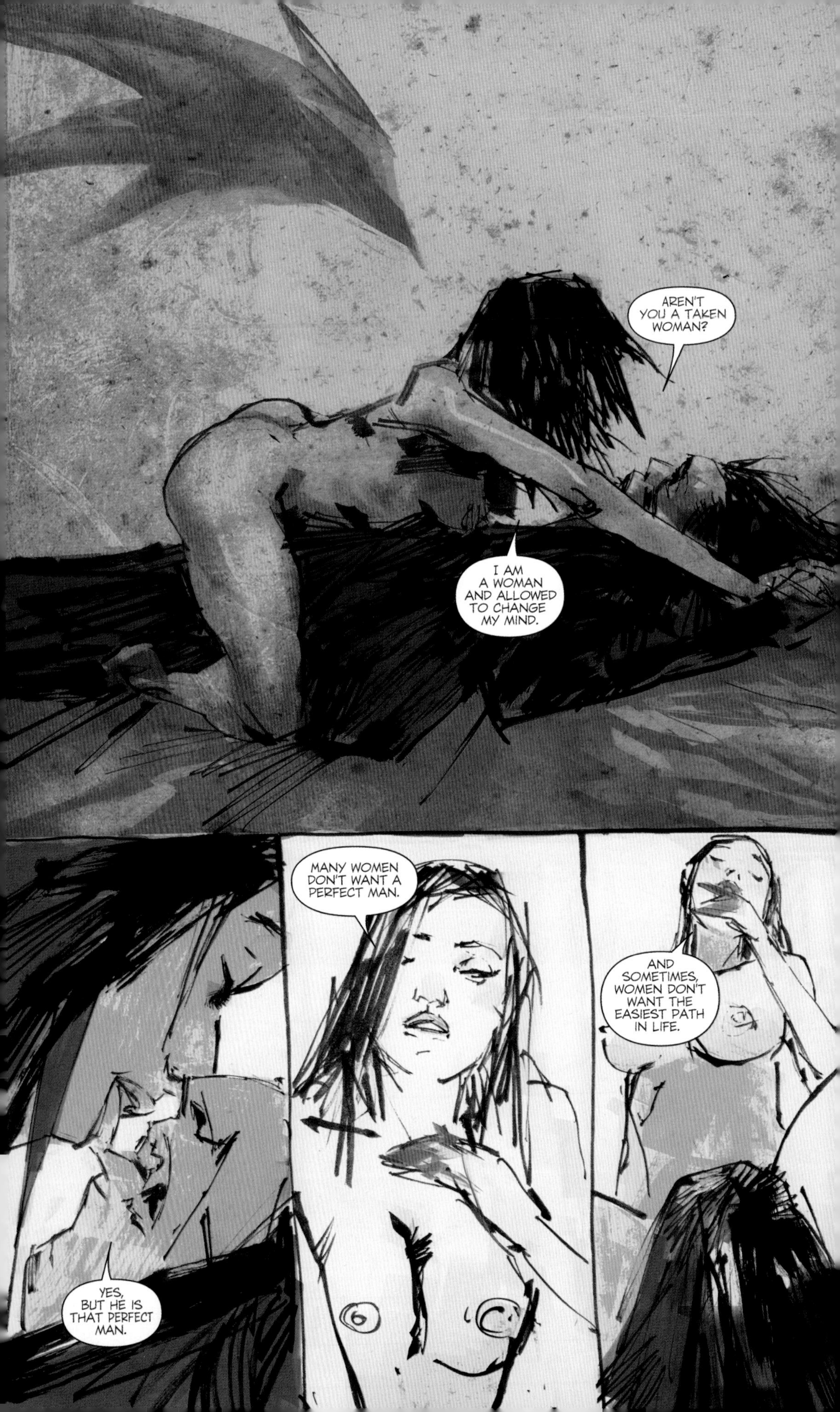
AREN'T YOU A TAKEN WOMAN?
I AM A WOMAN AND ALLOWED TO CHANGE MY MIND.
YES, BUT HE IS THAT PERFECT MAN.
MANY WOMEN DON'T WANT A PERFECT MAN.
AND SOMETIMES, WOMEN DON'T WANT THE EASIEST PATH IN LIFE.

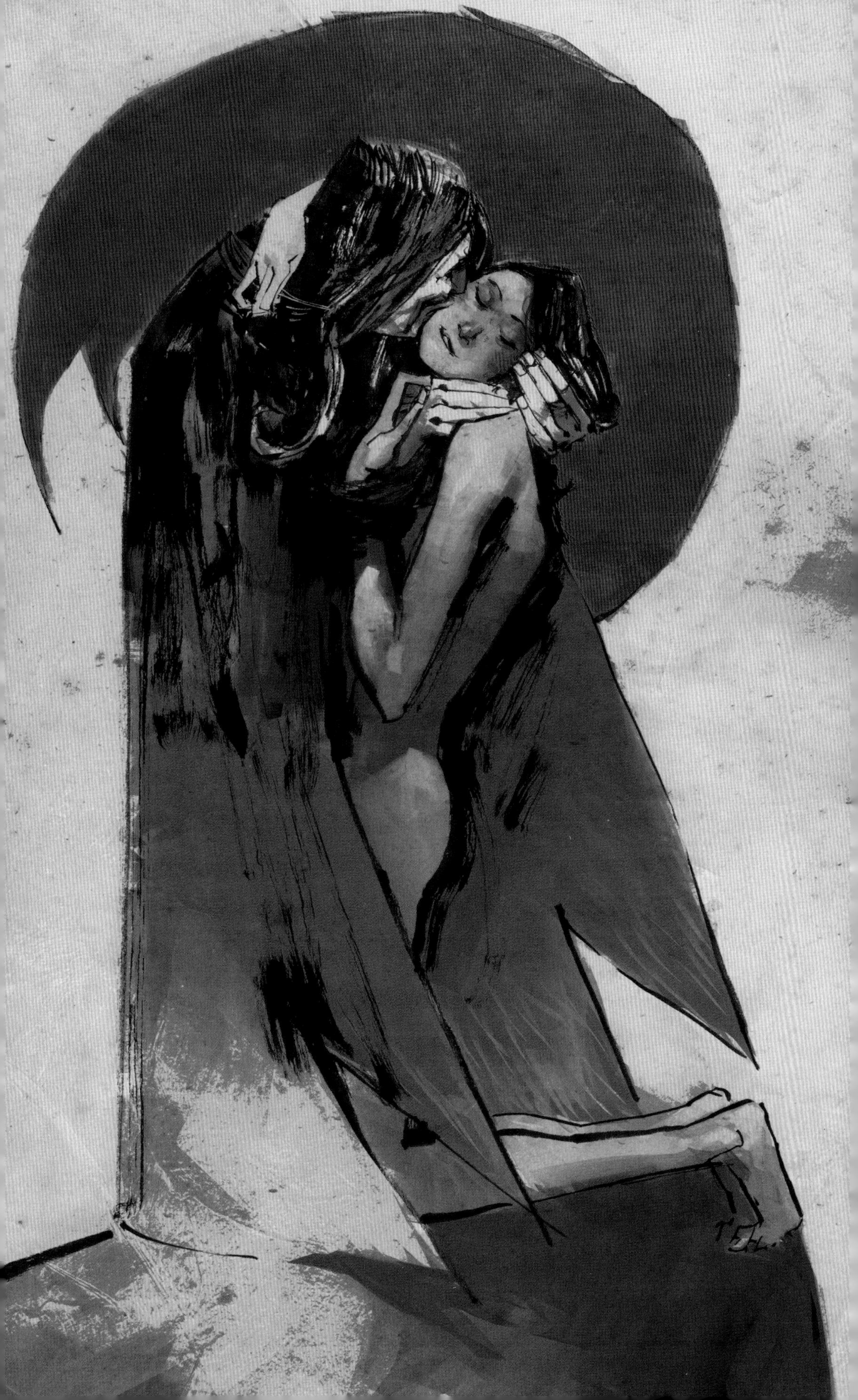

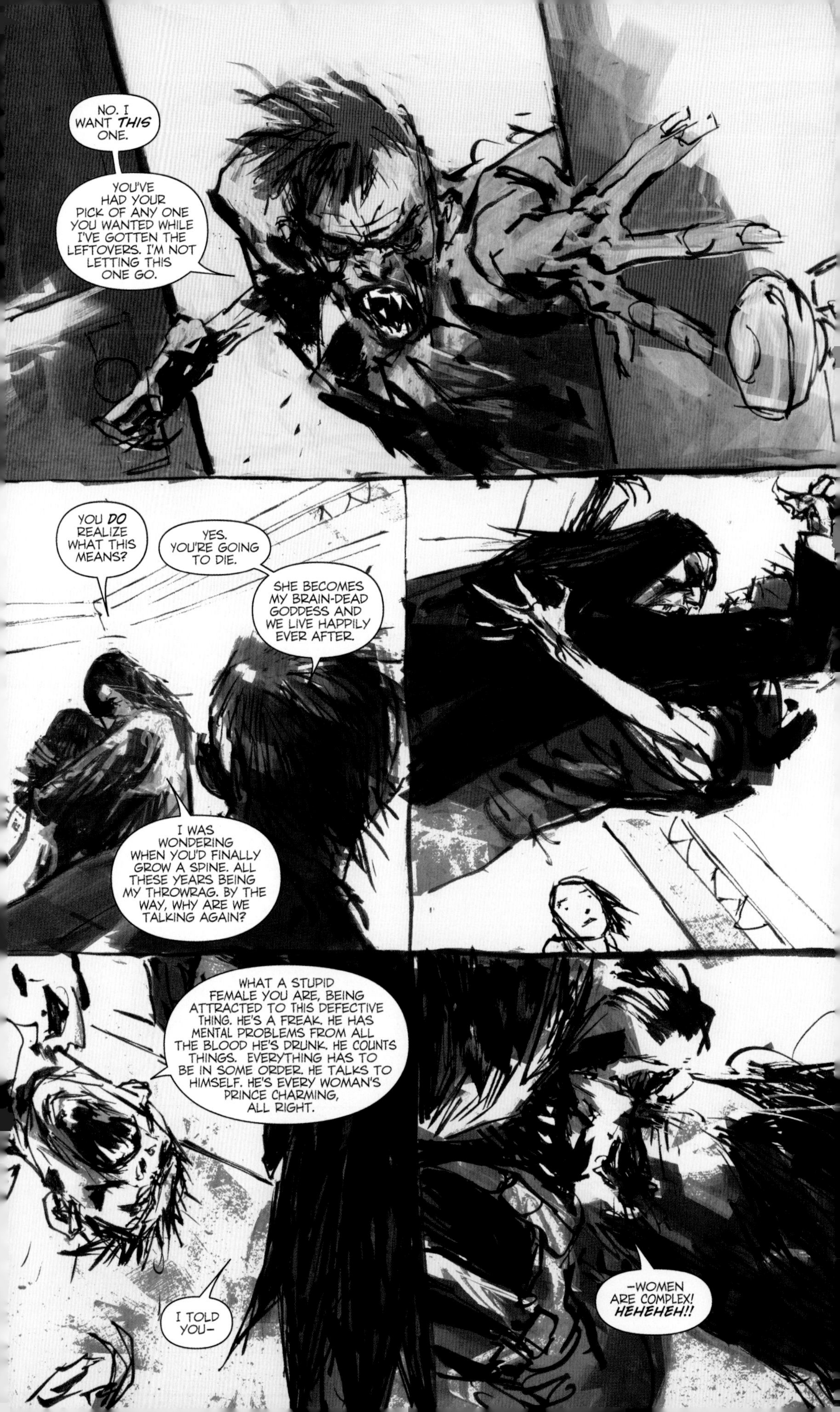
NO. I WANT *THIS* ONE.
YOU'VE HAD YOUR PICK OF ANY ONE YOU WANTED WHILE I'VE GOTTEN THE LEFTOVERS. I'M NOT LETTING THIS ONE GO.
YOU *DO* REALIZE WHAT THIS MEANS?
YES. YOU'RE GOING TO DIE.
SHE BECOMES MY BRAIN-DEAD GODDESS AND WE LIVE HAPPILY EVER AFTER.
I WAS WONDERING WHEN YOU'D FINALLY GROW A SPINE. ALL THESE YEARS BEING MY THROWRAG. BY THE WAY, WHY ARE WE TALKING AGAIN?
WHAT A STUPID FEMALE YOU ARE, BEING ATTRACTED TO THIS DEFECTIVE THING. HE'S A FREAK. HE HAS MENTAL PROBLEMS FROM ALL THE BLOOD HE'S DRUNK. HE COUNTS THINGS. EVERYTHING HAS TO BE IN SOME ORDER. HE TALKS TO HIMSELF. HE'S EVERY WOMAN'S PRINCE CHARMING, ALL RIGHT.
I TOLD YOU–
–WOMEN ARE COMPLEX! ***HEHEHEH!!***

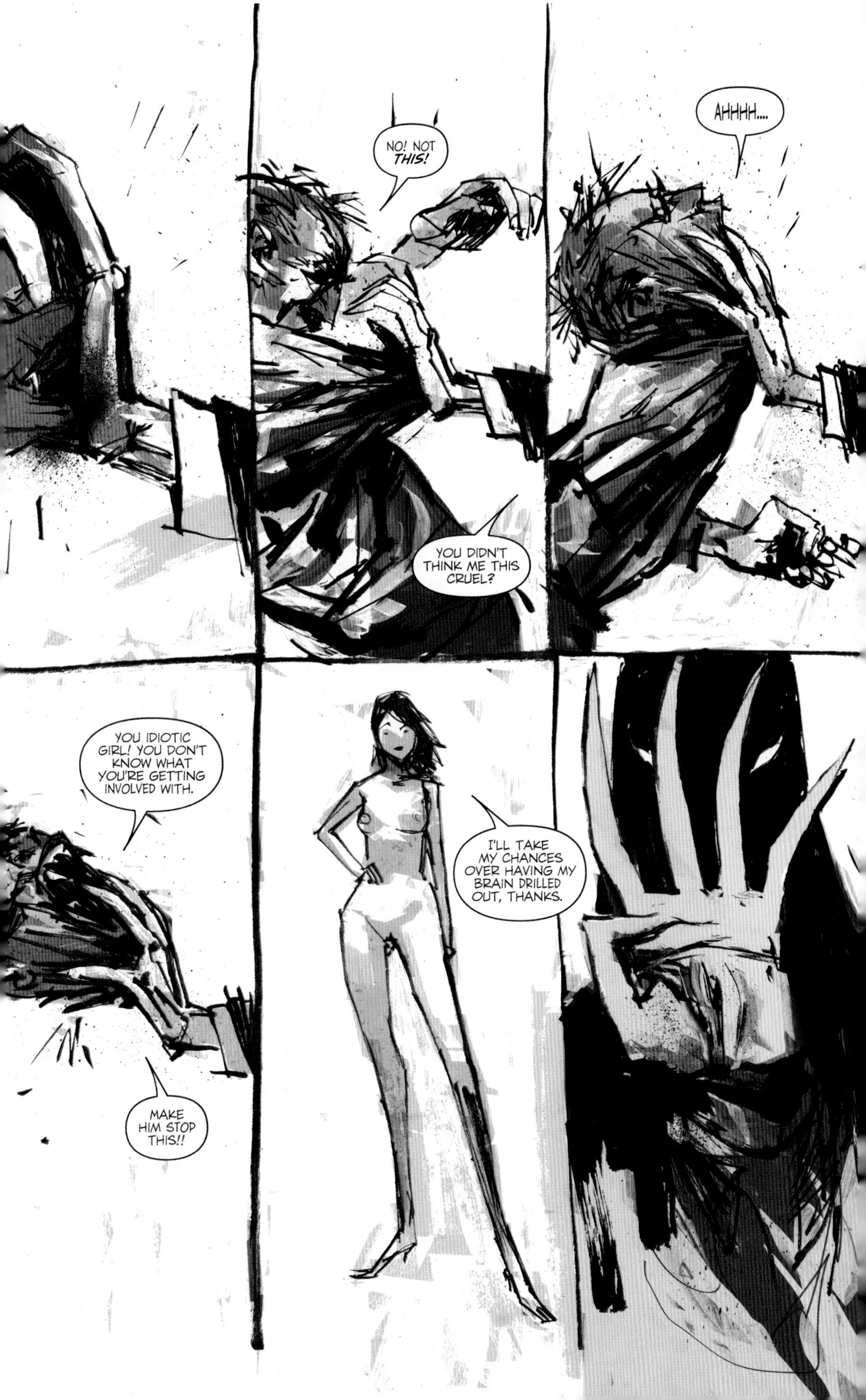
NO! NOT THIS!
YOU DIDN'T THINK ME THIS CRUEL?
AHHHH....
YOU IDIOTIC GIRL! YOU DON'T KNOW WHAT YOU'RE GETTING INVOLVED WITH.
MAKE HIM STOP THIS!!
I'LL TAKE MY CHANCES OVER HAVING MY BRAIN DRILLED OUT, THANKS.

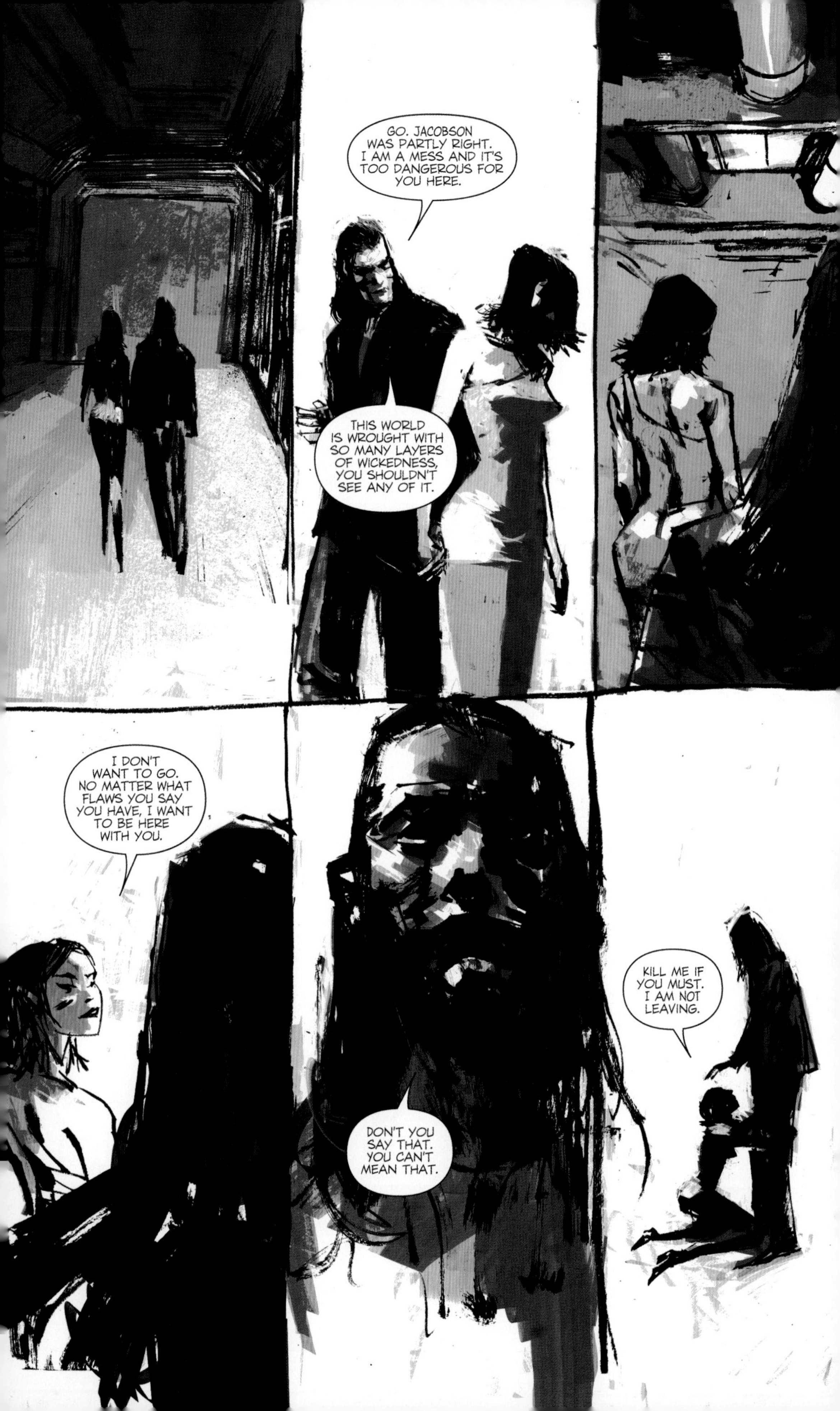
GO. JACOBSON WAS PARTLY RIGHT. I AM A MESS AND IT'S TOO DANGEROUS FOR YOU HERE.
THIS WORLD IS WROUGHT WITH SO MANY LAYERS OF WICKEDNESS, YOU SHOULDN'T SEE ANY OF IT.
I DON'T WANT TO GO. NO MATTER WHAT FLAWS YOU SAY YOU HAVE, I WANT TO BE HERE WITH YOU.
DON'T YOU SAY THAT. YOU CAN'T MEAN THAT.
KILL ME IF YOU MUST. I AM NOT LEAVING.

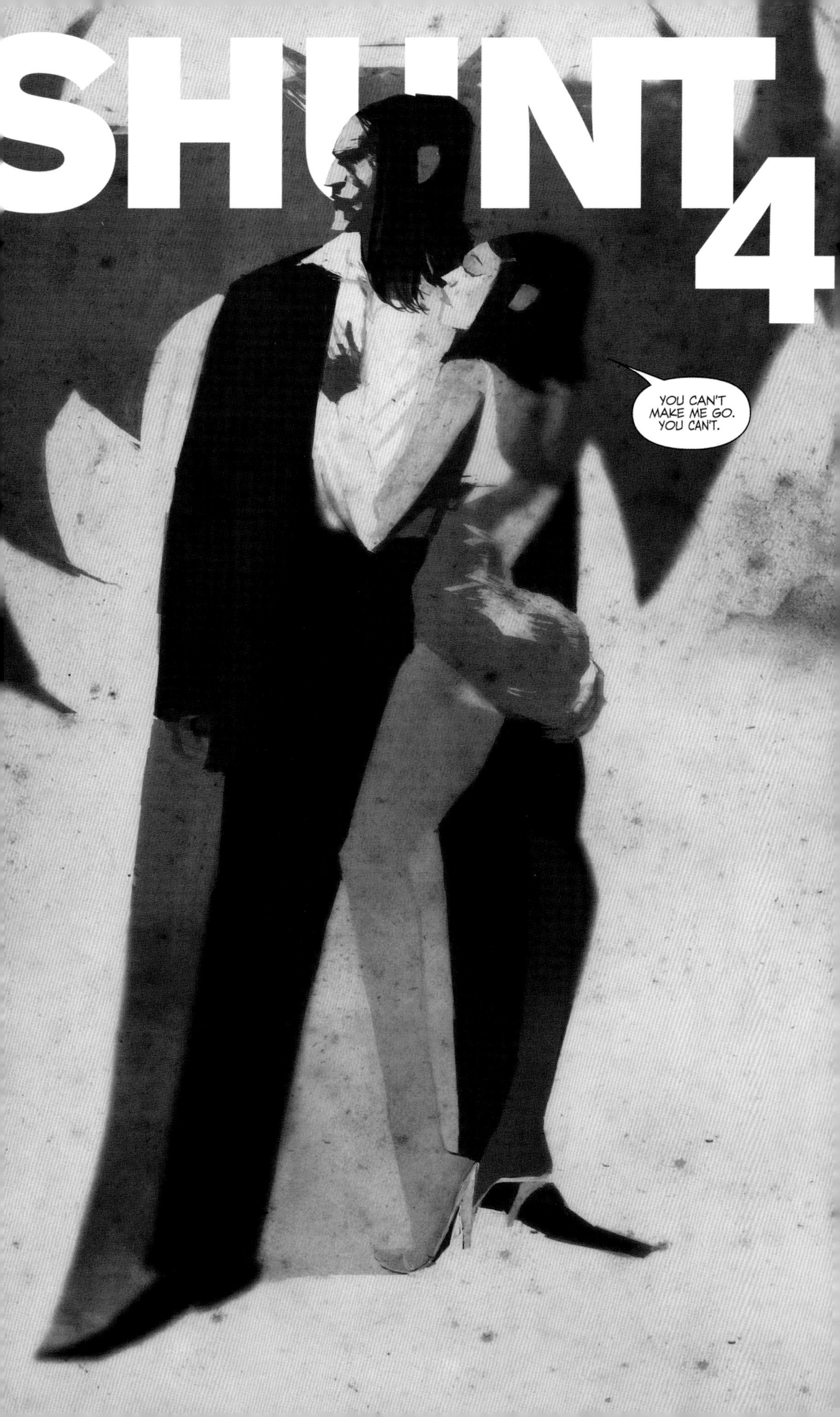
SHUNT 4
YOU CAN'T MAKE ME GO. YOU CAN'T.

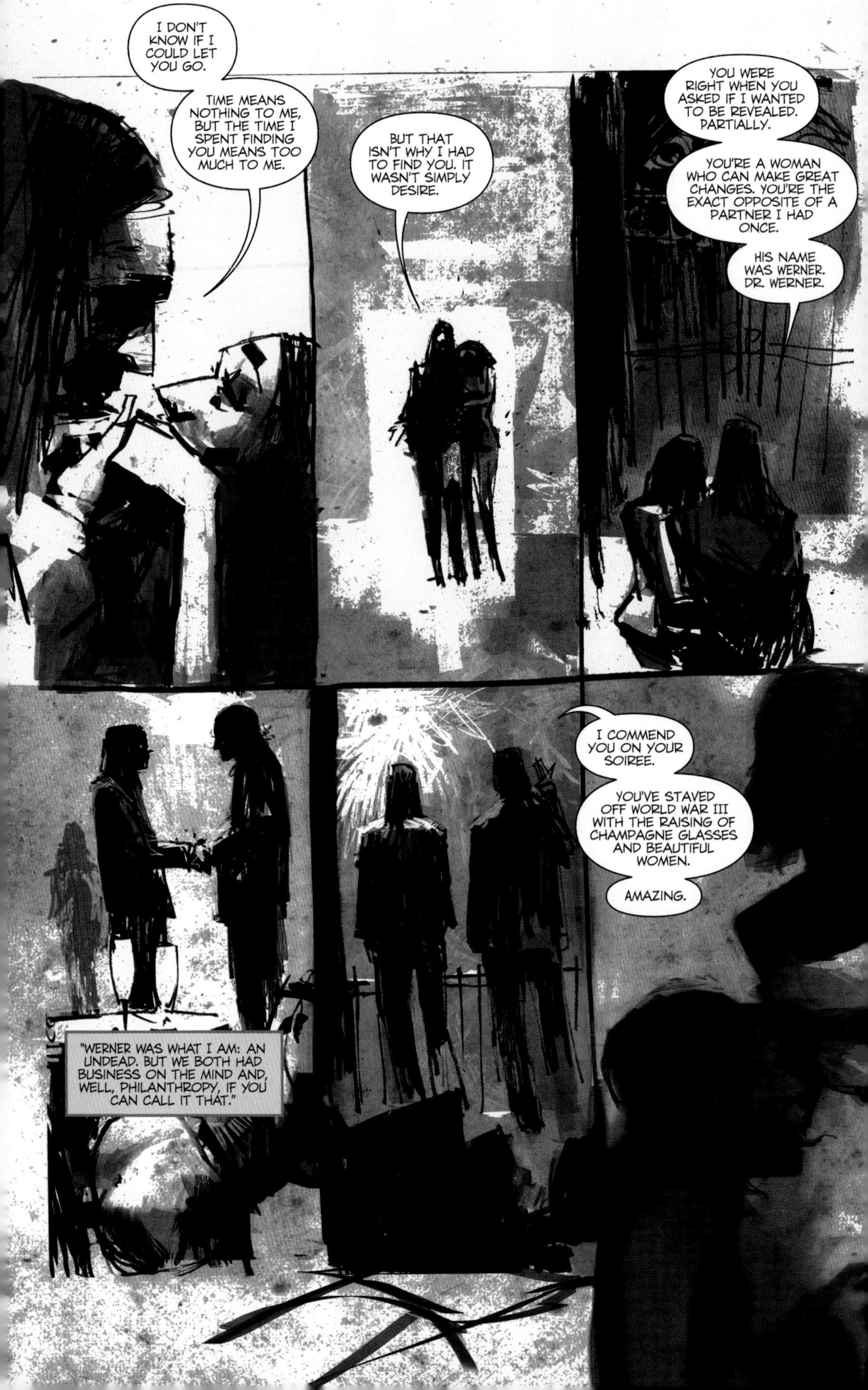
I DON'T KNOW IF I COULD LET YOU GO.
TIME MEANS NOTHING TO ME, BUT THE TIME I SPENT FINDING YOU MEANS TOO MUCH TO ME.
BUT THAT ISN'T WHY I HAD TO FIND YOU. IT WASN'T SIMPLY DESIRE.
YOU WERE RIGHT WHEN YOU ASKED IF I WANTED TO BE REVEALED. PARTIALLY.
YOU'RE A WOMAN WHO CAN MAKE GREAT CHANGES. YOU'RE THE EXACT OPPOSITE OF A PARTNER I HAD ONCE.
HIS NAME WAS WERNER. DR. WERNER.
"WERNER WAS WHAT I AM: AN UNDEAD. BUT WE BOTH HAD BUSINESS ON THE MIND AND, WELL, PHILANTHROPY, IF YOU CAN CALL IT THAT."
I COMMEND YOU ON YOUR SOIREE.
YOU'VE STAVED OFF WORLD WAR III WITH THE RAISING OF CHAMPAGNE GLASSES AND BEAUTIFUL WOMEN.
AMAZING.

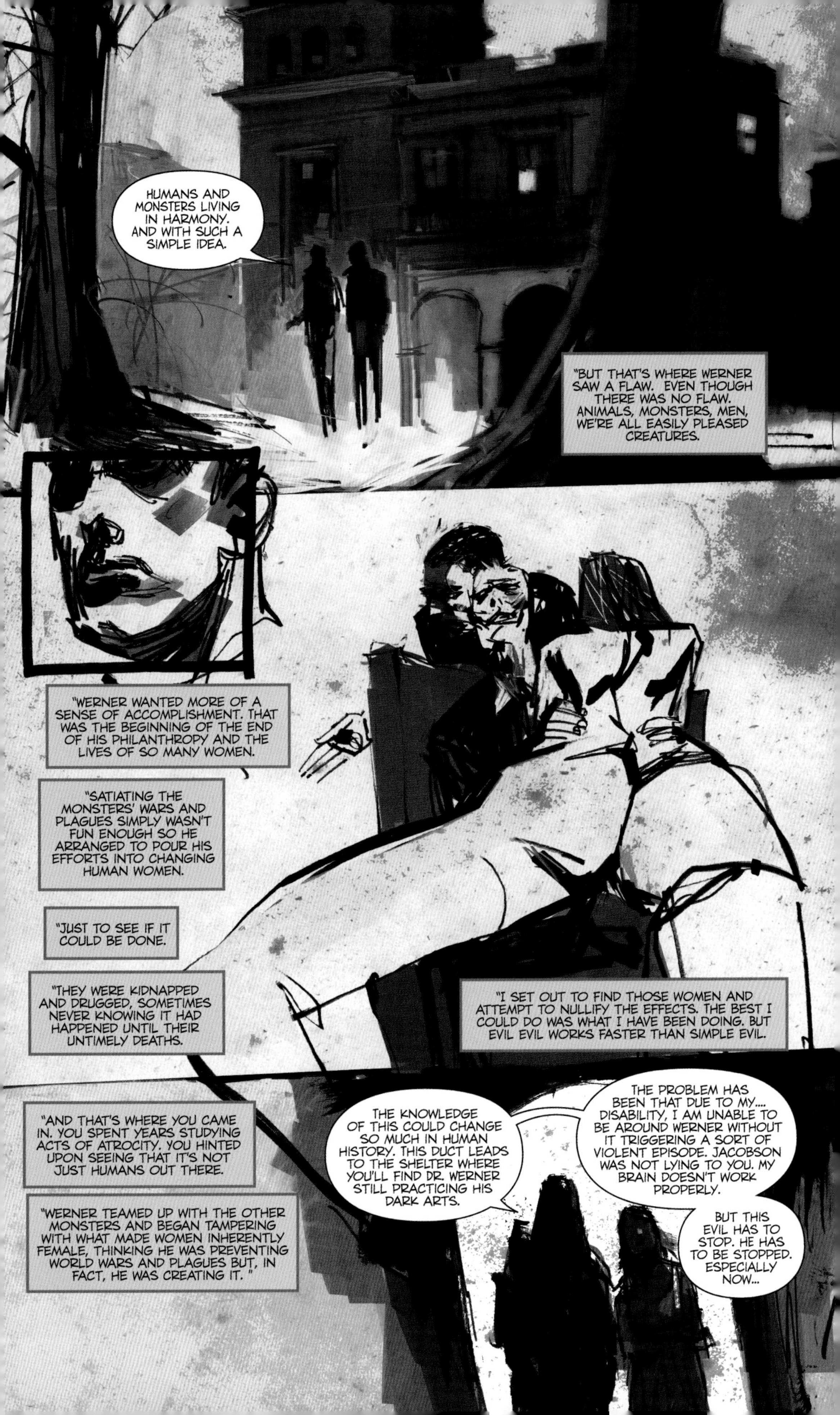
HUMANS AND MONSTERS LIVING IN HARMONY. AND WITH SUCH A SIMPLE IDEA.
"BUT THAT'S WHERE WERNER SAW A FLAW. EVEN THOUGH THERE WAS NO FLAW. ANIMALS, MONSTERS, MEN, WE'RE ALL EASILY PLEASED CREATURES.
"WERNER WANTED MORE OF A SENSE OF ACCOMPLISHMENT. THAT WAS THE BEGINNING OF THE END OF HIS PHILANTHROPY AND THE LIVES OF SO MANY WOMEN.
"SATIATING THE MONSTERS' WARS AND PLAGUES SIMPLY WASN'T FUN ENOUGH SO HE ARRANGED TO POUR HIS EFFORTS INTO CHANGING HUMAN WOMEN.
"JUST TO SEE IF IT COULD BE DONE.
"THEY WERE KIDNAPPED AND DRUGGED, SOMETIMES NEVER KNOWING IT HAD HAPPENED UNTIL THEIR UNTIMELY DEATHS.
"I SET OUT TO FIND THOSE WOMEN AND ATTEMPT TO NULLIFY THE EFFECTS. THE BEST I COULD DO WAS WHAT I HAVE BEEN DOING. BUT EVIL EVIL WORKS FASTER THAN SIMPLE EVIL.
"AND THAT'S WHERE YOU CAME IN. YOU SPENT YEARS STUDYING ACTS OF ATROCITY. YOU HINTED UPON SEEING THAT IT'S NOT JUST HUMANS OUT THERE.
"WERNER TEAMED UP WITH THE OTHER MONSTERS AND BEGAN TAMPERING WITH WHAT MADE WOMEN INHERENTLY FEMALE, THINKING HE WAS PREVENTING WORLD WARS AND PLAGUES BUT, IN FACT, HE WAS CREATING IT."
THE KNOWLEDGE OF THIS COULD CHANGE SO MUCH IN HUMAN HISTORY. THIS DUCT LEADS TO THE SHELTER WHERE YOU'LL FIND DR. WERNER STILL PRACTICING HIS DARK ARTS.
THE PROBLEM HAS BEEN THAT DUE TO MY.... DISABILITY, I AM UNABLE TO BE AROUND WERNER WITHOUT IT TRIGGERING A SORT OF VIOLENT EPISODE. JACOBSON WAS NOT LYING TO YOU. MY BRAIN DOESN'T WORK PROPERLY.
BUT THIS EVIL HAS TO STOP. HE HAS TO BE STOPPED. ESPECIALLY NOW...

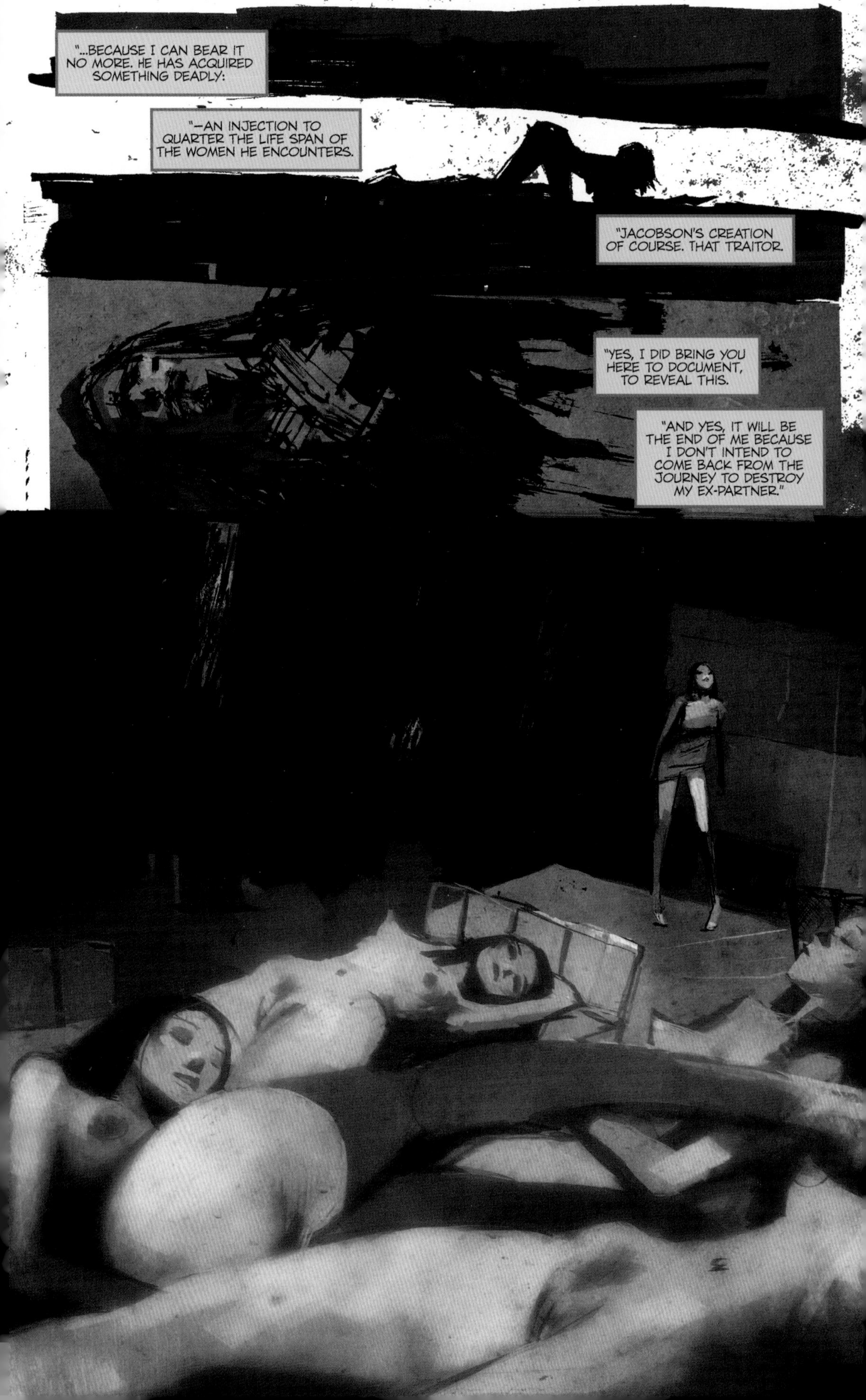
"...BECAUSE I CAN BEAR IT NO MORE. HE HAS ACQUIRED SOMETHING DEADLY:
"—AN INJECTION TO QUARTER THE LIFE SPAN OF THE WOMEN HE ENCOUNTERS.
"JACOBSON'S CREATION OF COURSE. THAT TRAITOR.
"YES, I DID BRING YOU HERE TO DOCUMENT, TO REVEAL THIS.
"AND YES, IT WILL BE THE END OF ME BECAUSE I DON'T INTEND TO COME BACK FROM THE JOURNEY TO DESTROY MY EX-PARTNER."

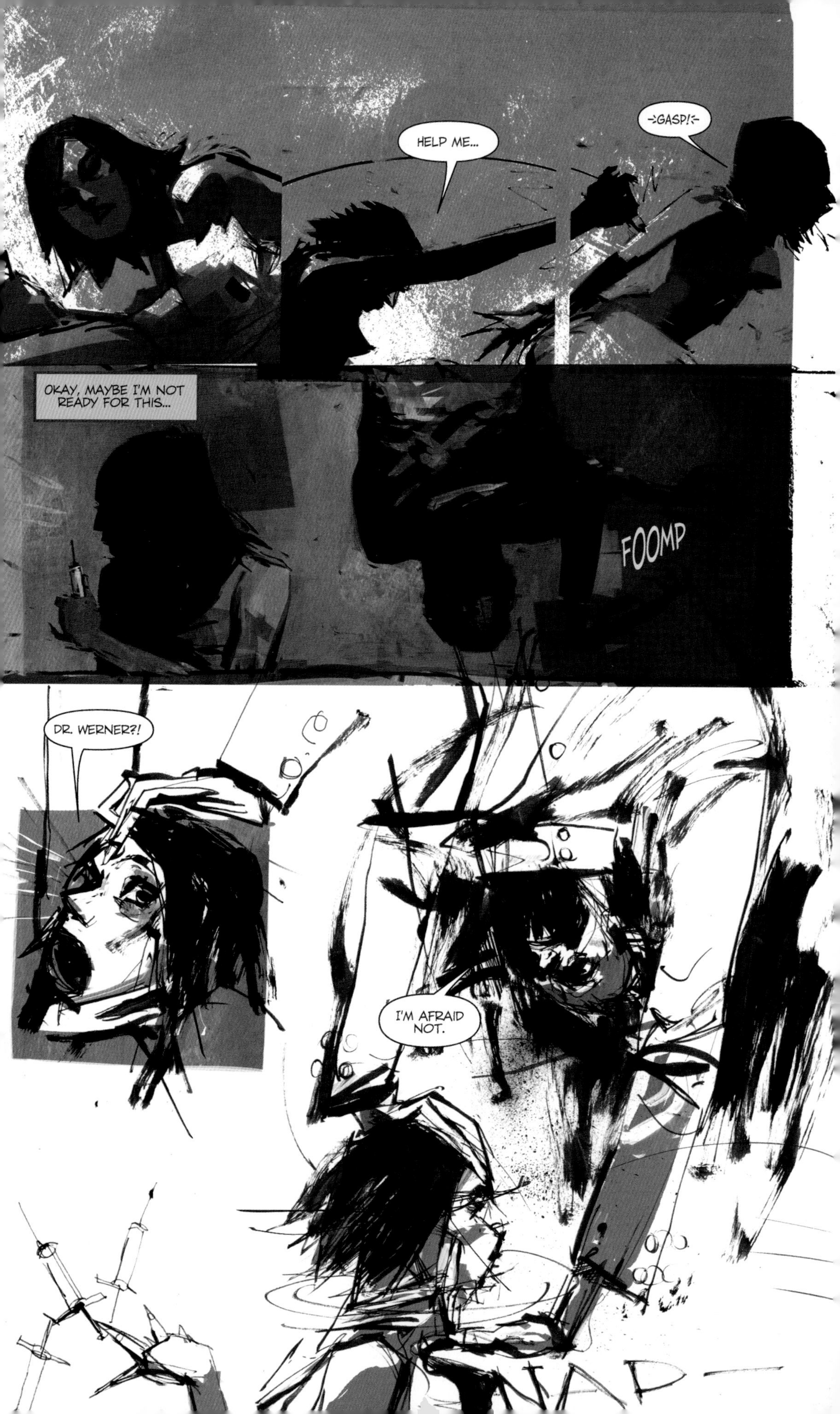
HELP ME...
-GASP!-
OKAY, MAYBE I'M NOT READY FOR THIS...
FOOMP
DR. WERNER?!
I'M AFRAID NOT.

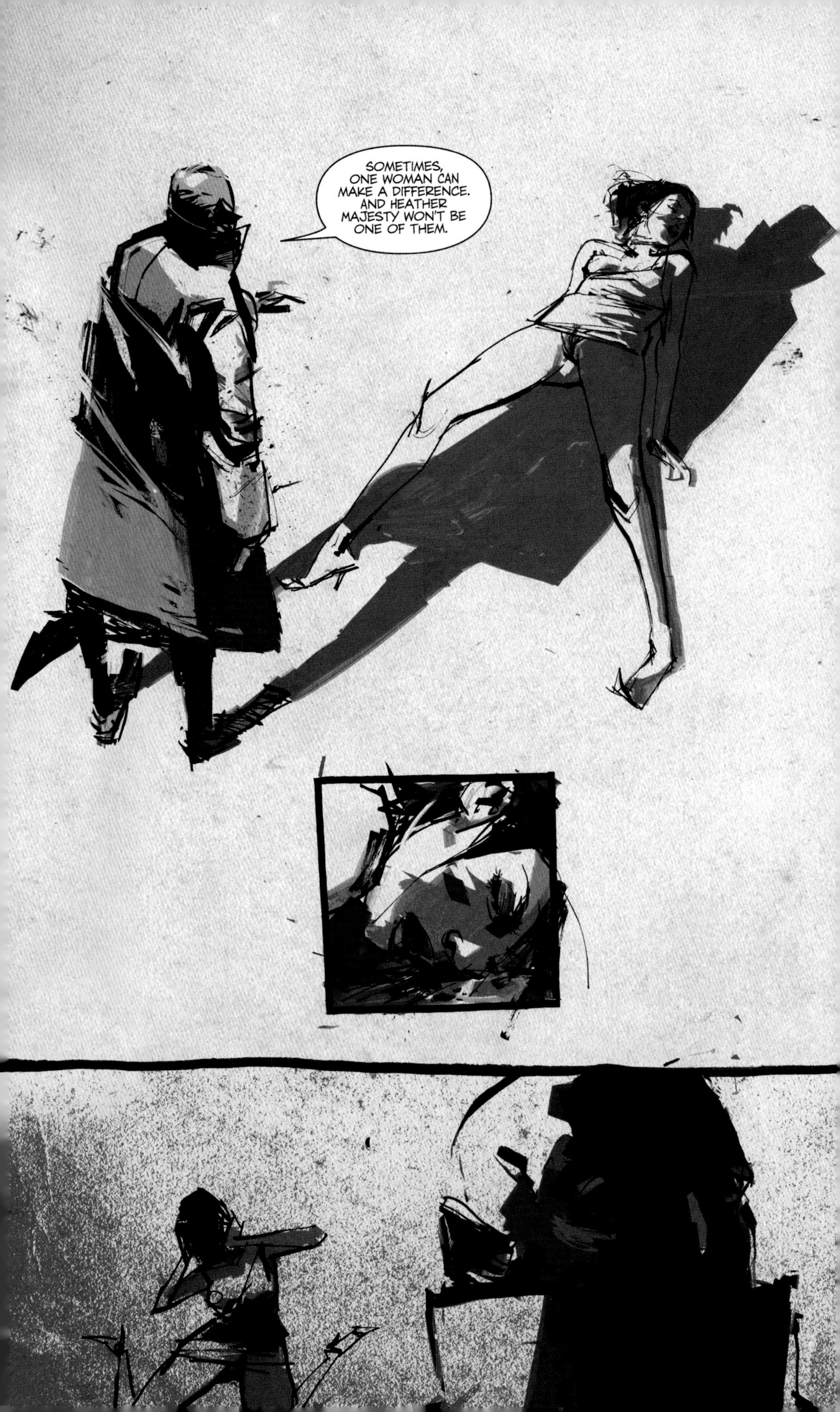
SOMETIMES, ONE WOMAN CAN MAKE A DIFFERENCE. AND HEATHER MAJESTY WON'T BE ONE OF THEM.

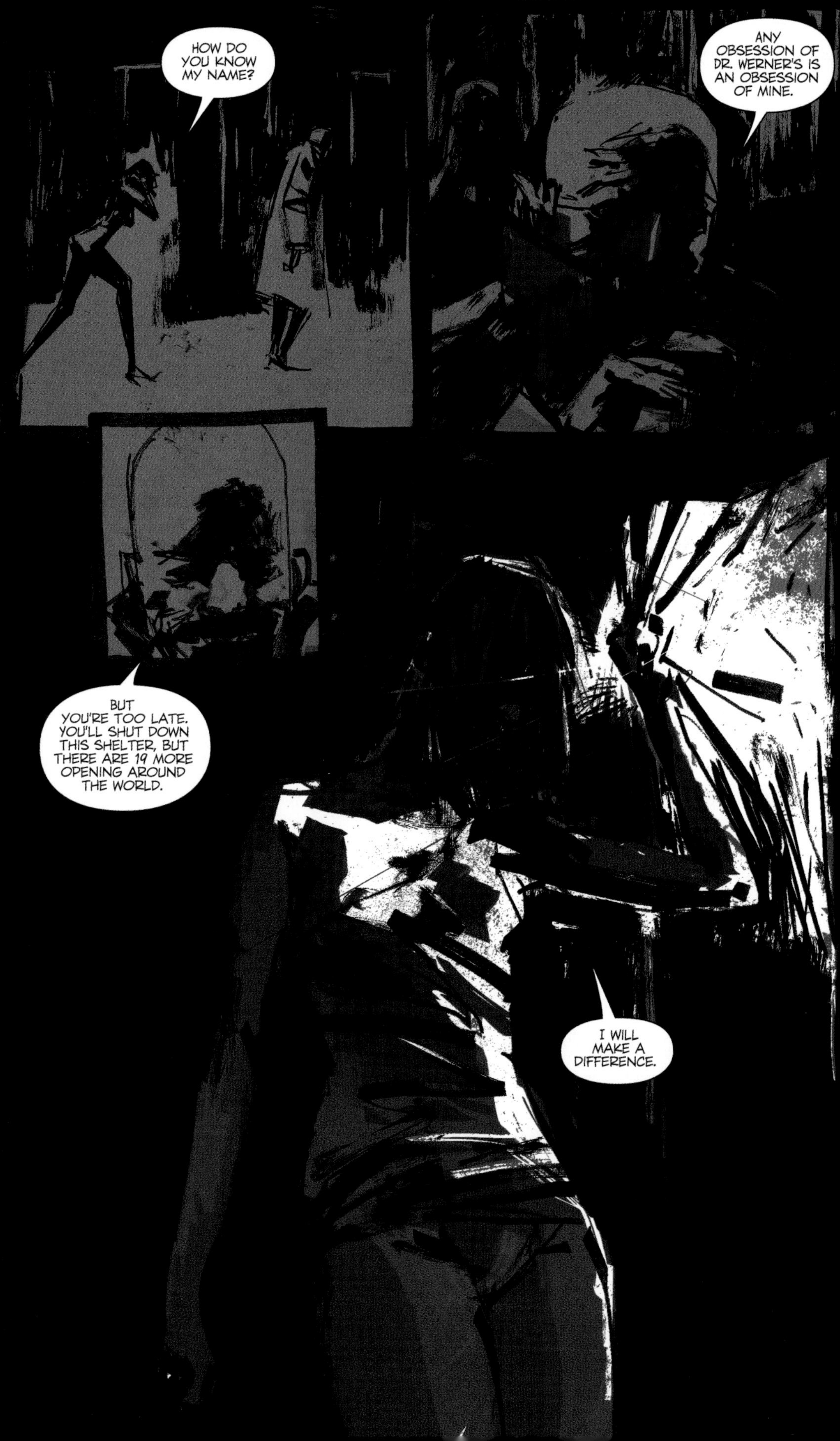
HOW DO YOU KNOW MY NAME?
ANY OBSESSION OF DR. WERNER'S IS AN OBSESSION OF MINE.
BUT YOU'RE TOO LATE. YOU'LL SHUT DOWN THIS SHELTER, BUT THERE ARE 19 MORE OPENING AROUND THE WORLD.
I WILL MAKE A DIFFERENCE.

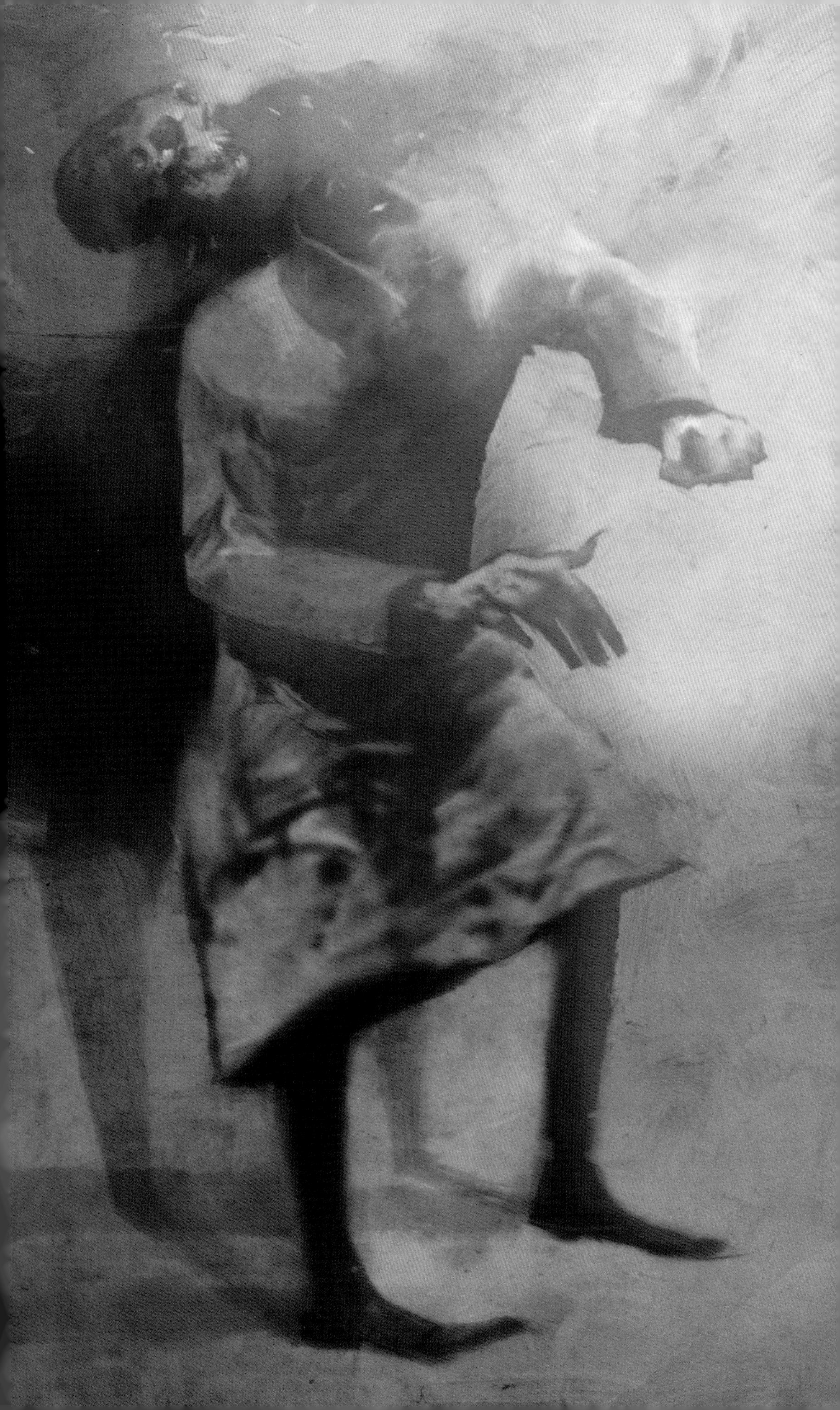

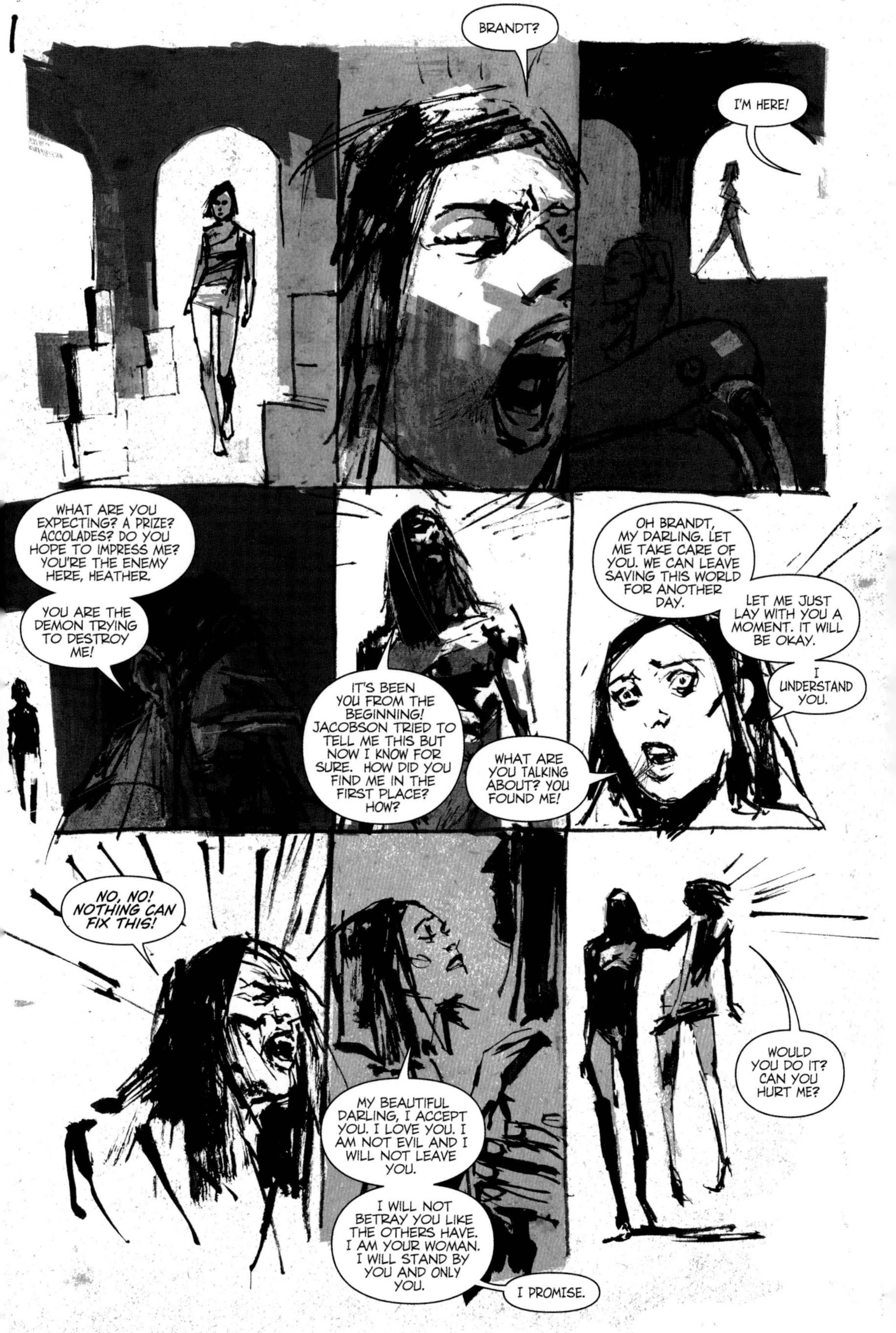
BRANDT?
I'M HERE!
WHAT ARE YOU EXPECTING? A PRIZE? ACCOLADES? DO YOU HOPE TO IMPRESS ME? YOU'RE THE ENEMY HERE, HEATHER.
YOU ARE THE DEMON TRYING TO DESTROY ME!
IT'S BEEN YOU FROM THE BEGINNING! JACOBSON TRIED TO TELL ME THIS BUT NOW I KNOW FOR SURE. HOW DID YOU FIND ME IN THE FIRST PLACE? HOW?
WHAT ARE YOU TALKING ABOUT? YOU FOUND ME!
OH BRANDT, MY DARLING. LET ME TAKE CARE OF YOU. WE CAN LEAVE SAVING THIS WORLD FOR ANOTHER DAY.
LET ME JUST LAY WITH YOU A MOMENT. IT WILL BE OKAY.
I UNDERSTAND YOU.
NO, NO! NOTHING CAN FIX THIS!
MY BEAUTIFUL DARLING, I ACCEPT YOU. I LOVE YOU. I AM NOT EVIL AND I WILL NOT LEAVE YOU.
I WILL NOT BETRAY YOU LIKE THE OTHERS HAVE. I AM YOUR WOMAN. I WILL STAND BY YOU AND ONLY YOU.
I PROMISE.
WOULD YOU DO IT? CAN YOU HURT ME?

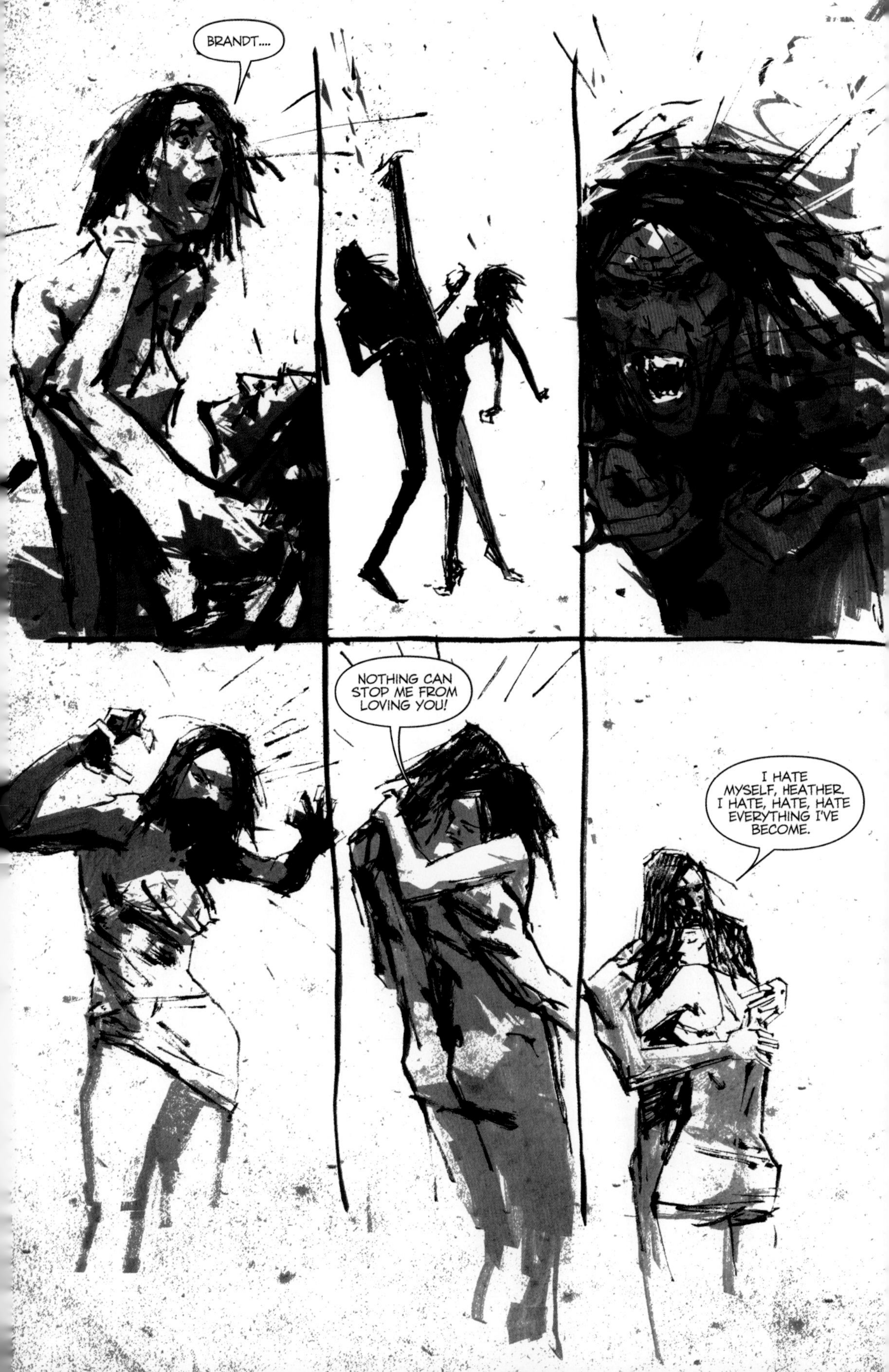
BRANDT....
NOTHING CAN STOP ME FROM LOVING YOU!
I HATE MYSELF, HEATHER. I HATE, HATE, HATE EVERYTHING I'VE BECOME.

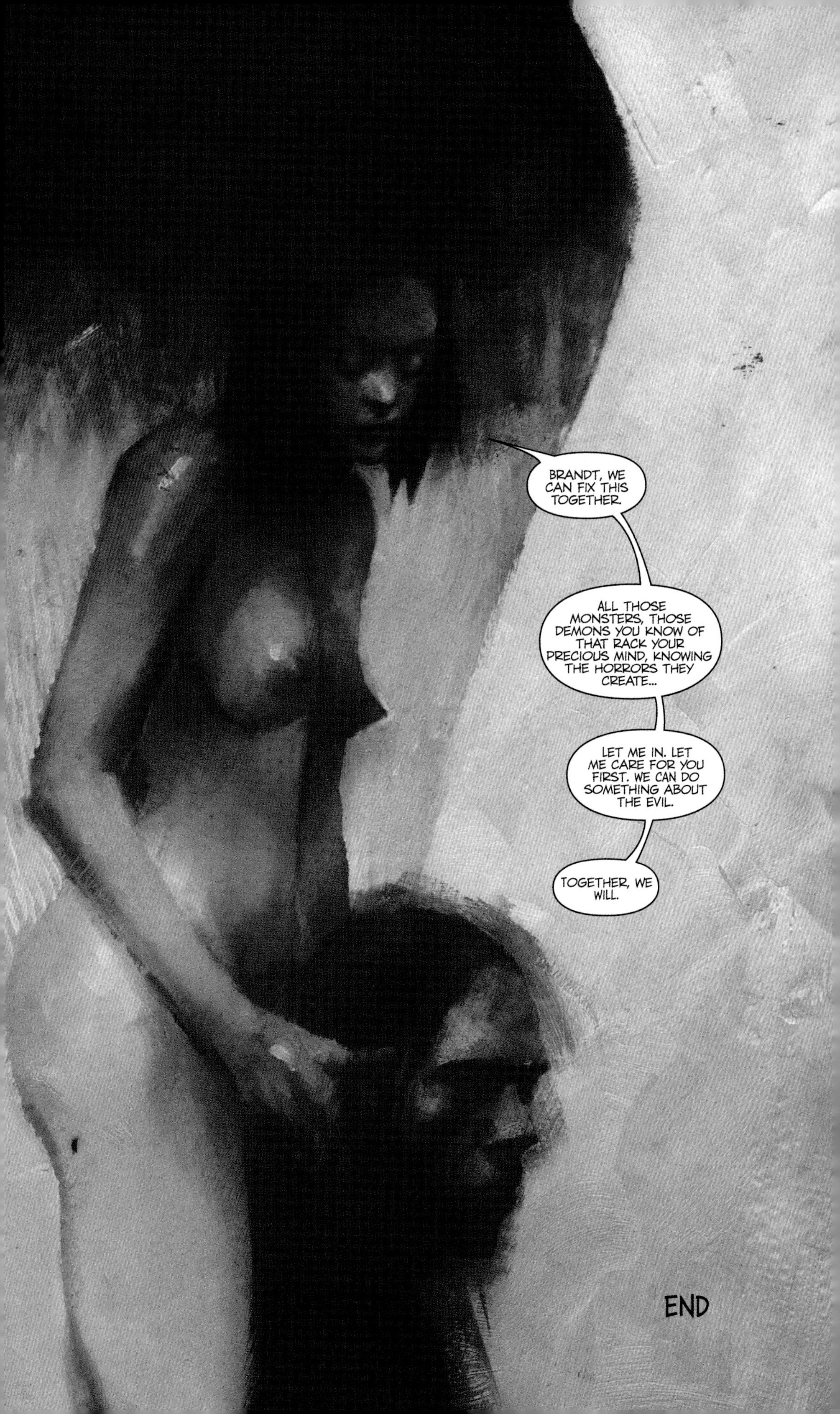
BRANDT, WE CAN FIX THIS TOGETHER.
ALL THOSE MONSTERS, THOSE DEMONS YOU KNOW OF THAT RACK YOUR PRECIOUS MIND, KNOWING THE HORRORS THEY CREATE...
LET ME IN. LET ME CARE FOR YOU FIRST. WE CAN DO SOMETHING ABOUT THE EVIL.
TOGETHER, WE WILL.
END

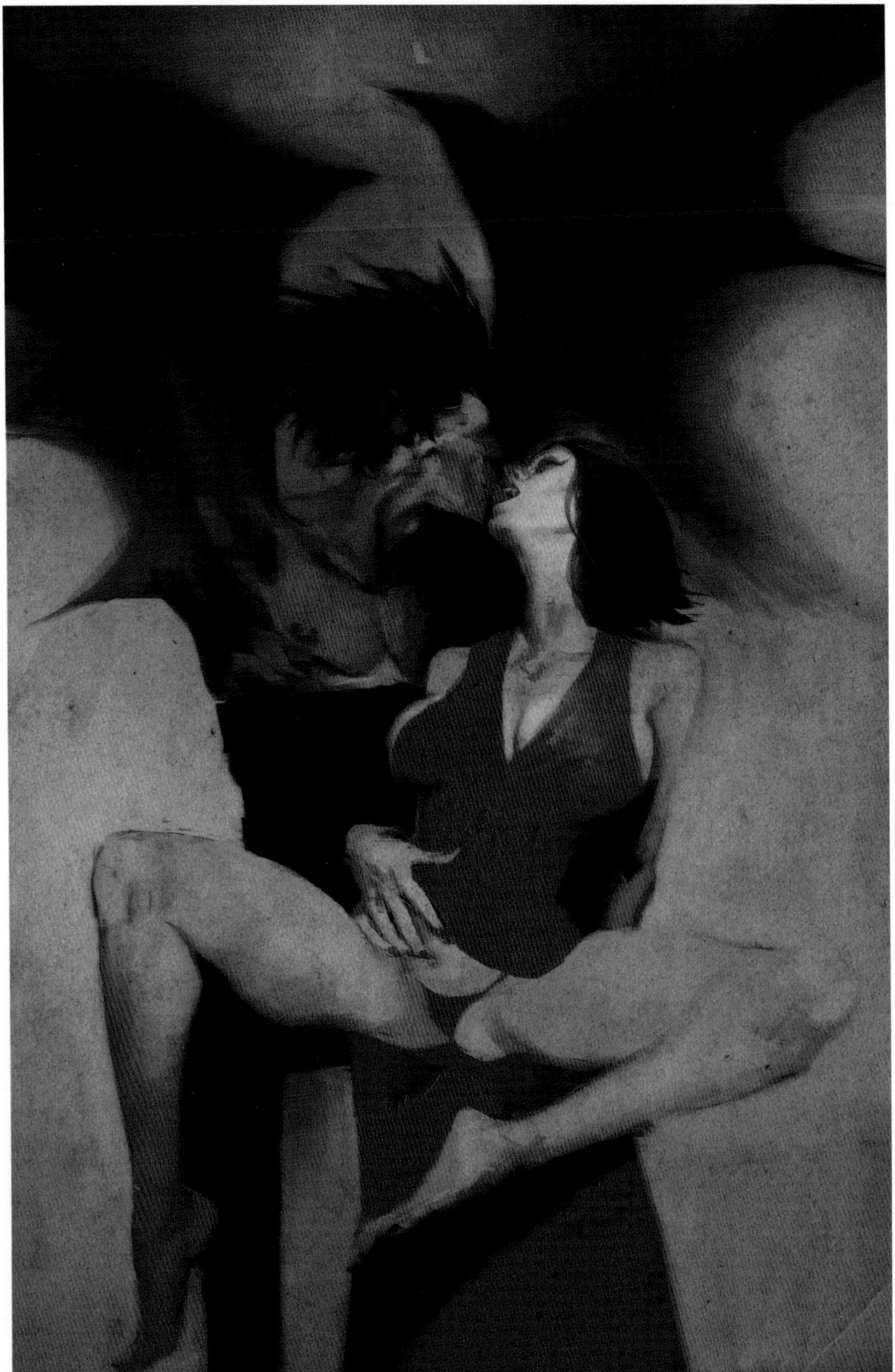

this page: issue 1 • opposite page: issue 2

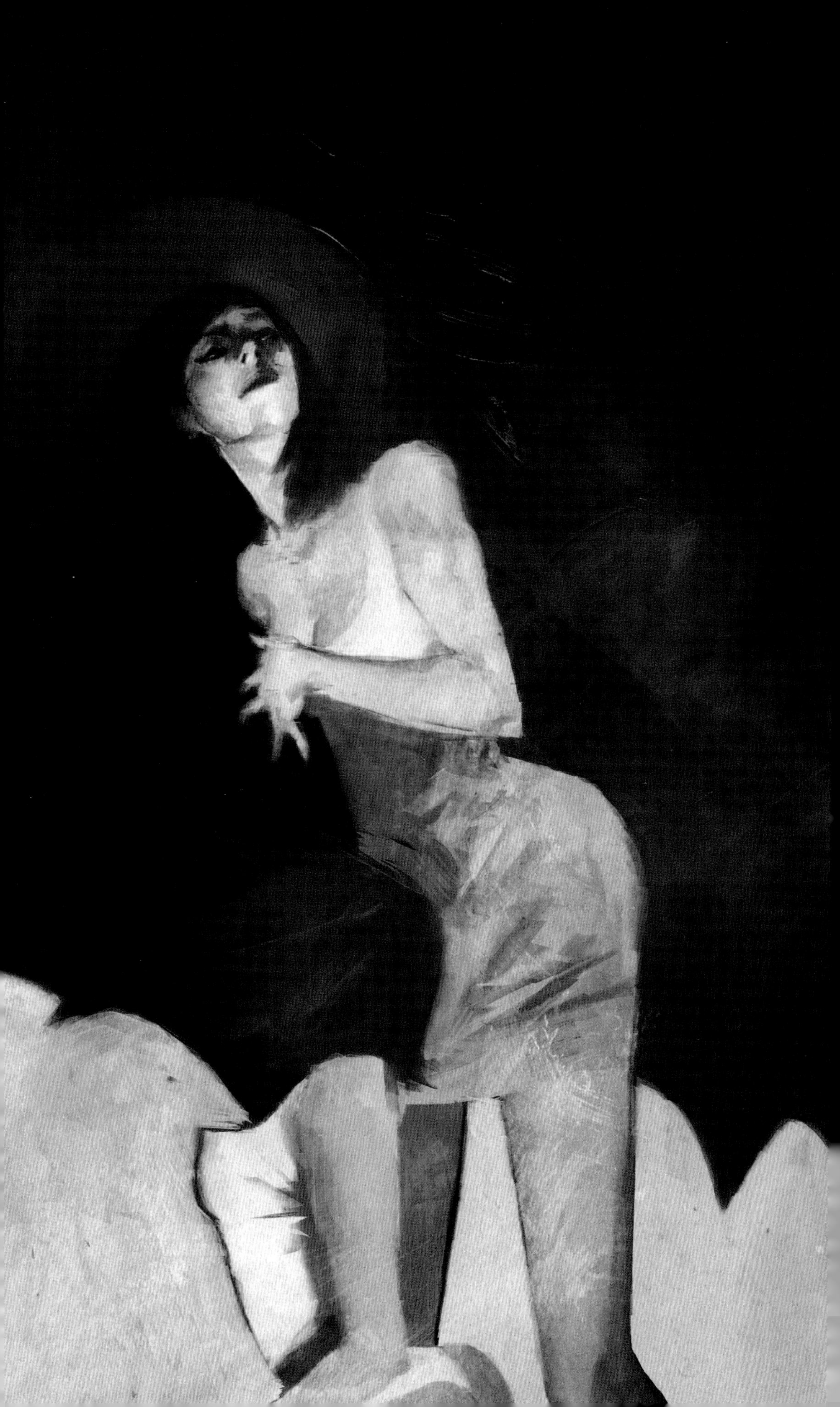

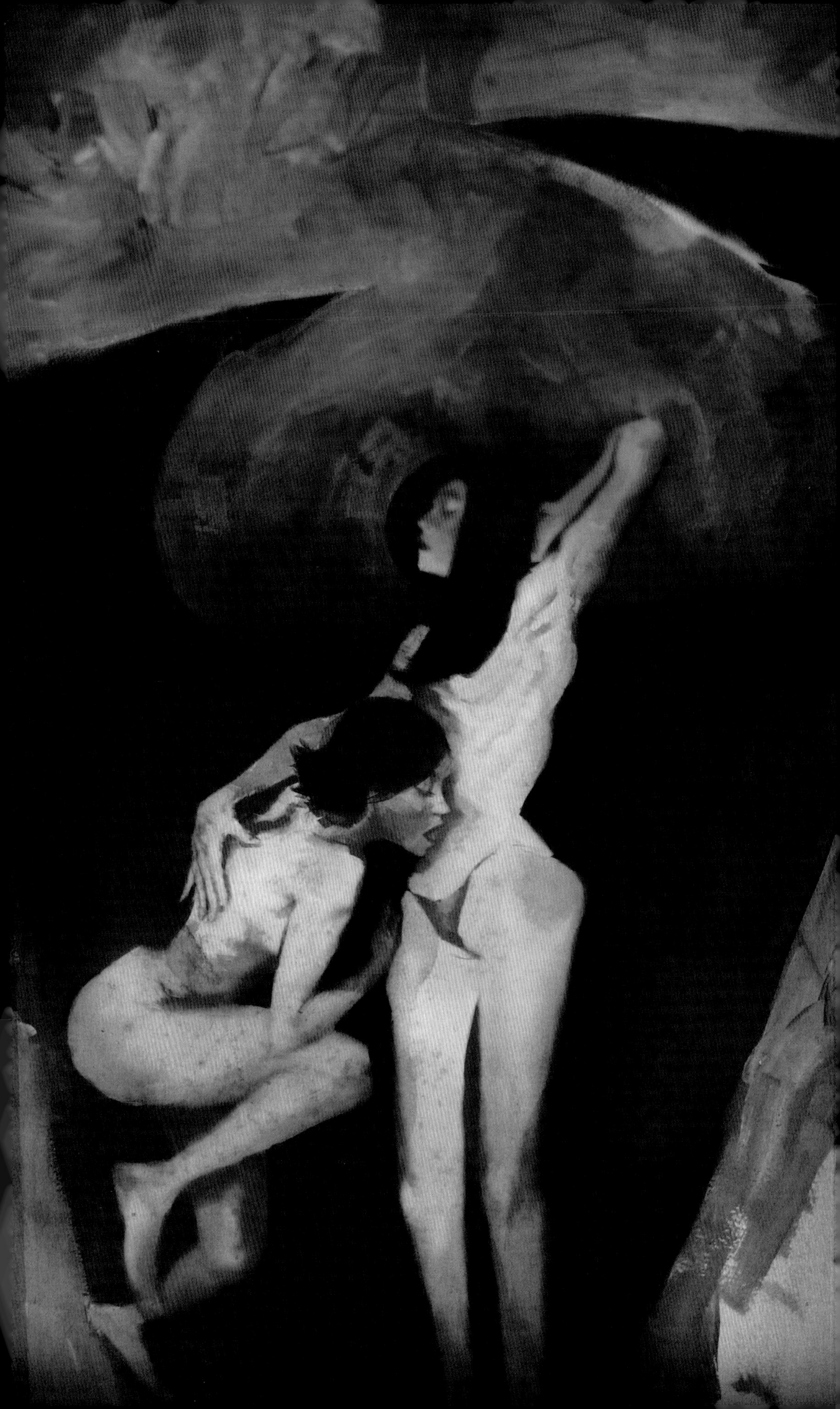

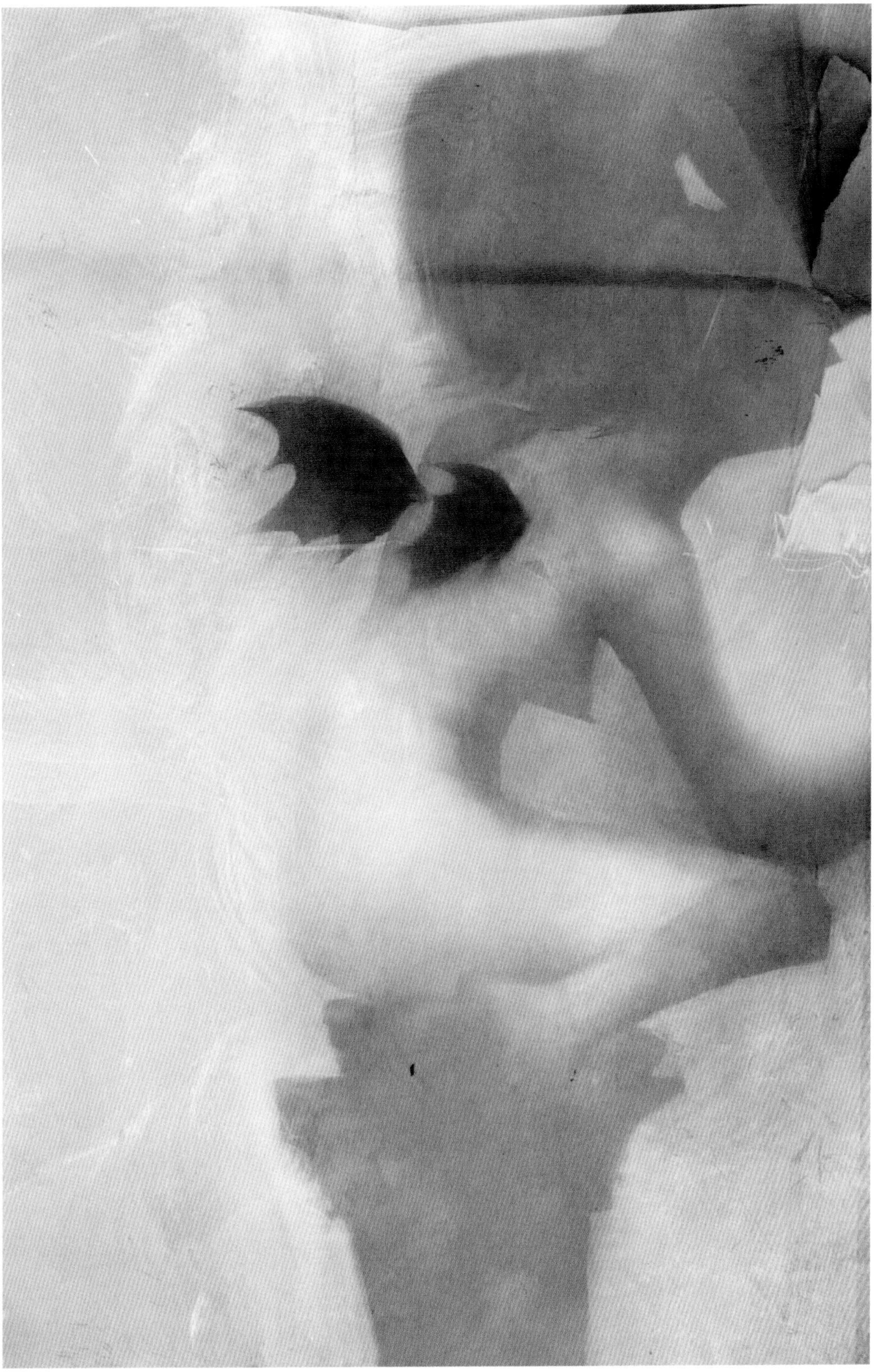

opposite page: issue 3 • this page: issue 4

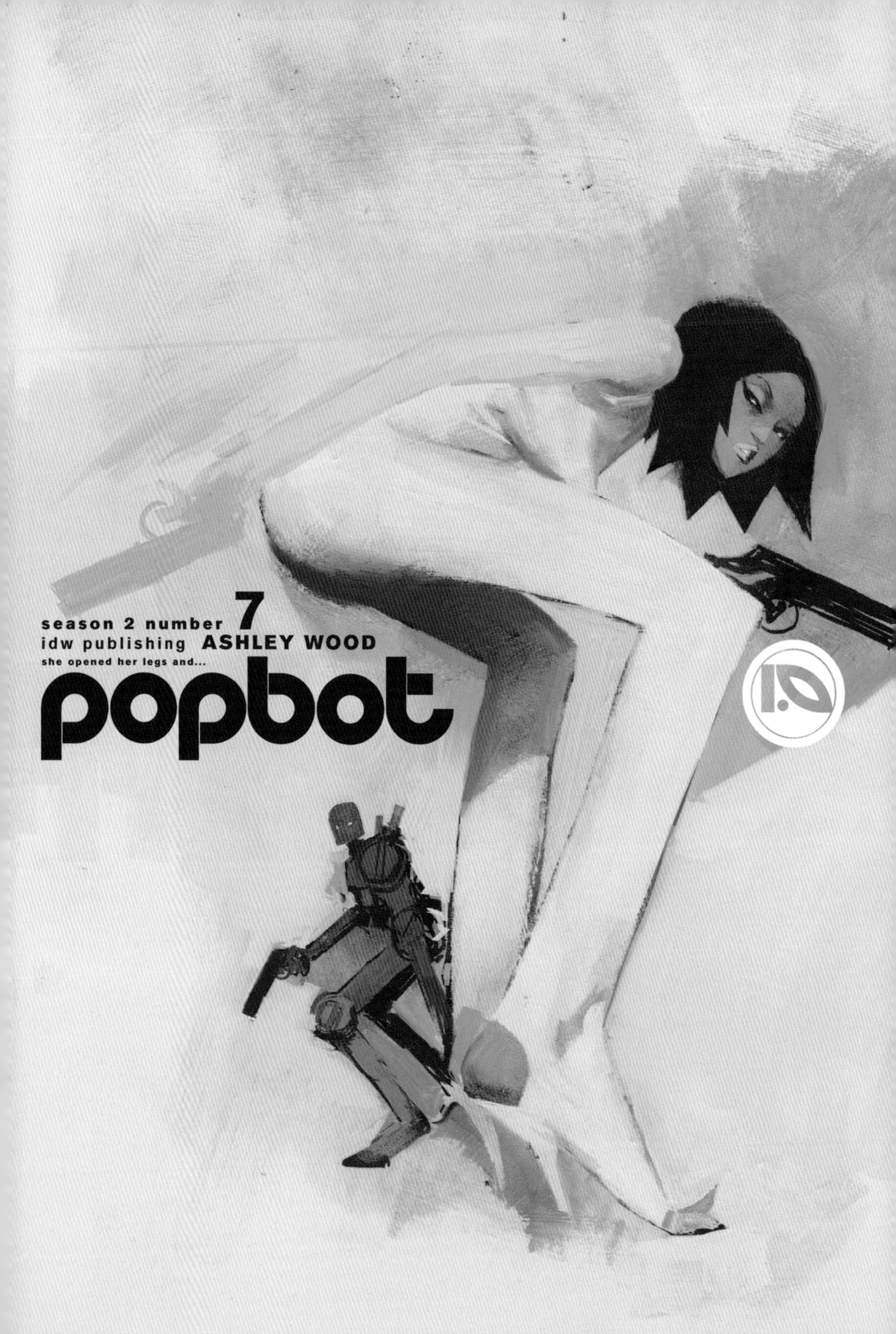
season 2 number 7
idw publishing ASHLEY WOOD
she opened her legs and...
popbot

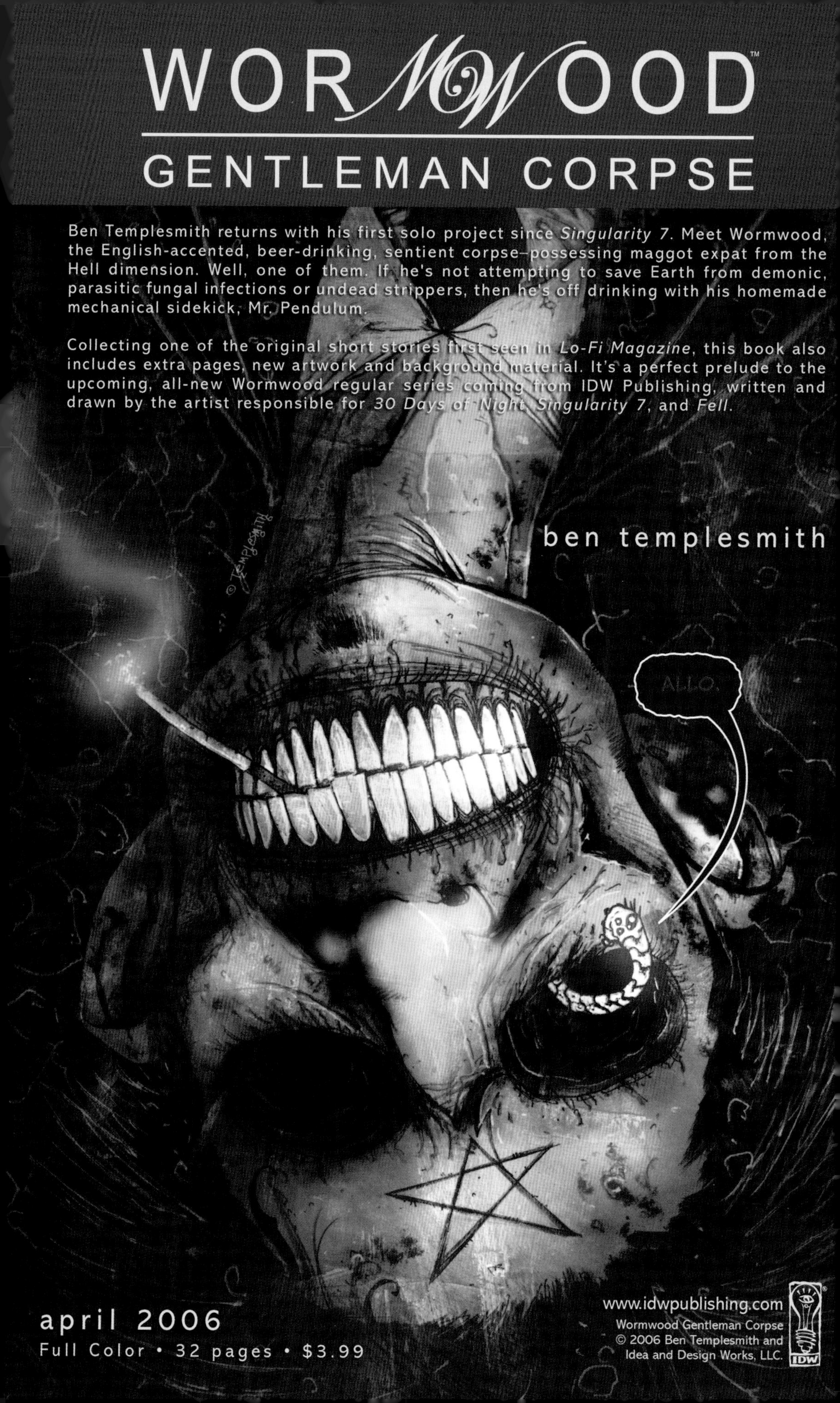

WORMWOOD™
GENTLEMAN CORPSE
Ben Templesmith returns with his first solo project since *Singularity 7*. Meet Wormwood, the English-accented, beer-drinking, sentient corpse–possessing maggot expat from the Hell dimension. Well, one of them. If he's not attempting to save Earth from demonic, parasitic fungal infections or undead strippers, then he's off drinking with his homemade mechanical sidekick, Mr. Pendulum.
Collecting one of the original short stories first seen in *Lo-Fi Magazine*, this book also includes extra pages, new artwork and background material. It's a perfect prelude to the upcoming, all-new Wormwood regular series coming from IDW Publishing, written and drawn by the artist responsible for *30 Days of Night*, *Singularity 7*, and *Fell*.
ben templesmith
ALLO.
april 2006
Full Color • 32 pages • $3.99
www.idwpublishing.com
Wormwood Gentleman Corpse
© 2006 Ben Templesmith and Idea and Design Works, LLC.

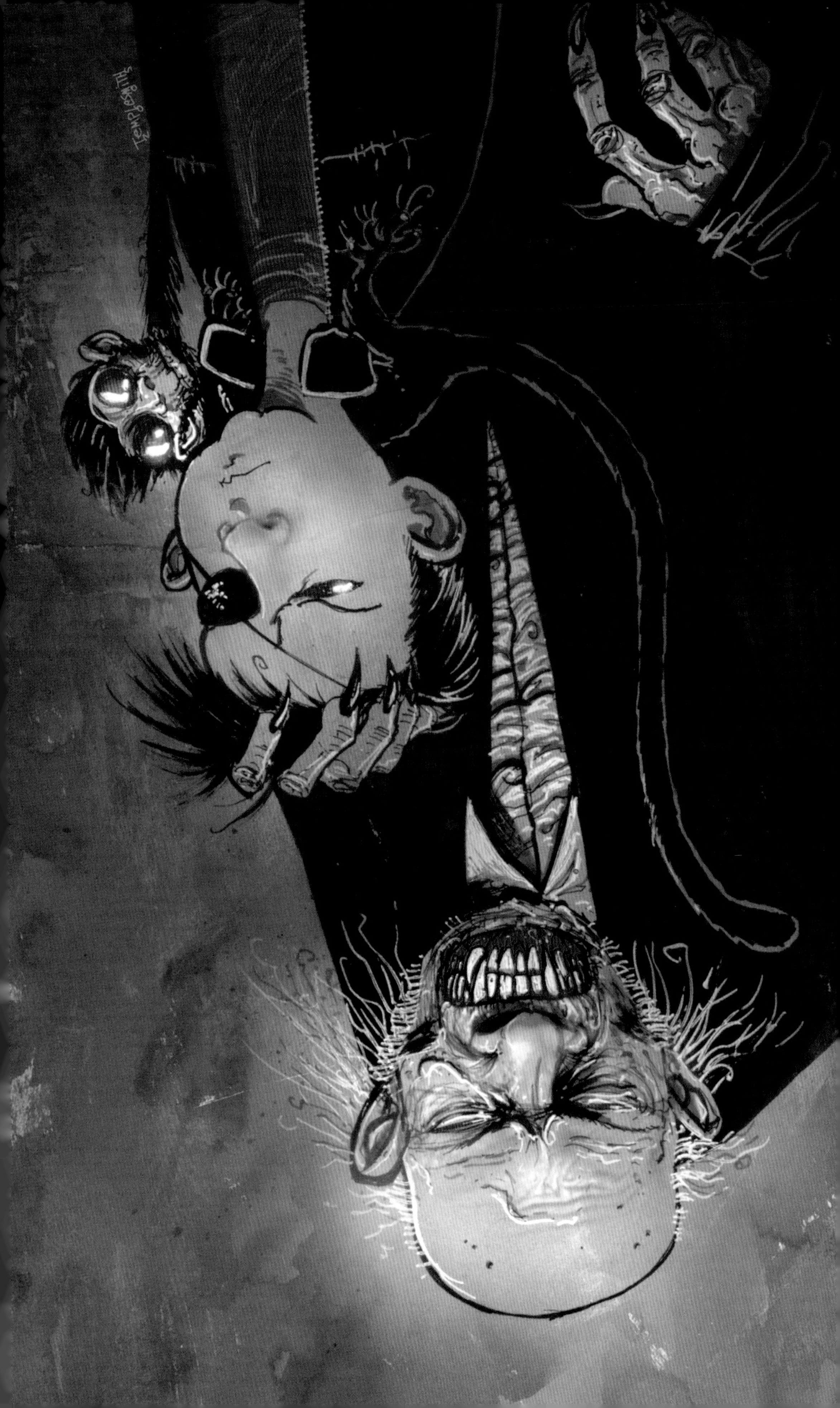

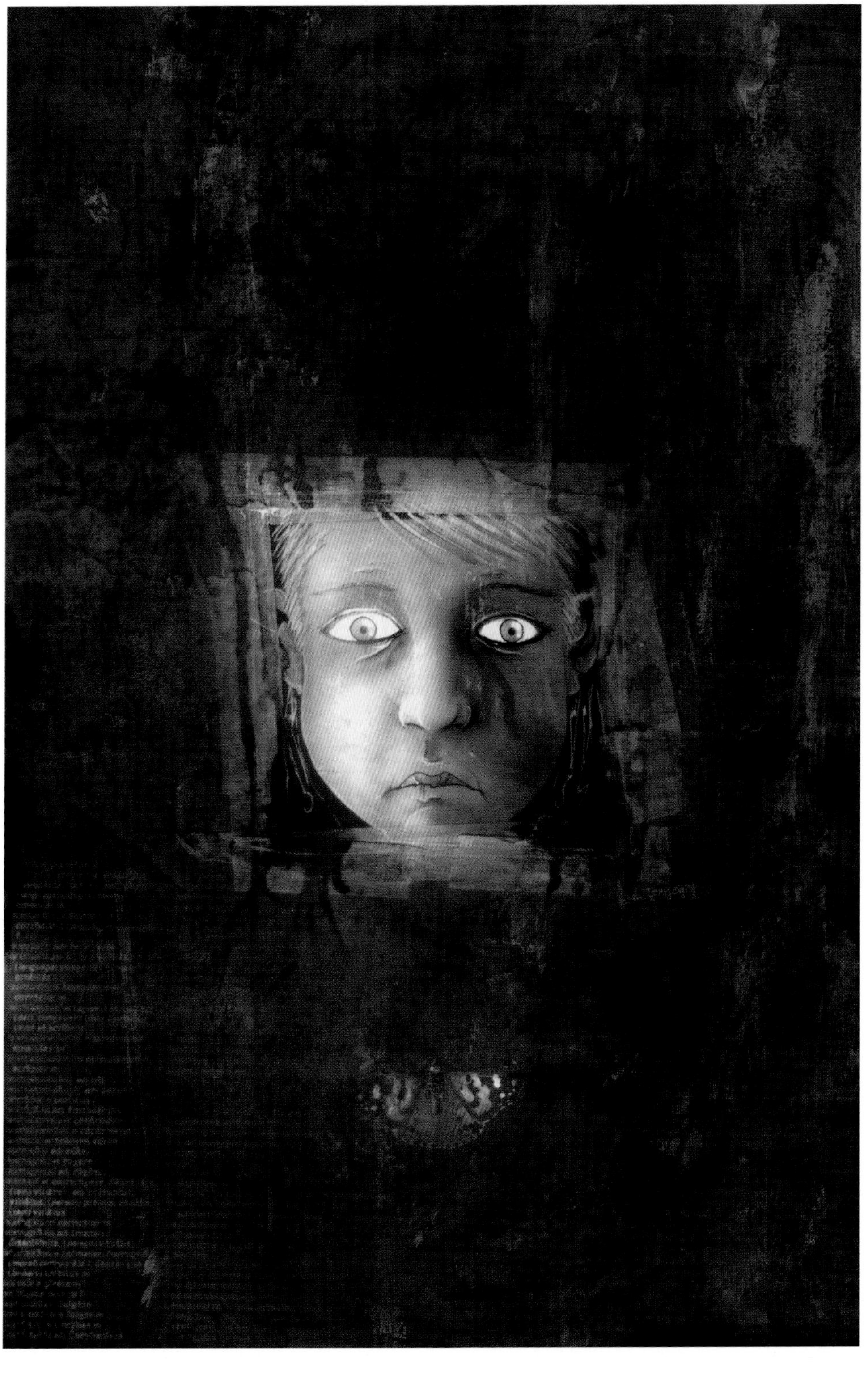

this page: issue 3 • opposite page: issue 4

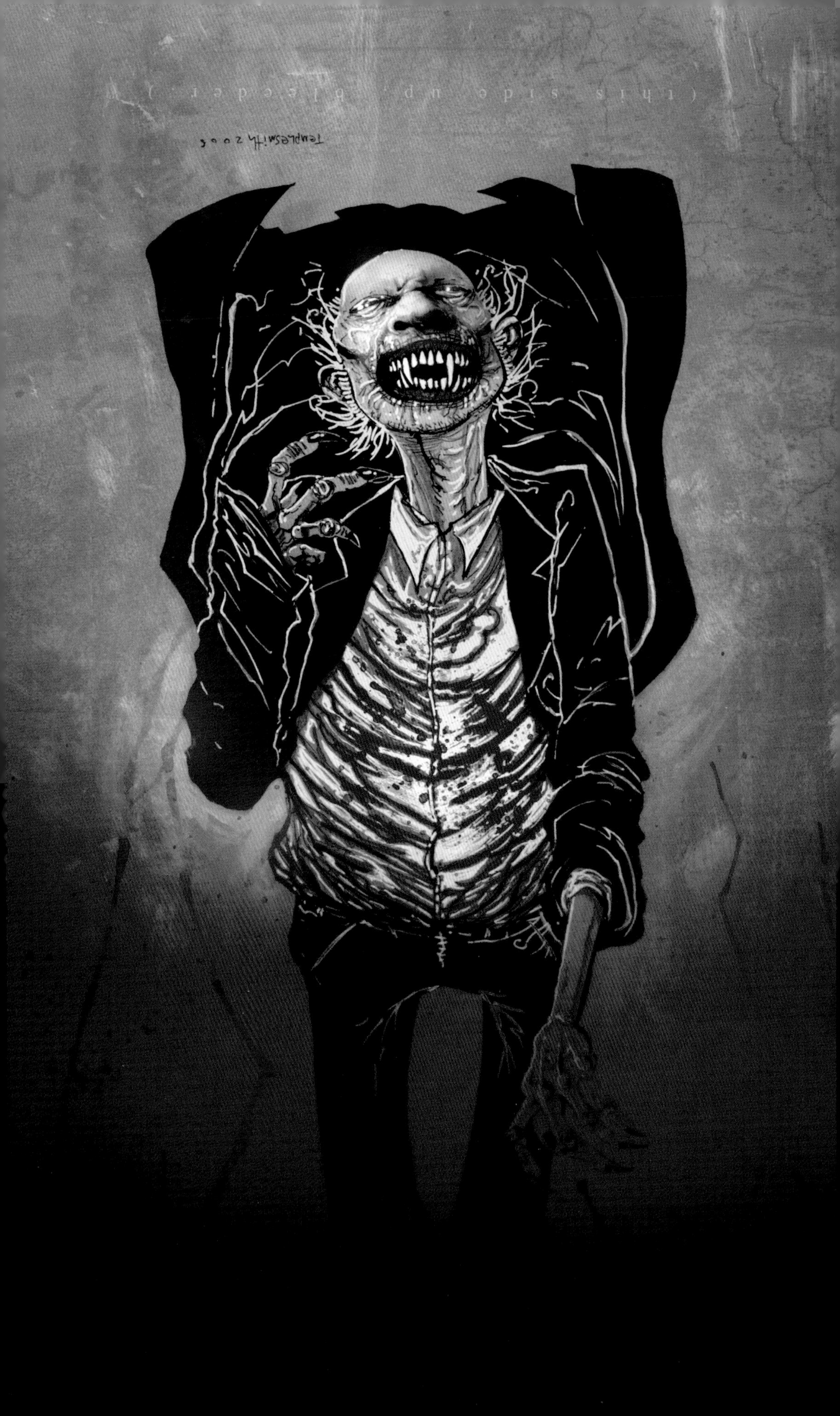
(this side up, bleeder.)
TEMPLESMITH 2006

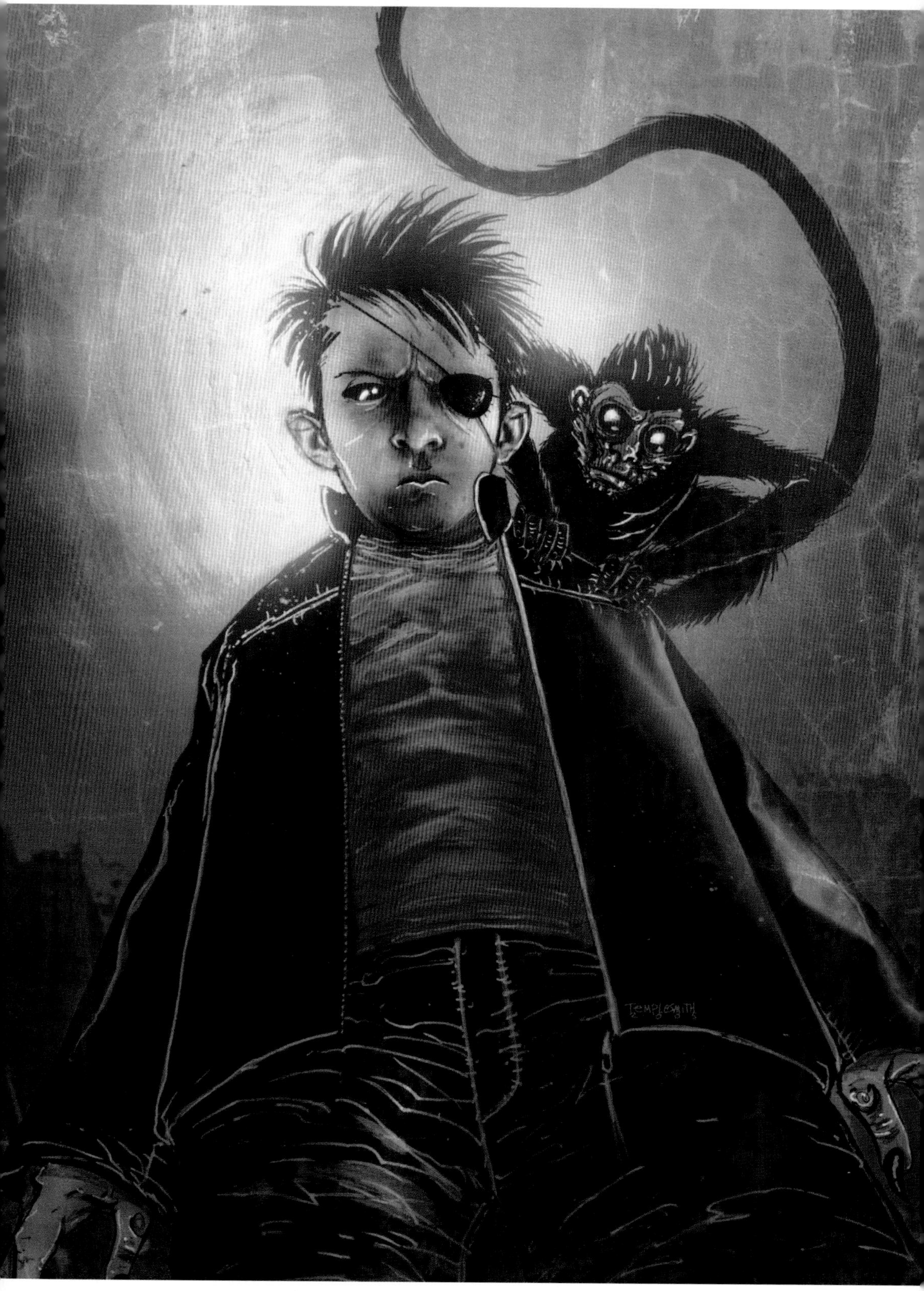
TEMPLESMITH

this page: issue 1 • opposite page: issue 2

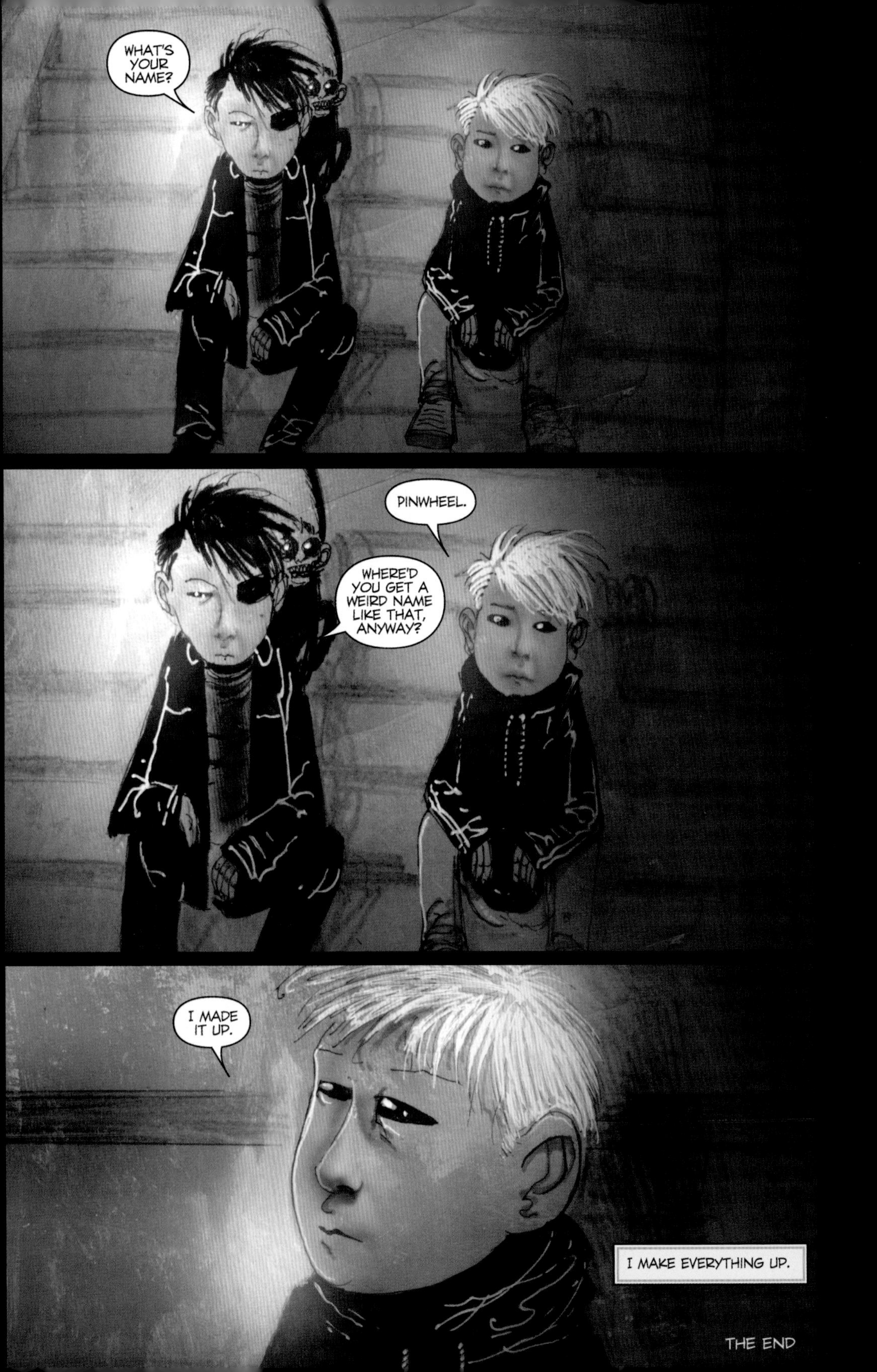
WHAT'S YOUR NAME?
PINWHEEL.
WHERE'D YOU GET A WEIRD NAME LIKE THAT, ANYWAY?
I MADE IT UP.
I MAKE EVERYTHING UP.
THE END

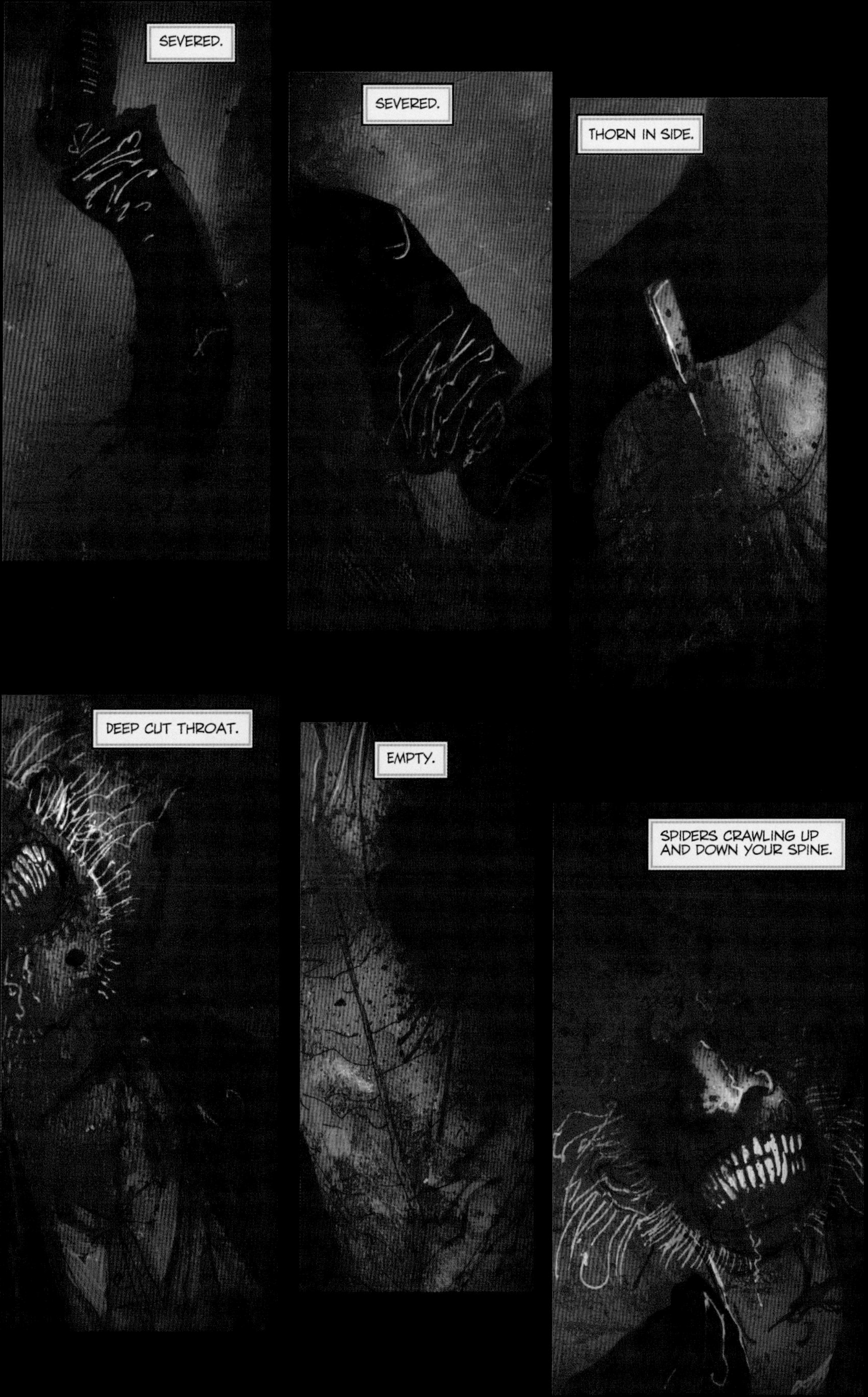
SEVERED.
SEVERED.
THORN IN SIDE.
DEEP CUT THROAT.
EMPTY.
SPIDERS CRAWLING UP AND DOWN YOUR SPINE.

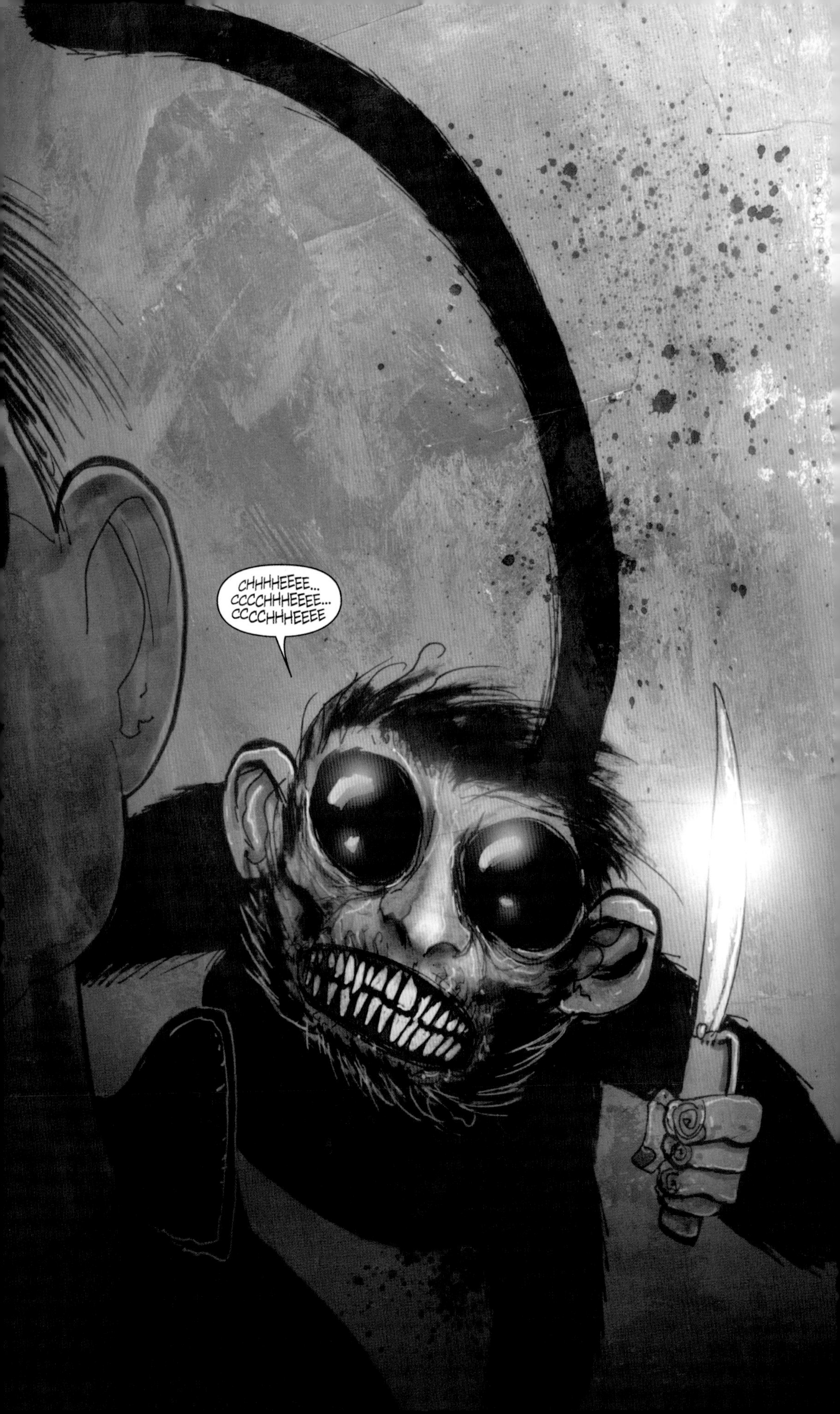
CHHHHEEEE... CCCCHHHEEEE... CCCCHHHEEEE

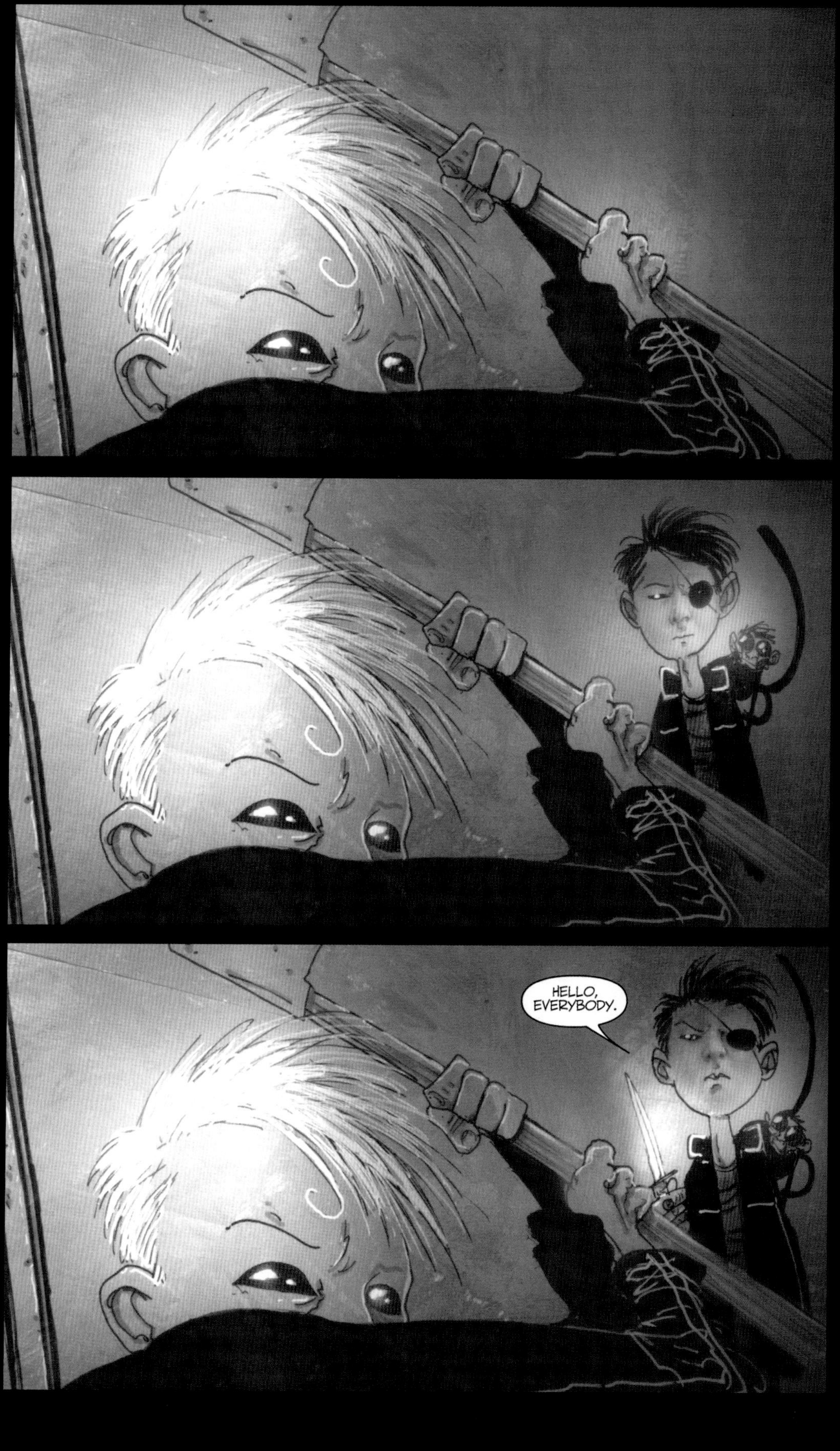
HELLO, EVERYBODY.

MOOOORRSEEELLL!

NOPE. BUT I'LL GIVE YOU TWO MORE GUESSES. JUST TO BE FAIR, KINDA.

MORSEL?

Grrreeeaak!

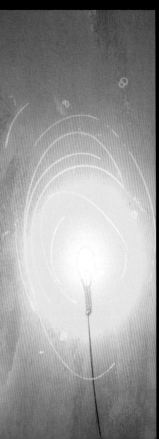

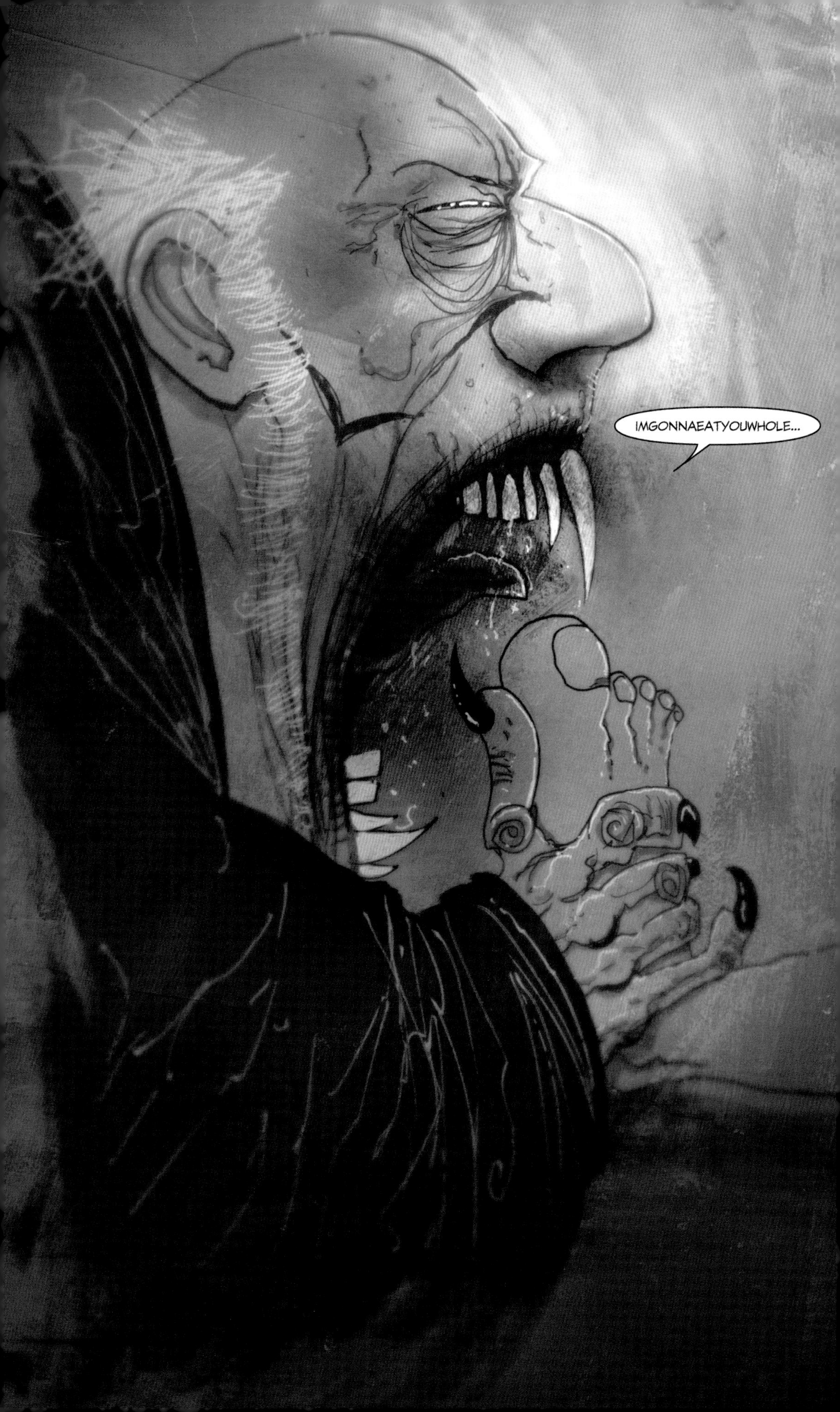
IMGONNAEATYOUWHOLE...

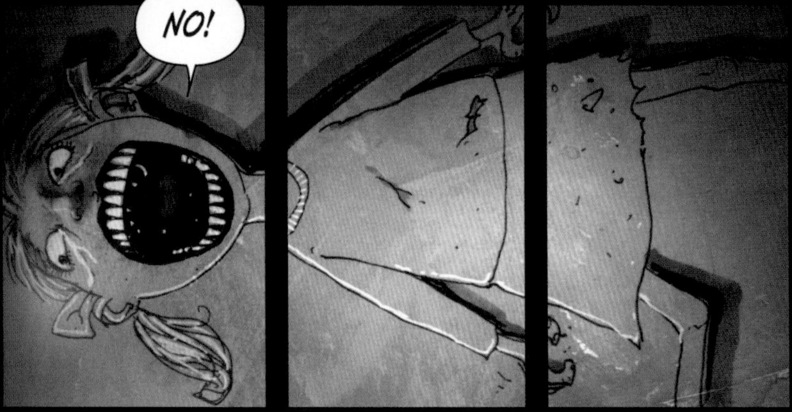
NO!

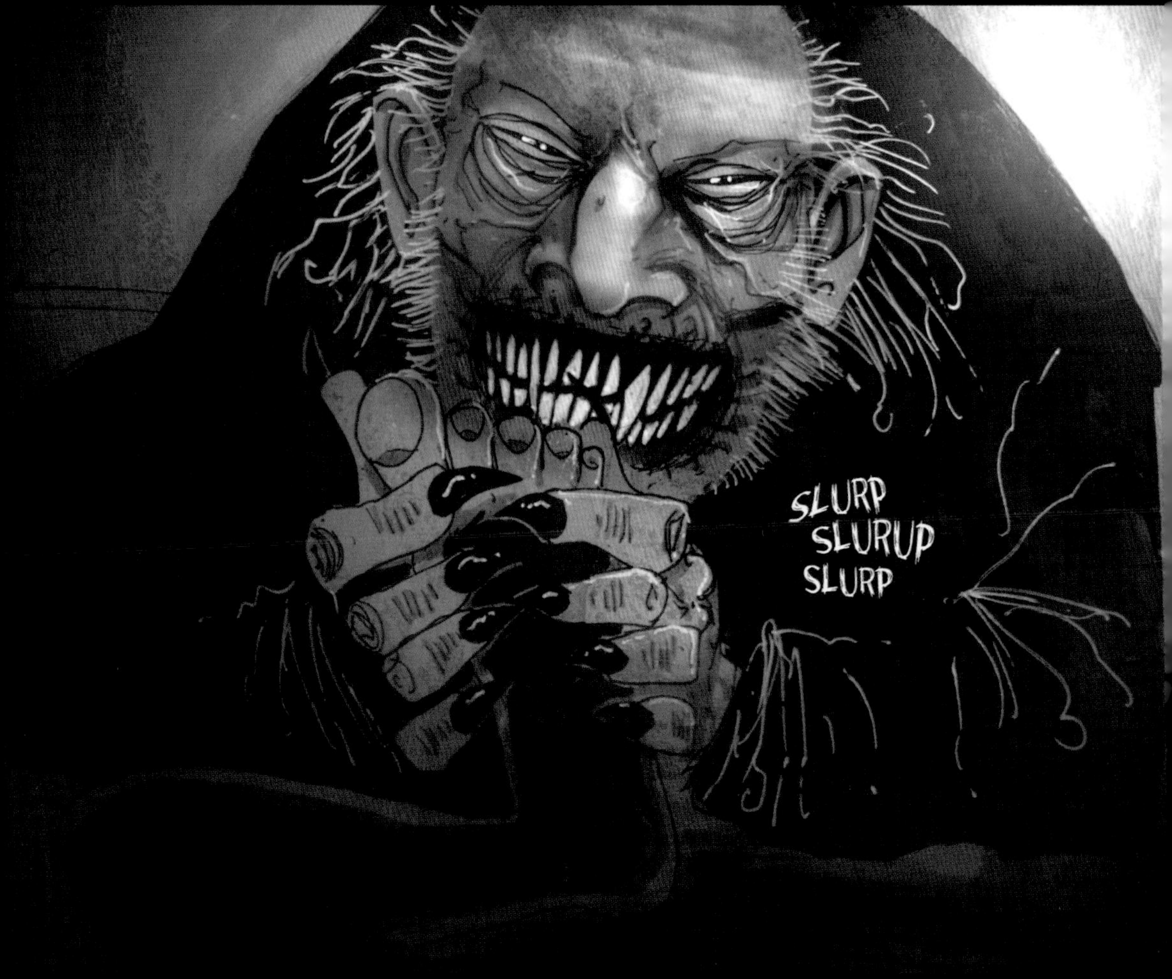
SLURP
SLURUP
SLURP

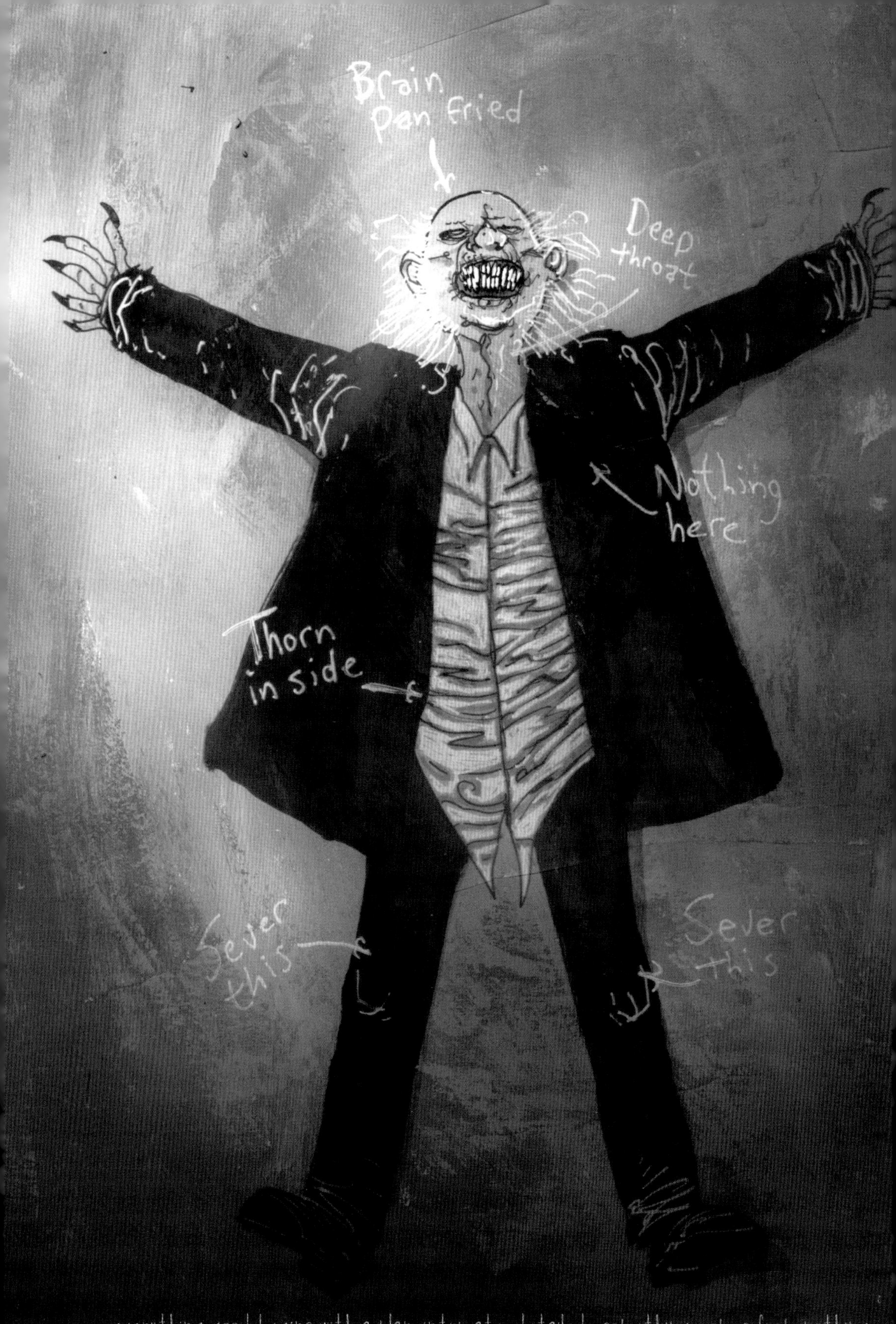
Brain pan fried
Deep throat
Nothing here
Thorn in side
Sever this
Sever this

everything good begins with a plan intricate, detailed... something comes from nothing...
sometimes... when i was a little boy my heart stopped beating in my chest...
i cheated and won the war, but lost every battle... i wish things were different...
i wish i were better... i wish you loved me more... i wish i loved you more...

WHEN THE PAST IS DEAD...

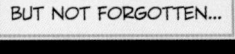

BUT NOT FORGOTTEN...

YOU MUST ARISE FROM THE ASHES...

SHINY AND NEW.

CREUNCH
CREUNCH
CREUNCH
I'M SORRY, MOMMY.
I'M SORRY.
I CAN'T LIVE IF YOU SURVIVE...

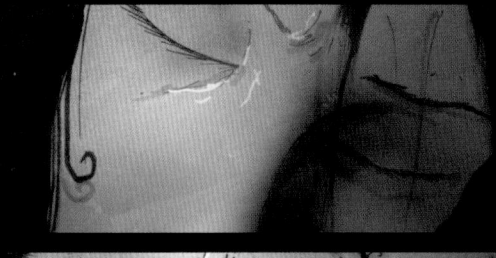

YOU CAN NEVER
ERASE THE PAST.

IT'S ALWAYS
WITH YOU.

NO MATTER HOW
FAR AWAY YOU GO.

OR HOW CHANGED
YOU BECOME.

DEMON FATHER JOHN'S
PINWHEEL BLUES PART
FOUR
Amber Benson
Ben Templesmith

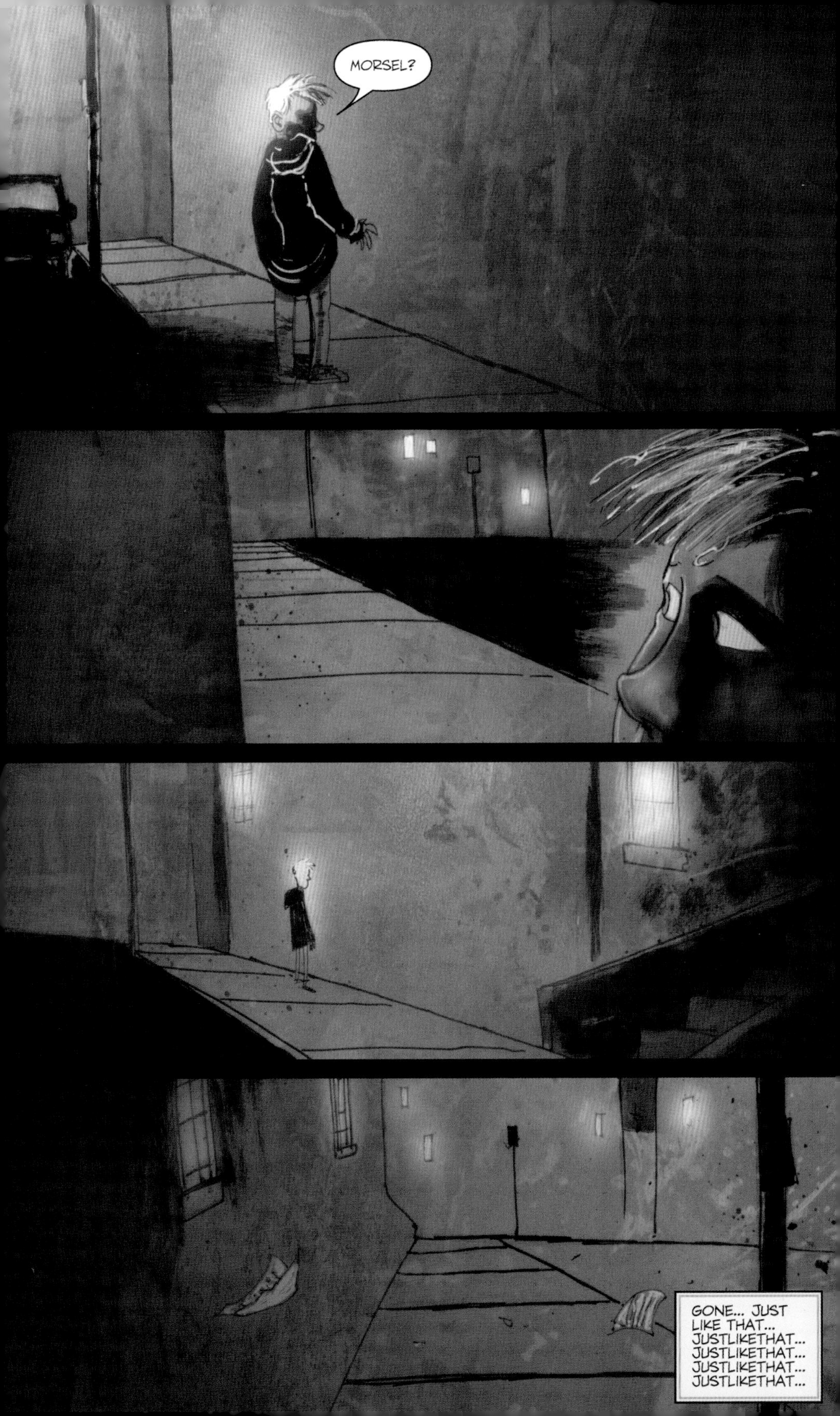
MORSEL?
GONE... JUST
LIKE THAT...
JUSTLIKETHAT...
JUSTLIKETHAT...
JUSTLIKETHAT...
JUSTLIKETHAT...

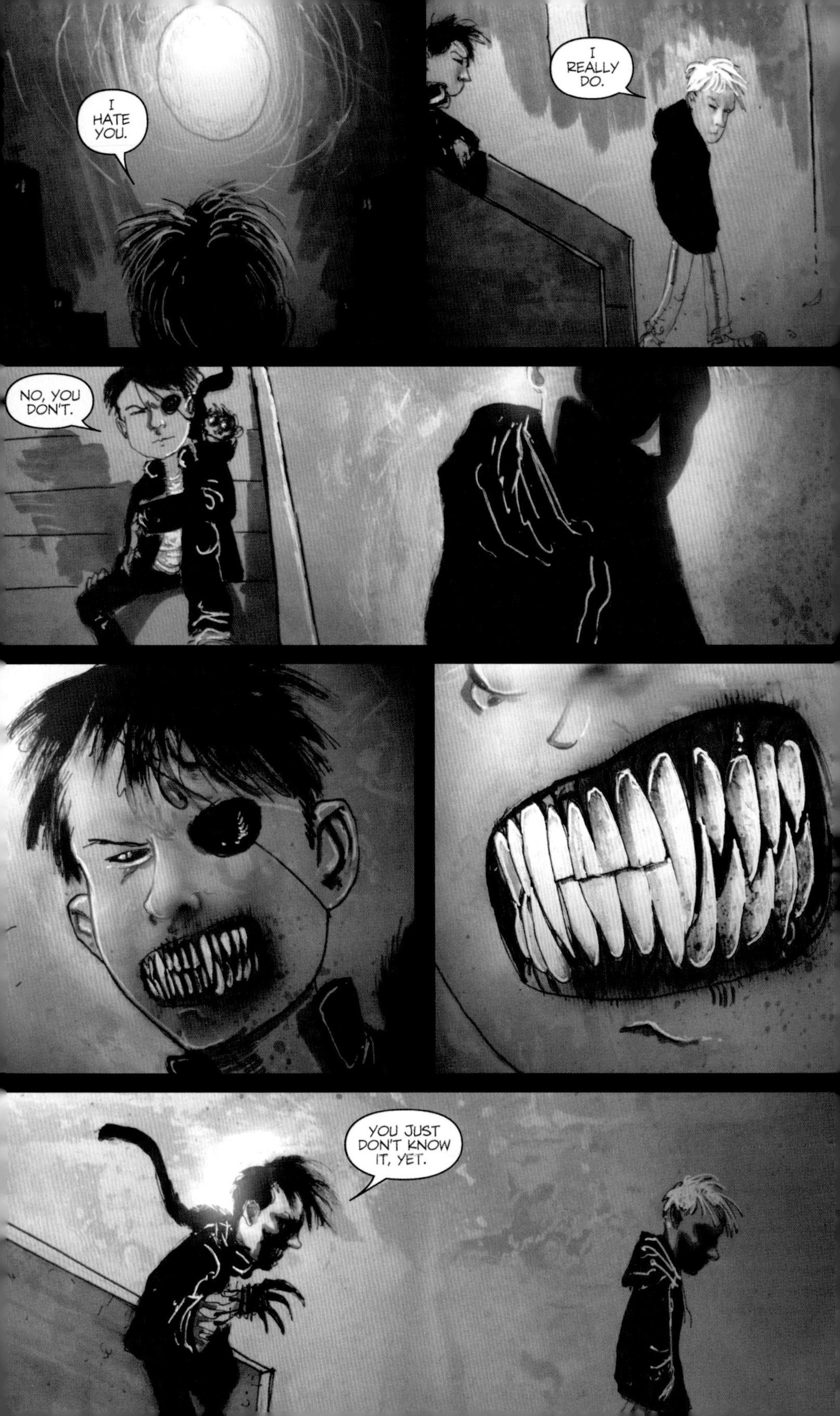
I HATE YOU.
I REALLY DO.
NO, YOU DON'T.
YOU JUST DON'T KNOW IT, YET.

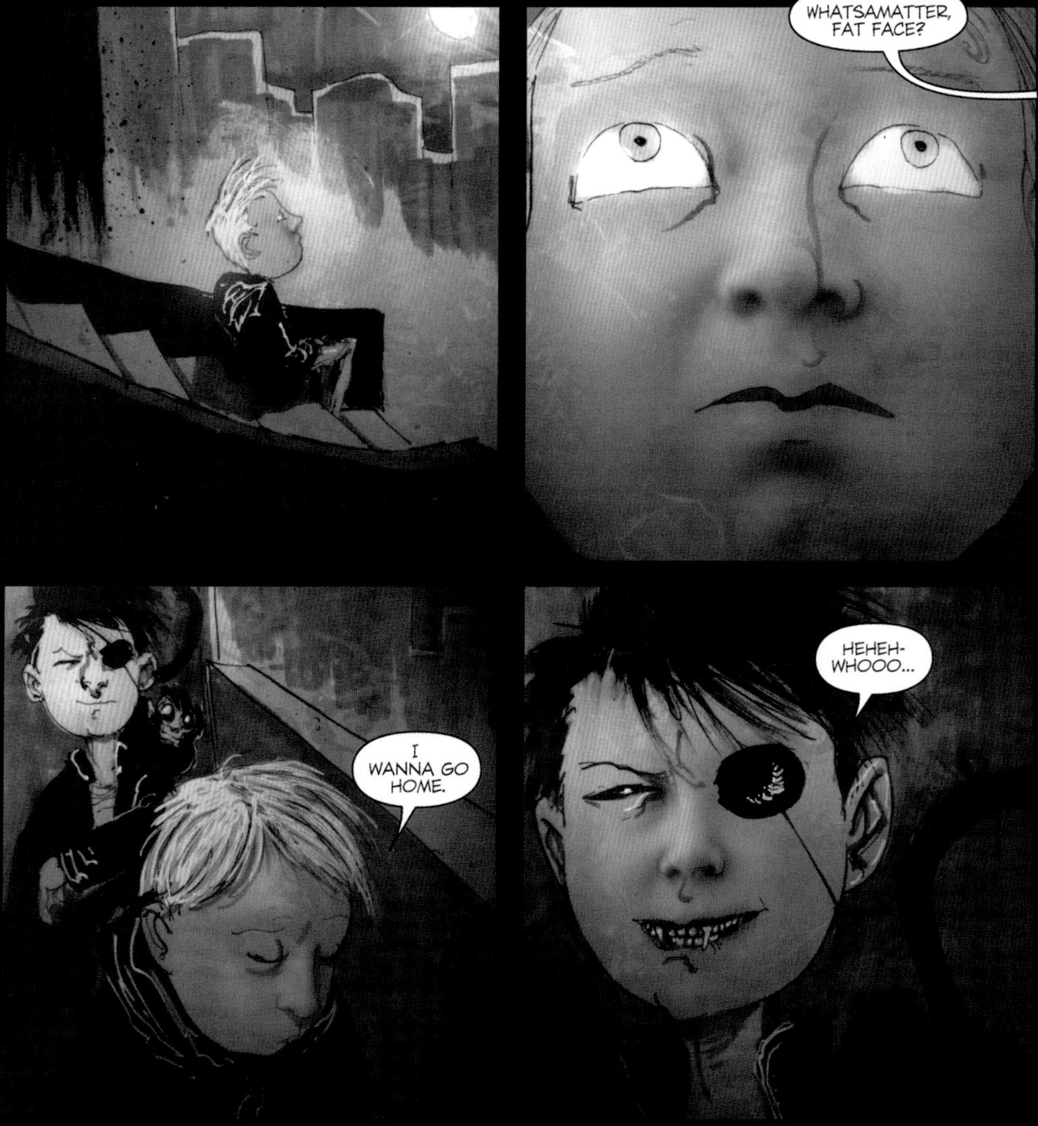
WHATSAMATTER, FAT FACE?
I WANNA GO HOME.
HEHEH-WHOOO...

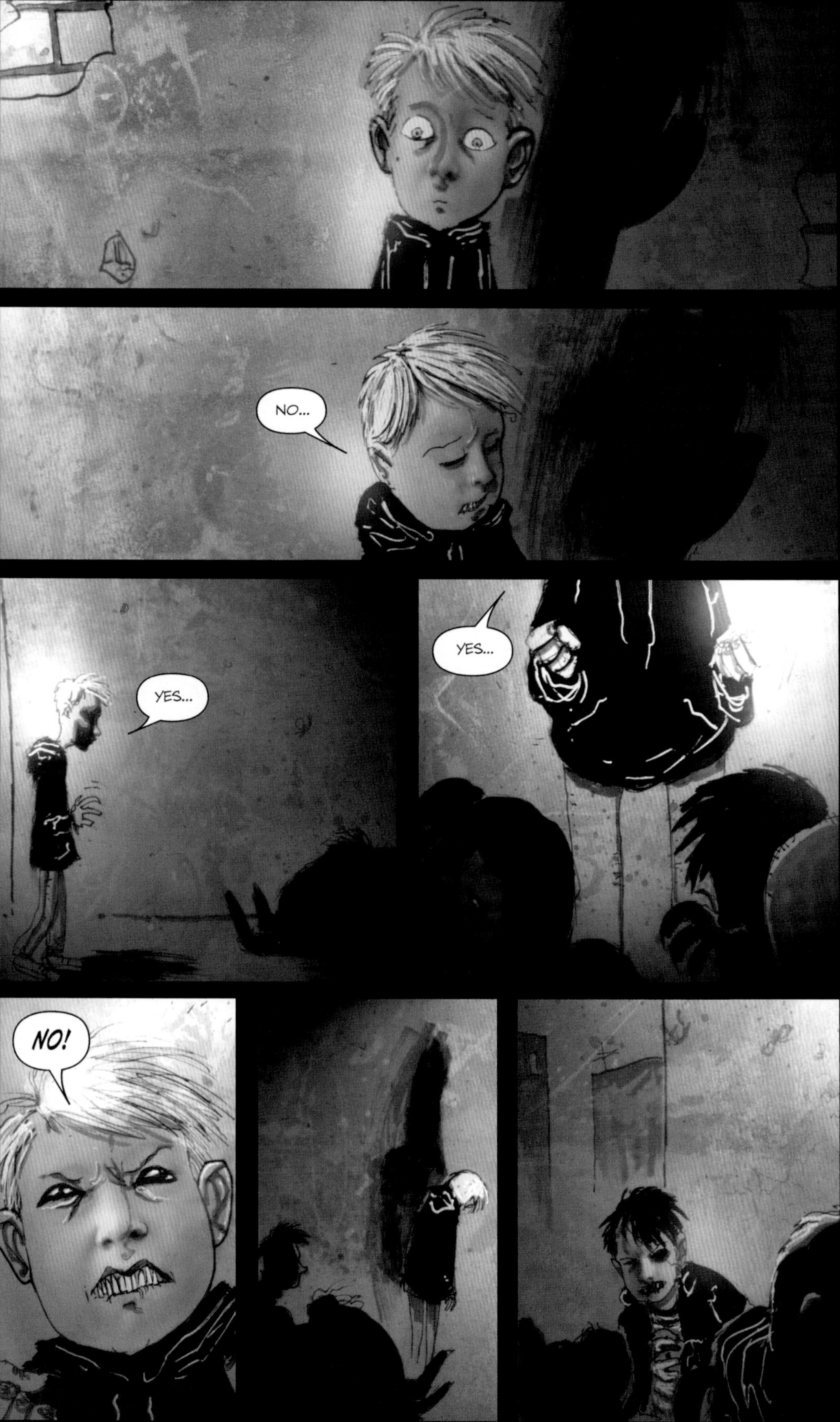
NO...
YES...
YES...
NO!

SCHLURP
SQUELCH
CRACK
SPLISH

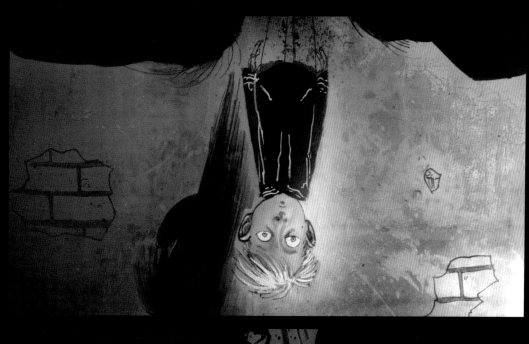

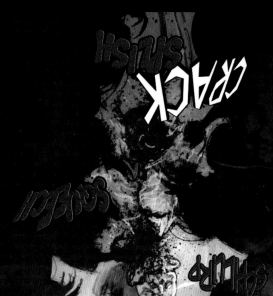

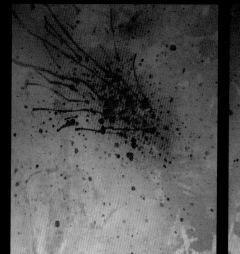

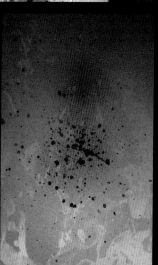

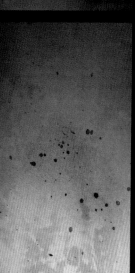

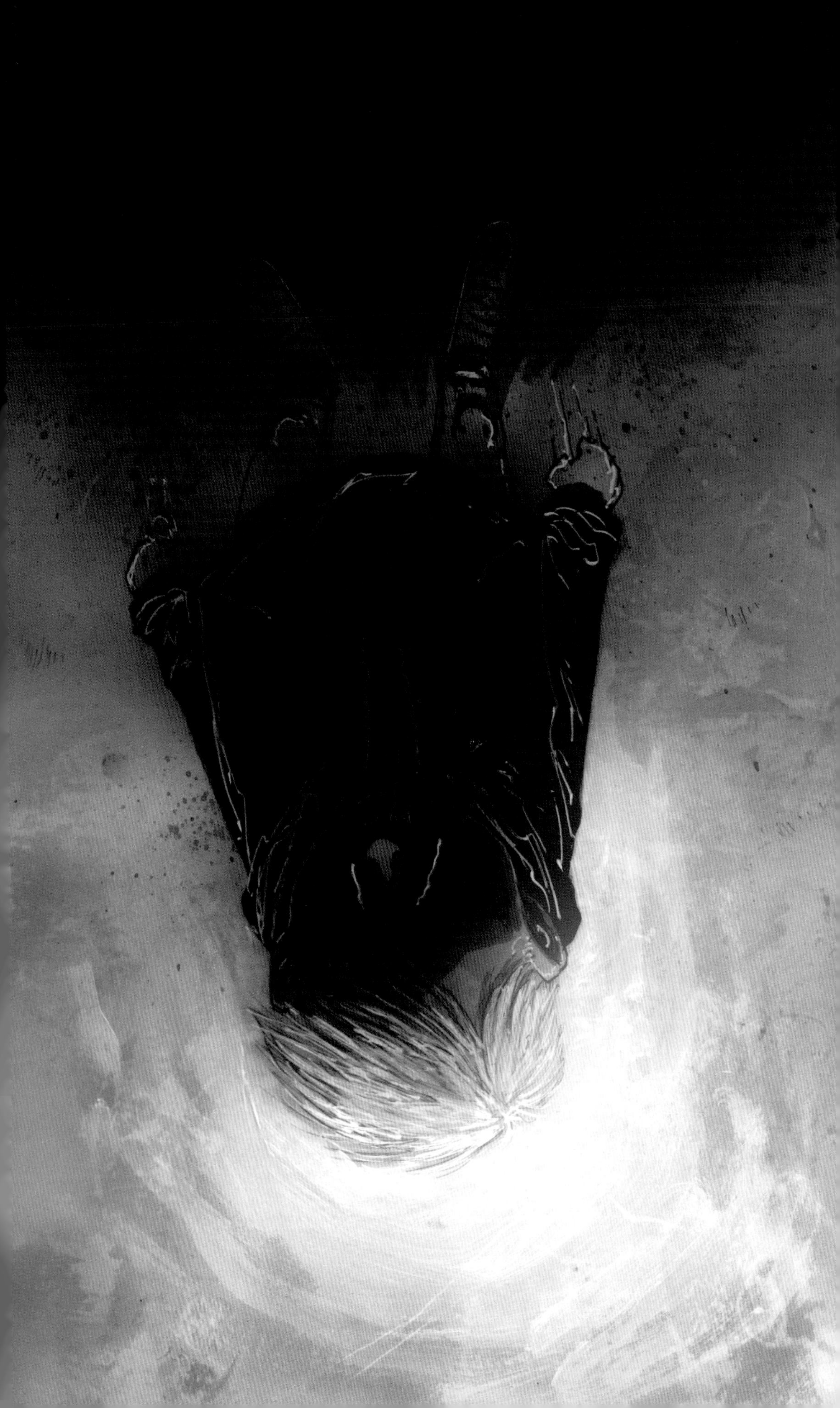

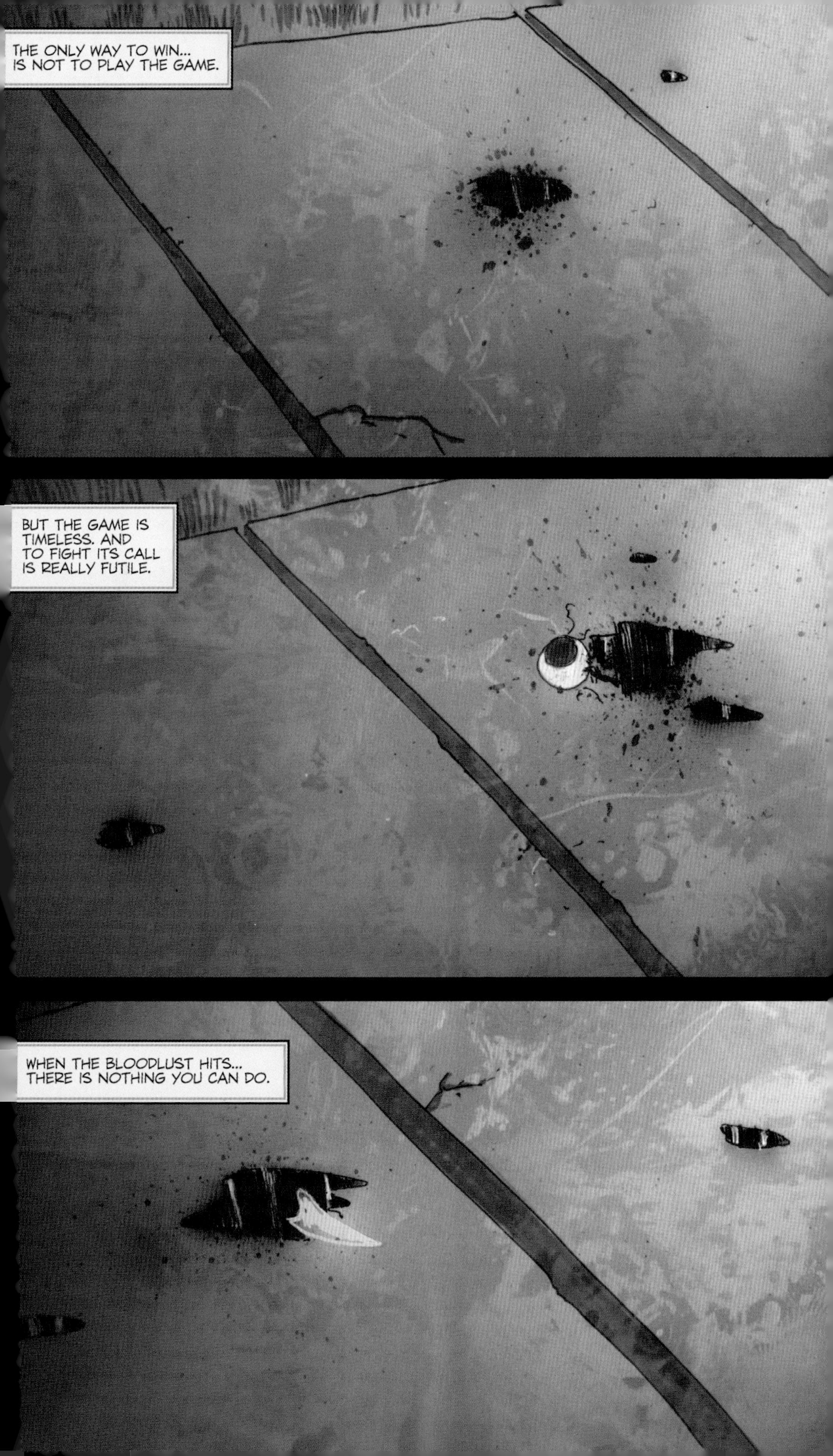
THE ONLY WAY TO WIN... IS NOT TO PLAY THE GAME.
BUT THE GAME IS TIMELESS. AND TO FIGHT ITS CALL IS REALLY FUTILE.
WHEN THE BLOODLUST HITS... THERE IS NOTHING YOU CAN DO.

SNIFF... SNIFF... SNIFF...
WHAT THE... NO!
SHOO!
GET LOST!
YOU HEARD ME! GET OUTTA HERE!
GO... A... WAY!

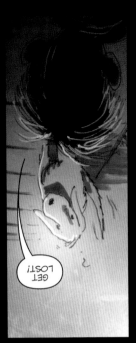

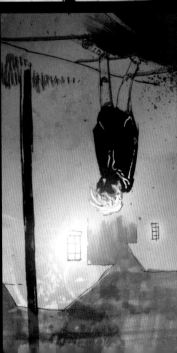

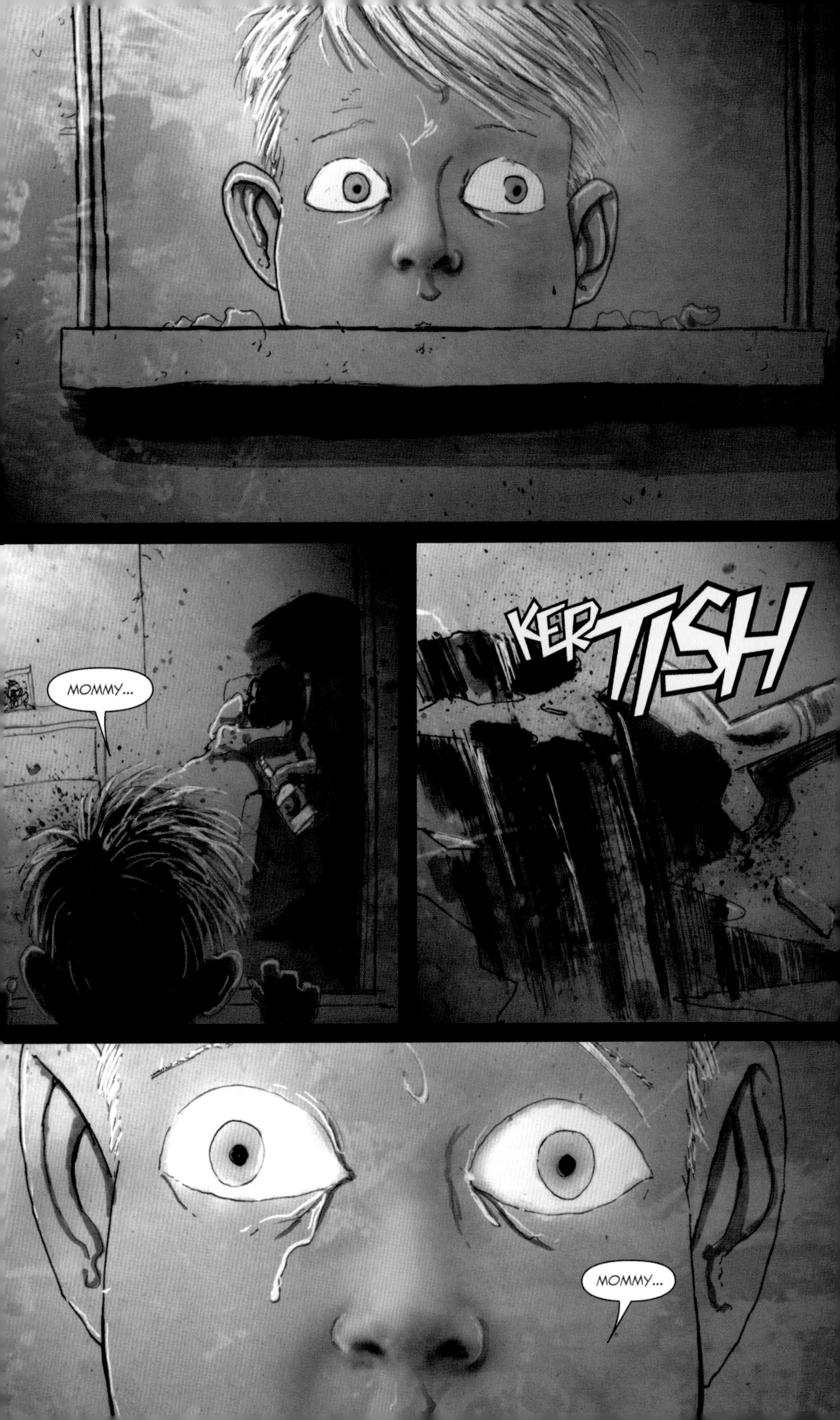
MOMMY...
KERTISH
MOMMY...

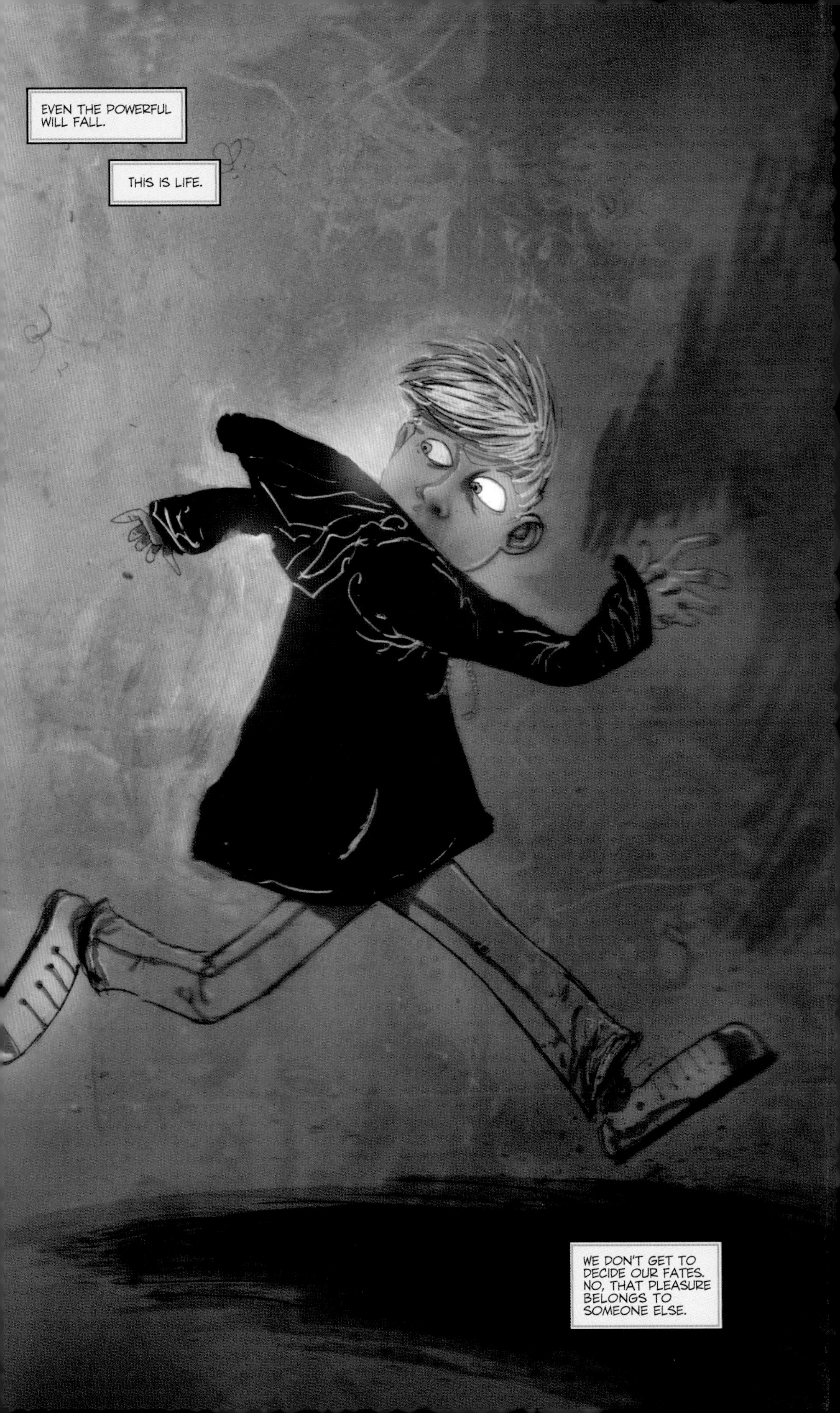
EVEN THE POWERFUL WILL FALL.
THIS IS LIFE.
WE DON'T GET TO DECIDE OUR FATES. NO, THAT PLEASURE BELONGS TO SOMEONE ELSE.

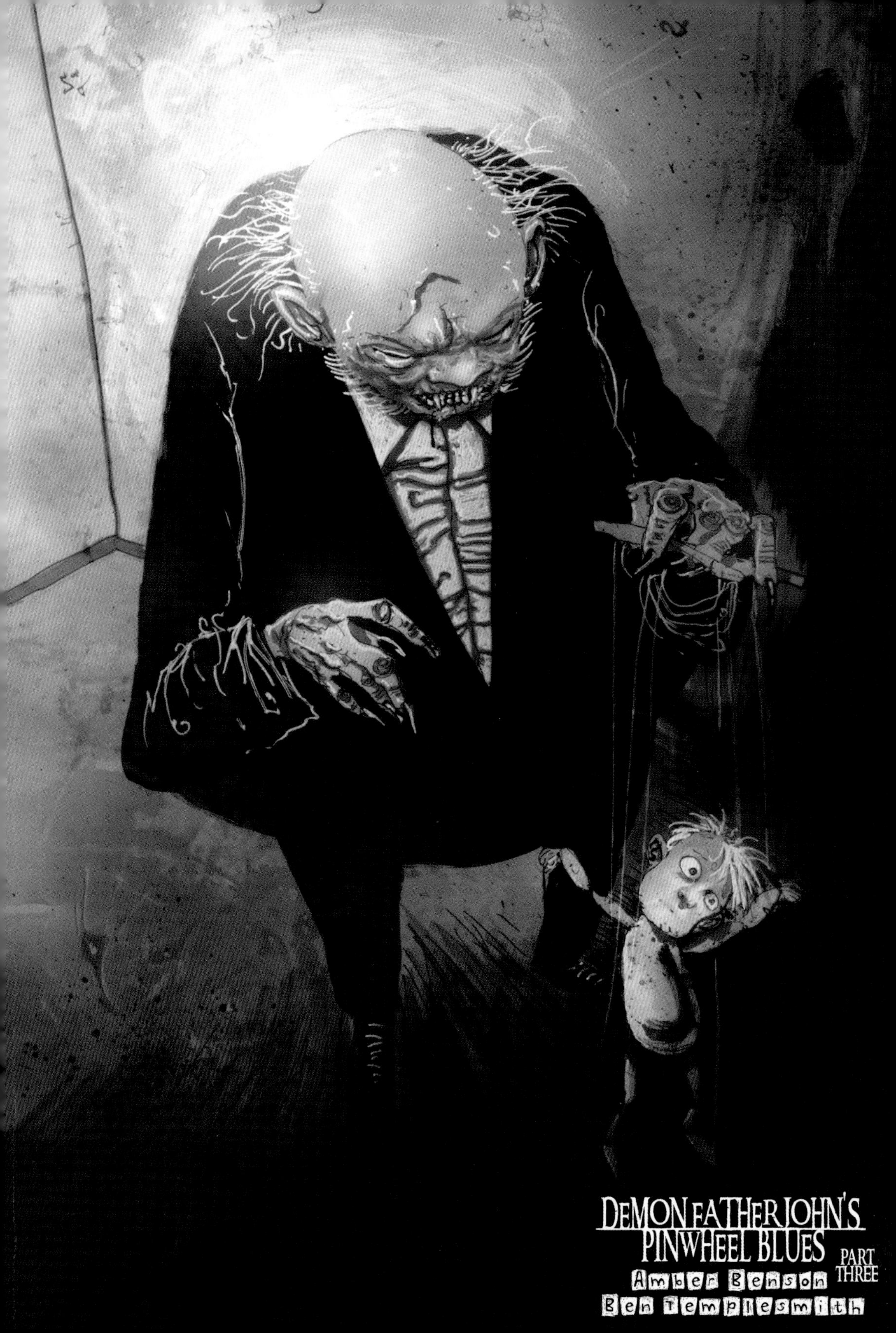

DEMON FATHER JOHN'S
PINWHEEL BLUES
PART THREE
Amber Benson
Ben Templesmith

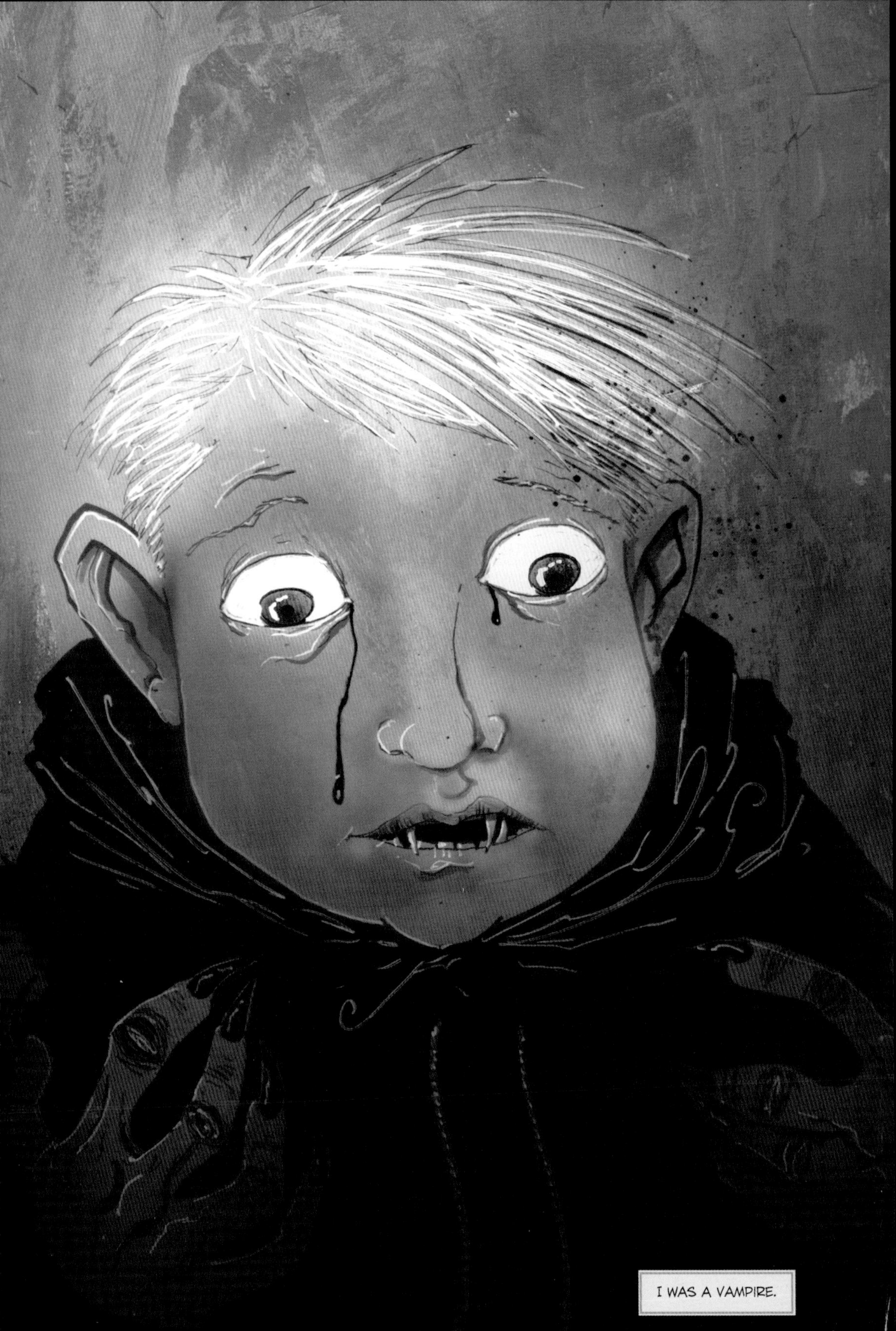
I WAS A VAMPIRE.

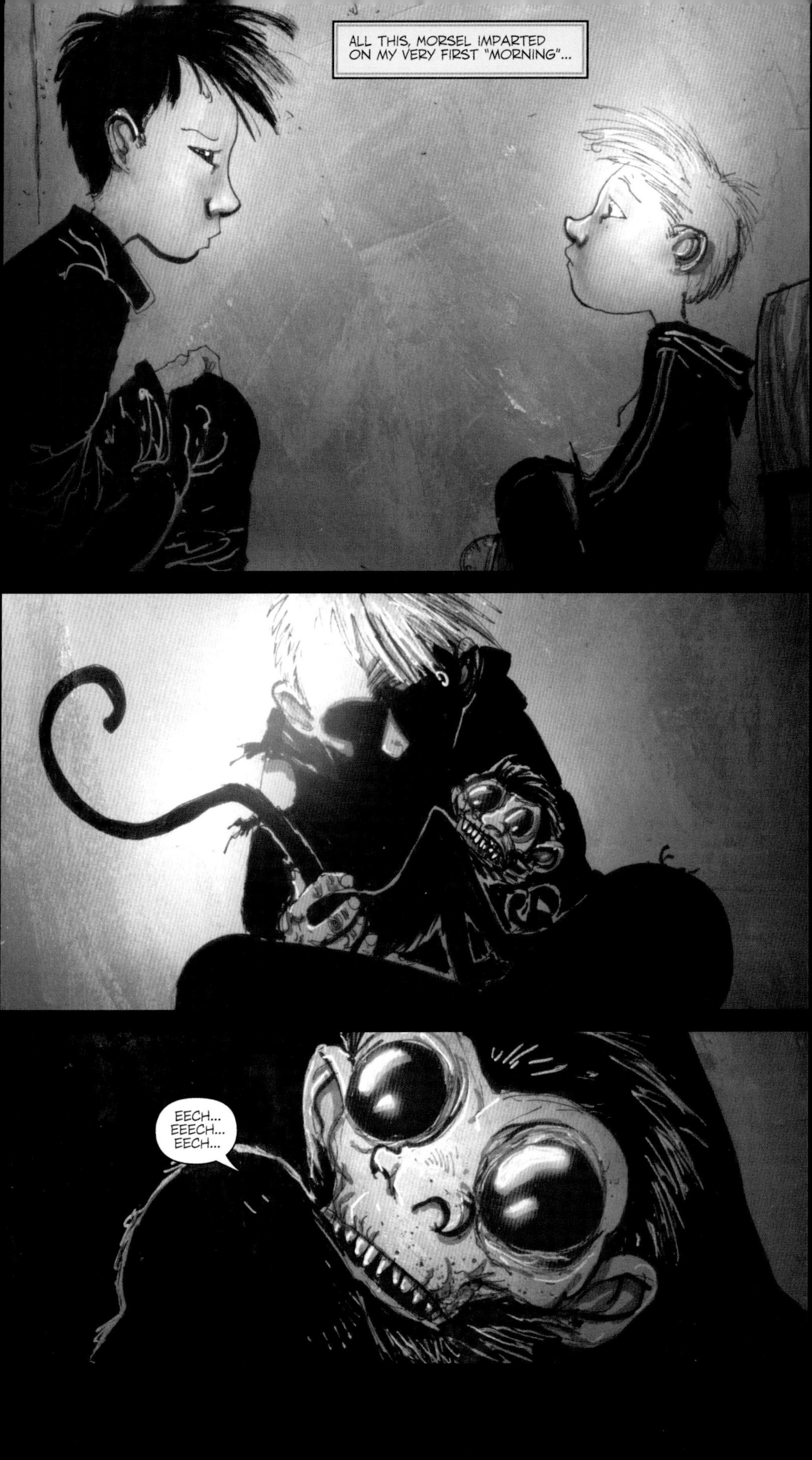
ALL THIS, MORSEL IMPARTED ON MY VERY FIRST "MORNING"...
EECH... EEECH... EECH...

Ben Templesmith

Amber Benson

SHADOWPLAY™

IDW Publishing
Robbie Robbins, Preside...
Chris Ryall, Publisher/Editor-in-Chi...
Ted Adams, Vice Preside...
Kris Oprisko, Vice Preside...
Neil Uyetake, Art Direct...
Dan Taylor, Edit...
Aaron Myers, Distribution Manag...
Tom B. Long, Design...
Chance Boren, Editorial Assist...
Matthew Ruzicka, CPA, Contro...
Alex Garner, Creative Direct...
Yumiko Miyano, Business Developme...
Rick Privman, Business Developme...

www.idwpublishing.com

ISBN: 1-933239-84-0

5 4 3 2 1 06 07 08 09

SHADOWPLAY™

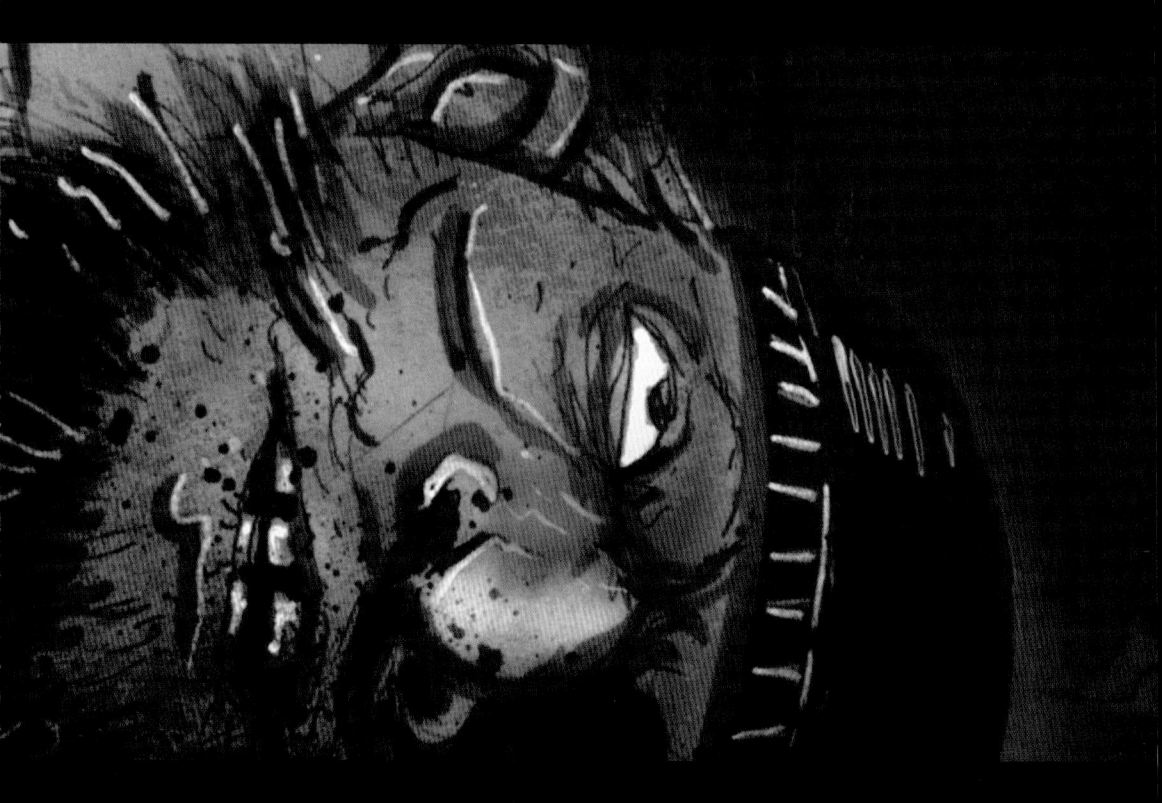

Demon Father John's Pinwheel Blues

story: **Amber Bensen**

art: **Ben Templesmith**

letters: **Tom B. Long**

editor: **Chris Ryall**

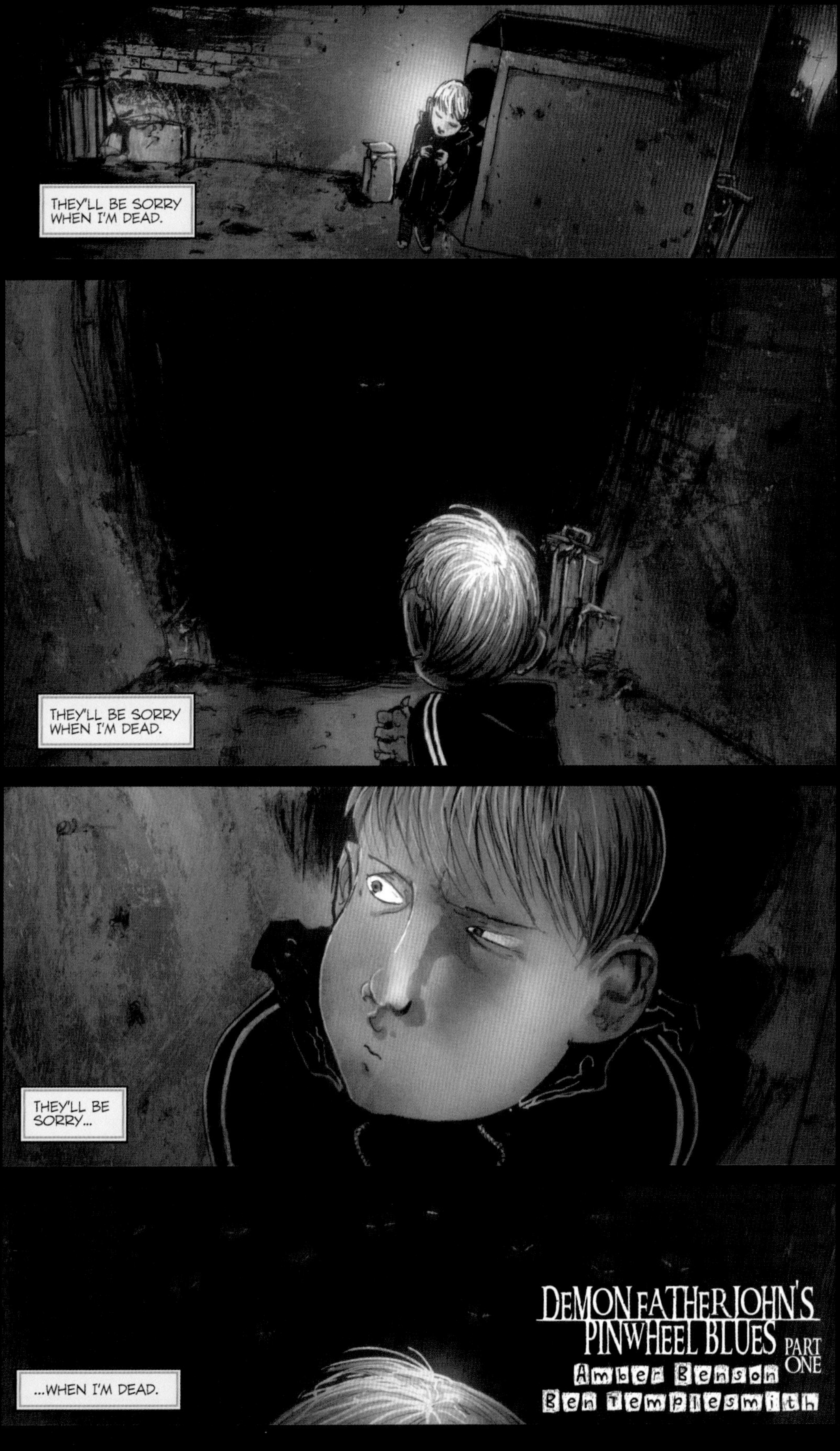
THEY'LL BE SORRY WHEN I'M DEAD.
THEY'LL BE SORRY WHEN I'M DEAD.
THEY'LL BE SORRY...
...WHEN I'M DEAD.
DEMON FATHER JOHN'S PINWHEEL BLUES PART ONE
Amber Benson
Ben Templesmith

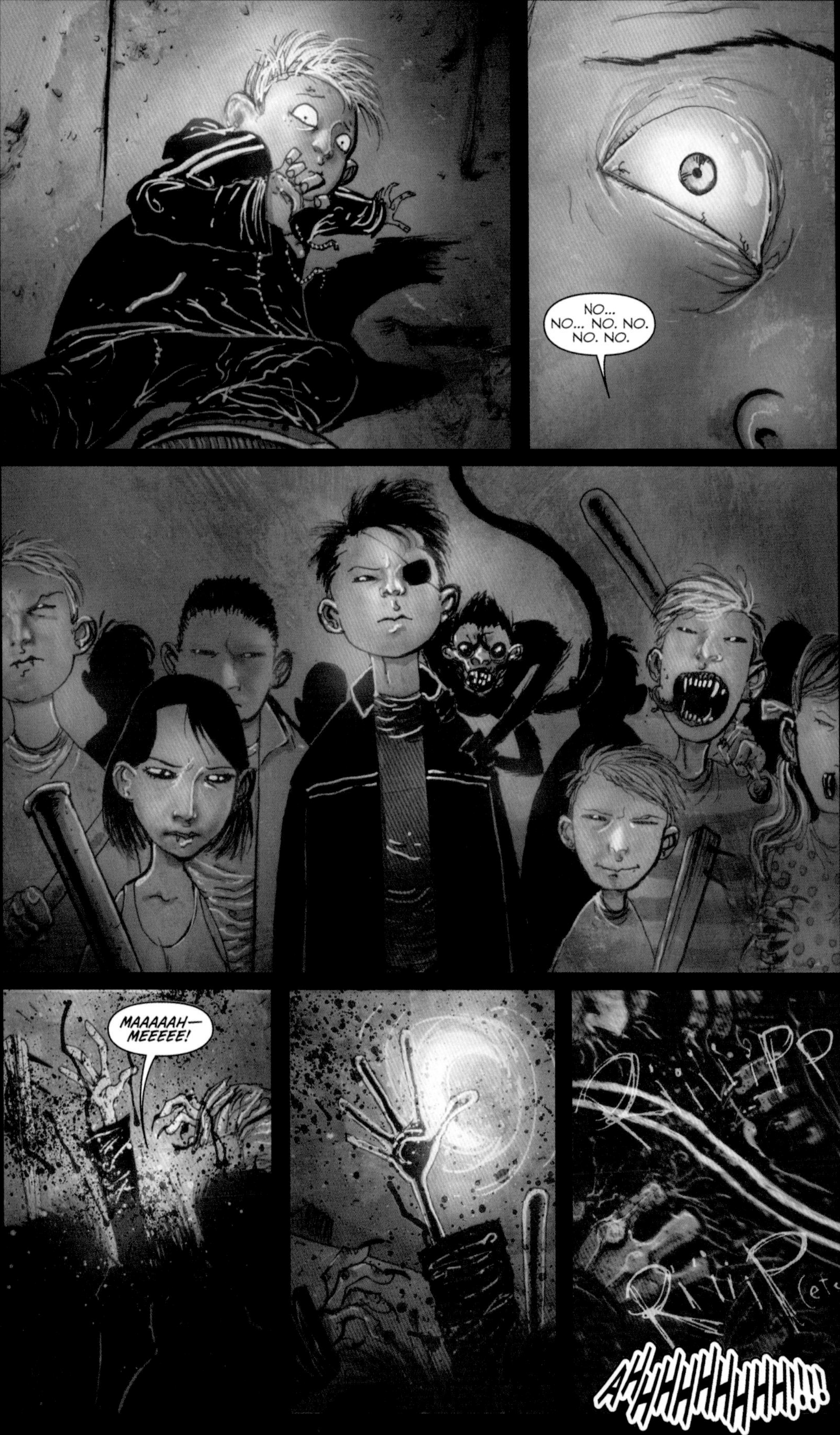
NO...
NO... NO. NO.
NO. NO.
MAAAAAH—
MEEEEE!
AHHHHHHHHHH!!!!

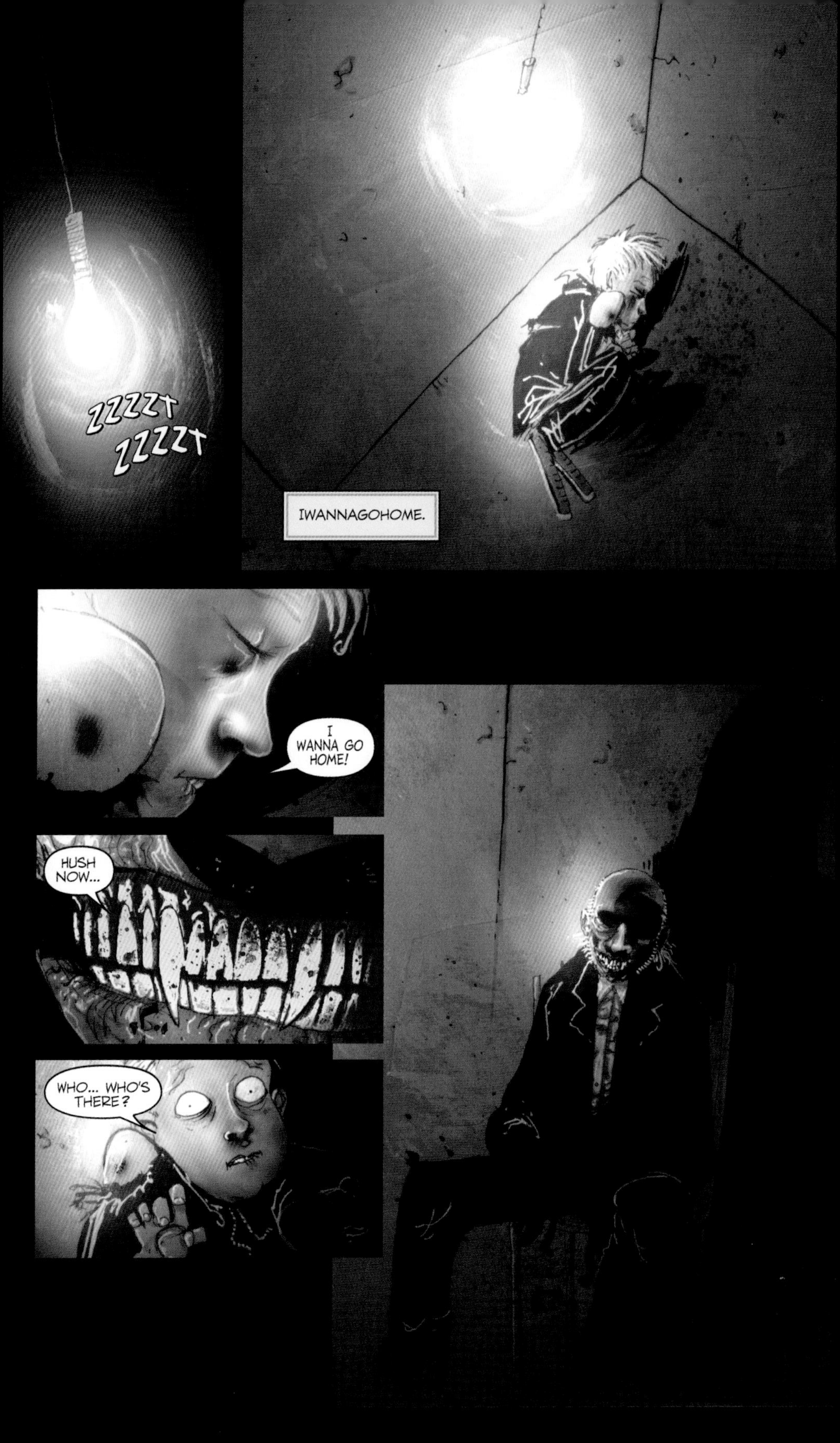

ZZZZT
ZZZZT
IWANNAGOHOME.
I WANNA GO HOME!
HUSH NOW...
WHO... WHO'S THERE?

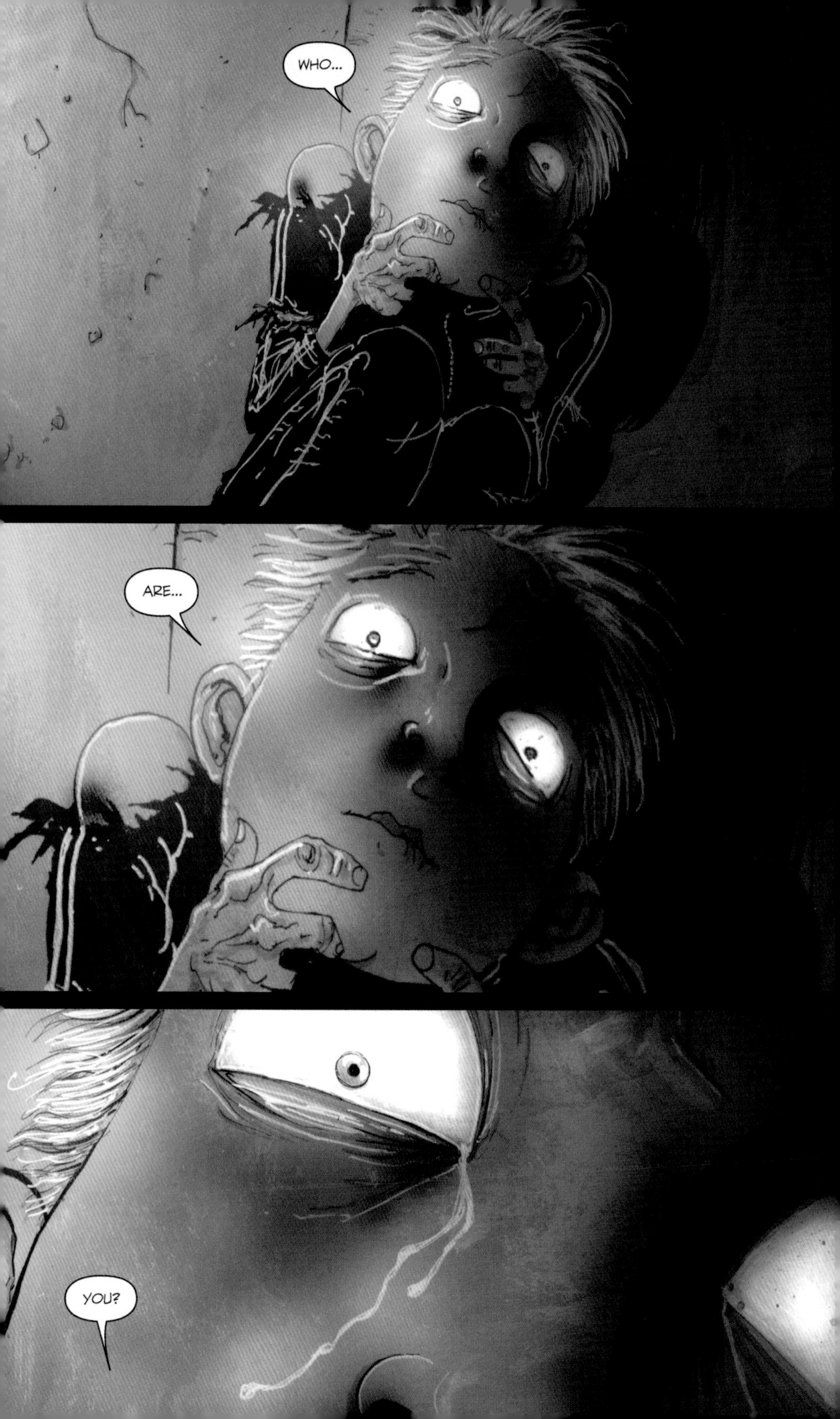
WHO...
ARE...
YOU?

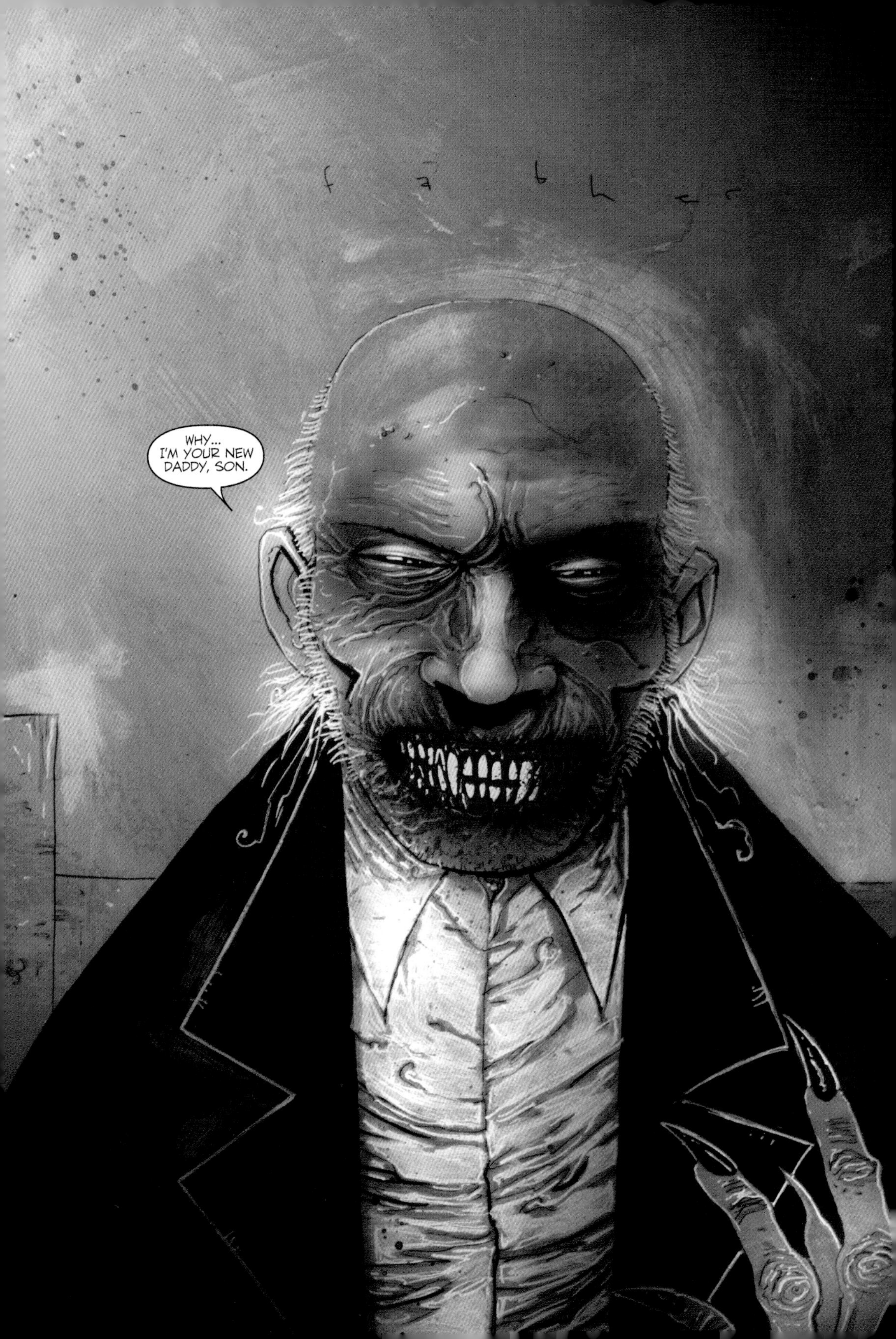
WHY... I'M YOUR NEW DADDY, SON.

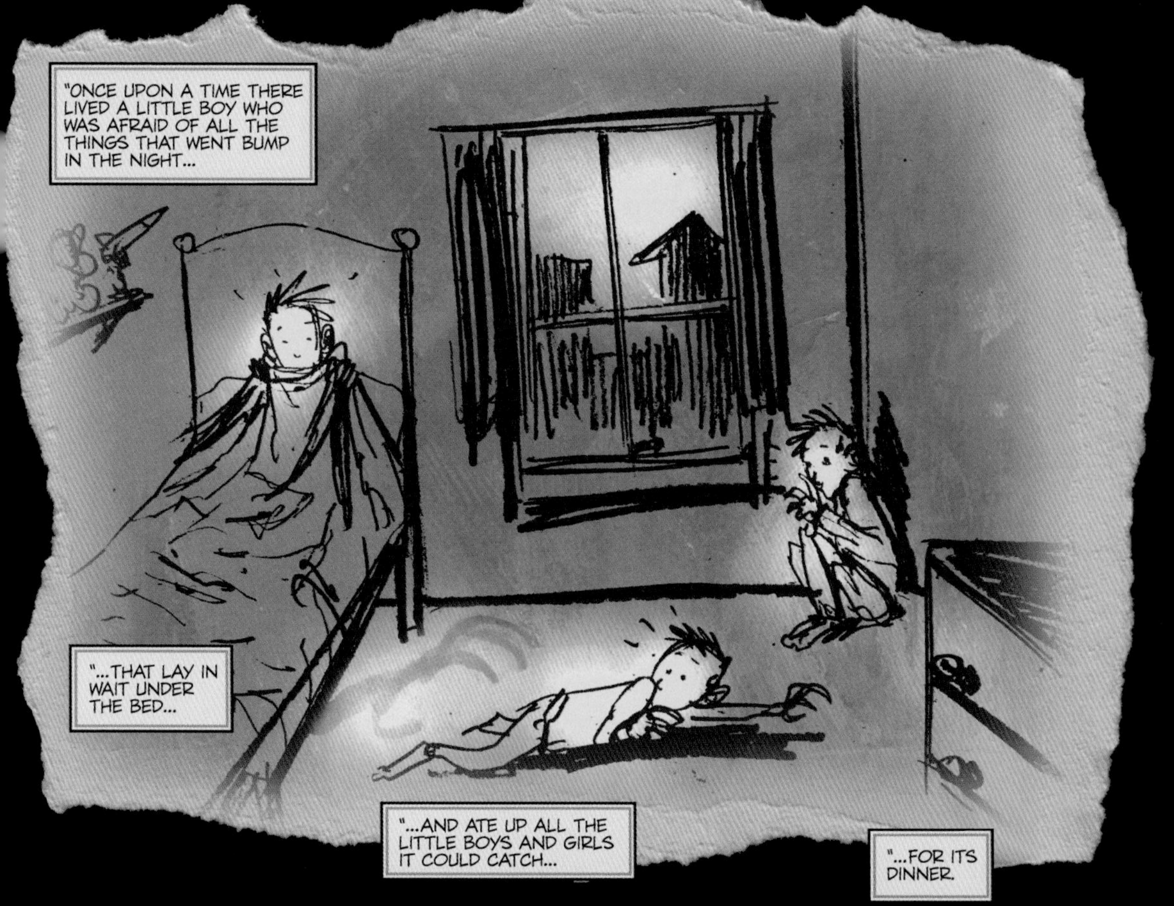
"ONCE UPON A TIME THERE LIVED A LITTLE BOY WHO WAS AFRAID OF ALL THE THINGS THAT WENT BUMP IN THE NIGHT...
"...THAT LAY IN WAIT UNDER THE BED...
"...AND ATE UP ALL THE LITTLE BOYS AND GIRLS IT COULD CATCH...
"...FOR ITS DINNER.

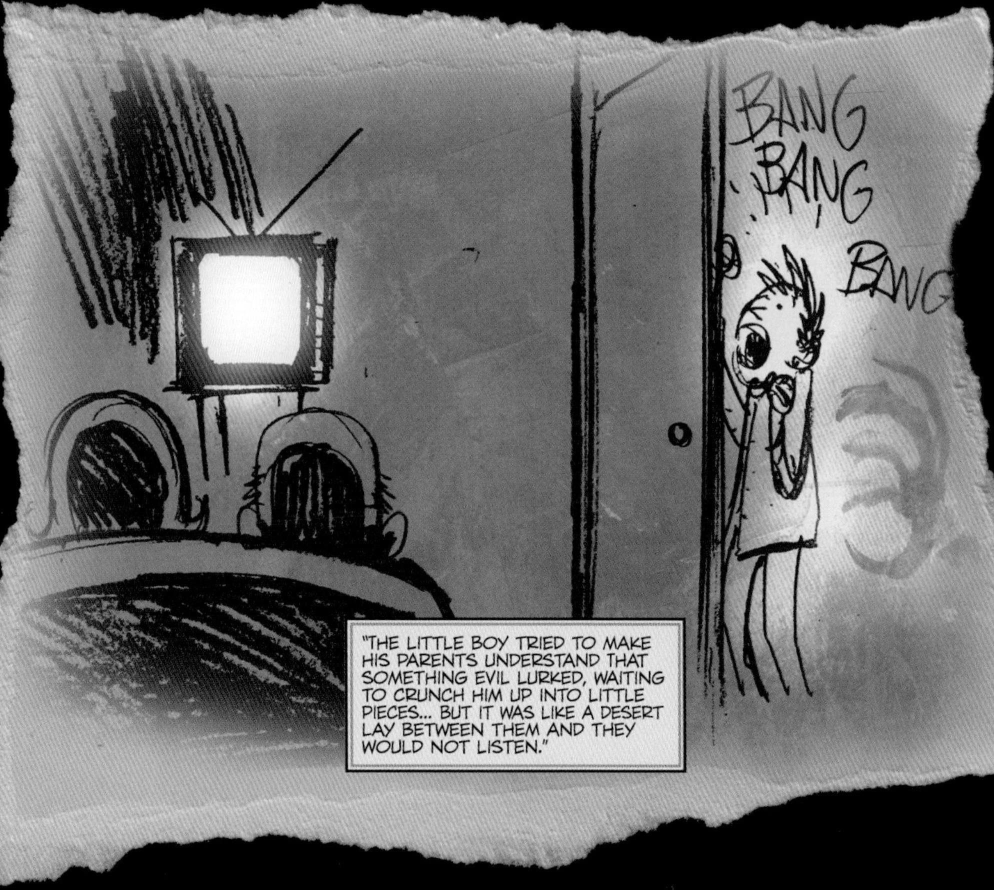
BANG
BANG
BANG
"THE LITTLE BOY TRIED TO MAKE HIS PARENTS UNDERSTAND THAT SOMETHING EVIL LURKED, WAITING TO CRUNCH HIM UP INTO LITTLE PIECES... BUT IT WAS LIKE A DESERT LAY BETWEEN THEM AND THEY WOULD NOT LISTEN."

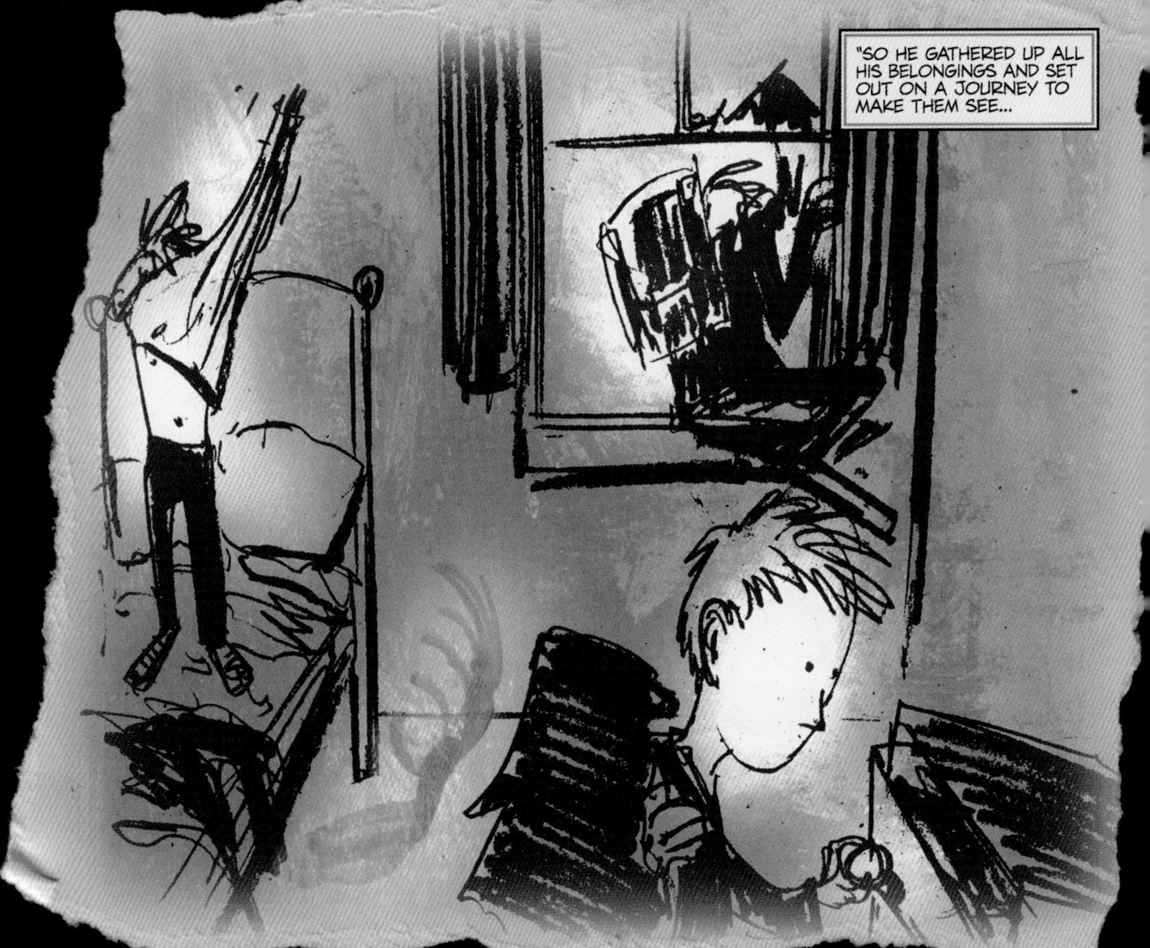
"SO HE GATHERED UP ALL HIS BELONGINGS AND SET OUT ON A JOURNEY TO MAKE THEM SEE...

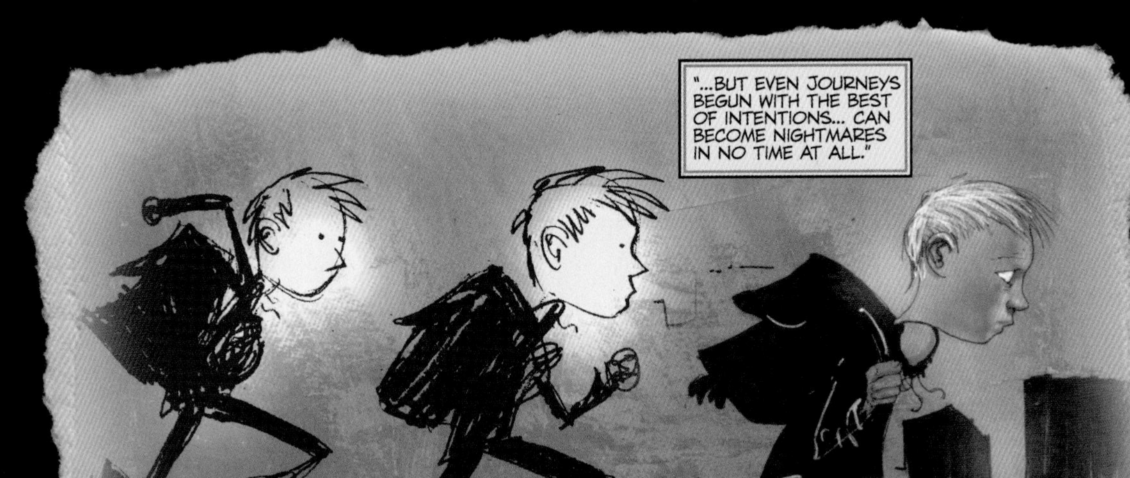
"...BUT EVEN JOURNEYS BEGUN WITH THE BEST OF INTENTIONS... CAN BECOME NIGHTMARES IN NO TIME AT ALL."

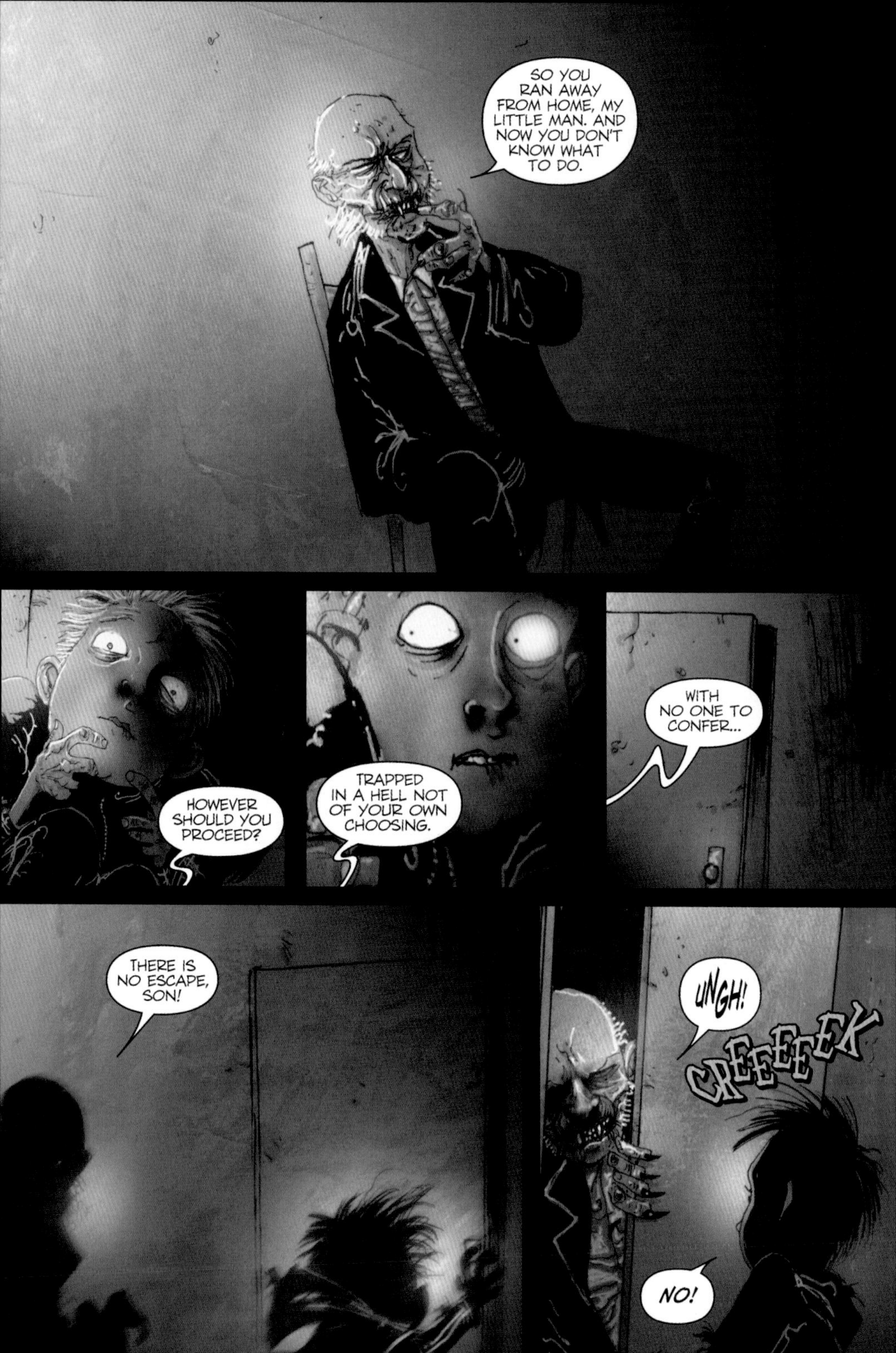
SO YOU RAN AWAY FROM HOME, MY LITTLE MAN. AND NOW YOU DON'T KNOW WHAT TO DO.
HOWEVER SHOULD YOU PROCEED?
TRAPPED IN A HELL NOT OF YOUR OWN CHOOSING.
WITH NO ONE TO CONFER...
THERE IS NO ESCAPE, SON!
UNGH!
CREEEEEK
NO!

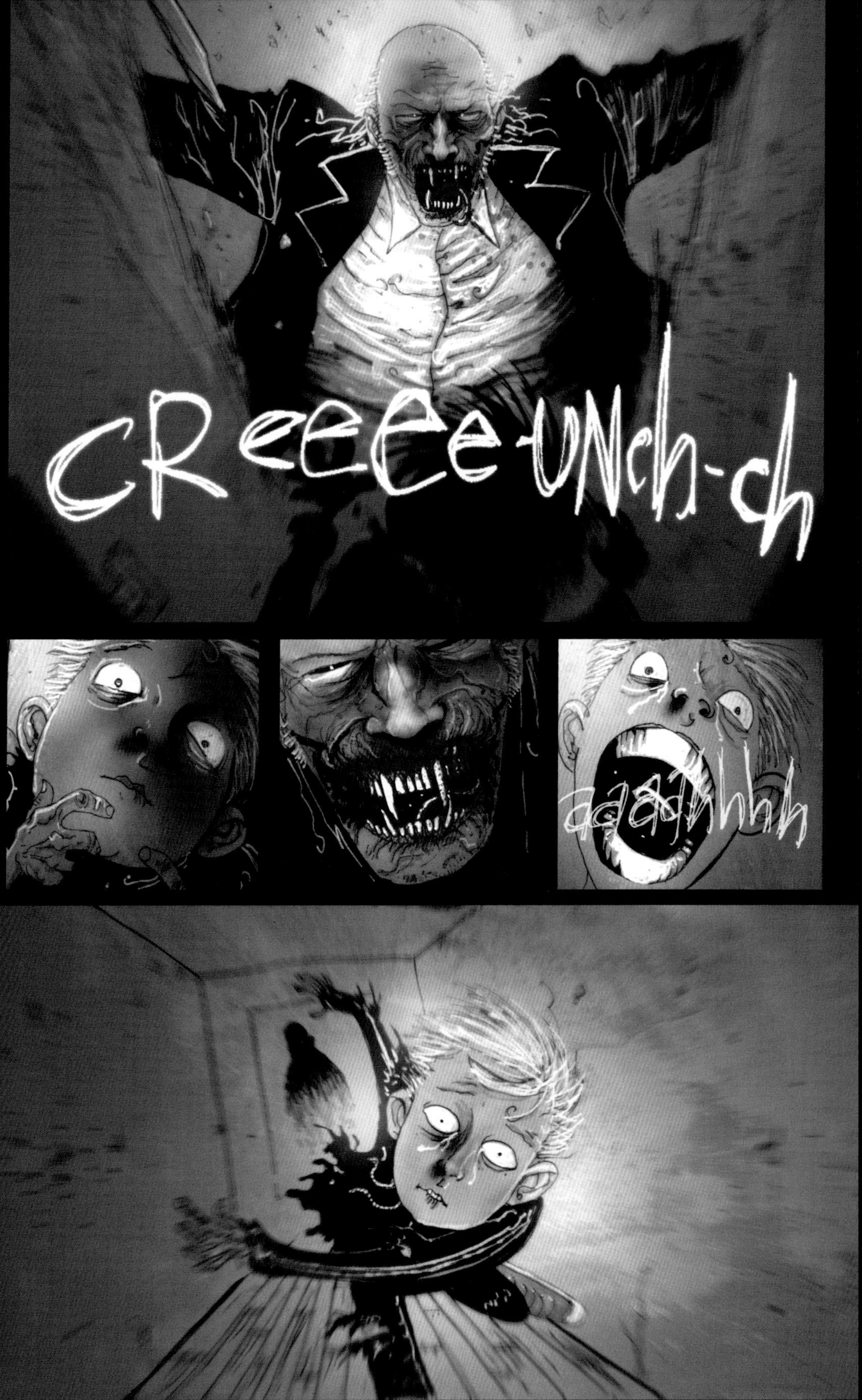
CReeee-uNch-ch
aaaahhhh

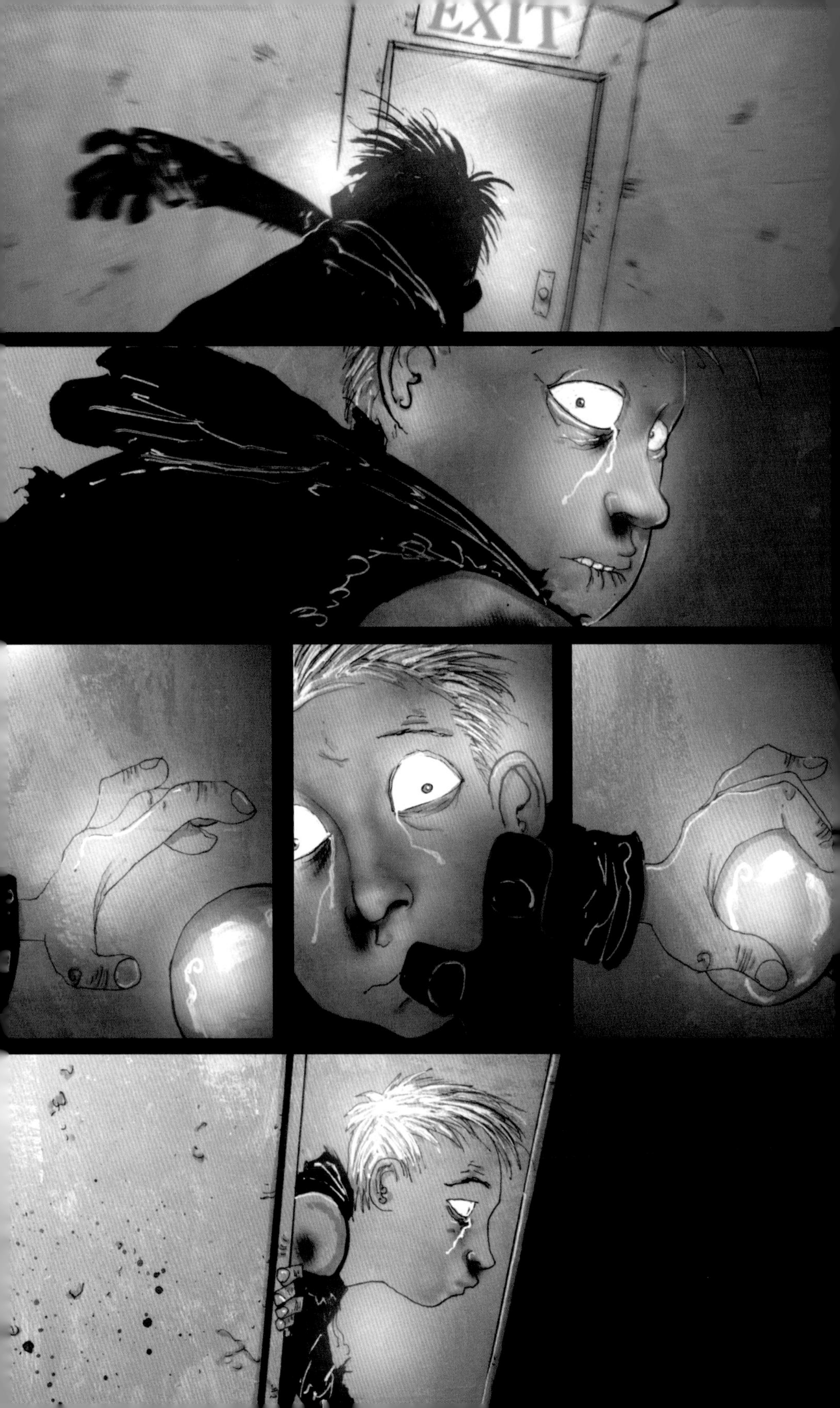
EXIT

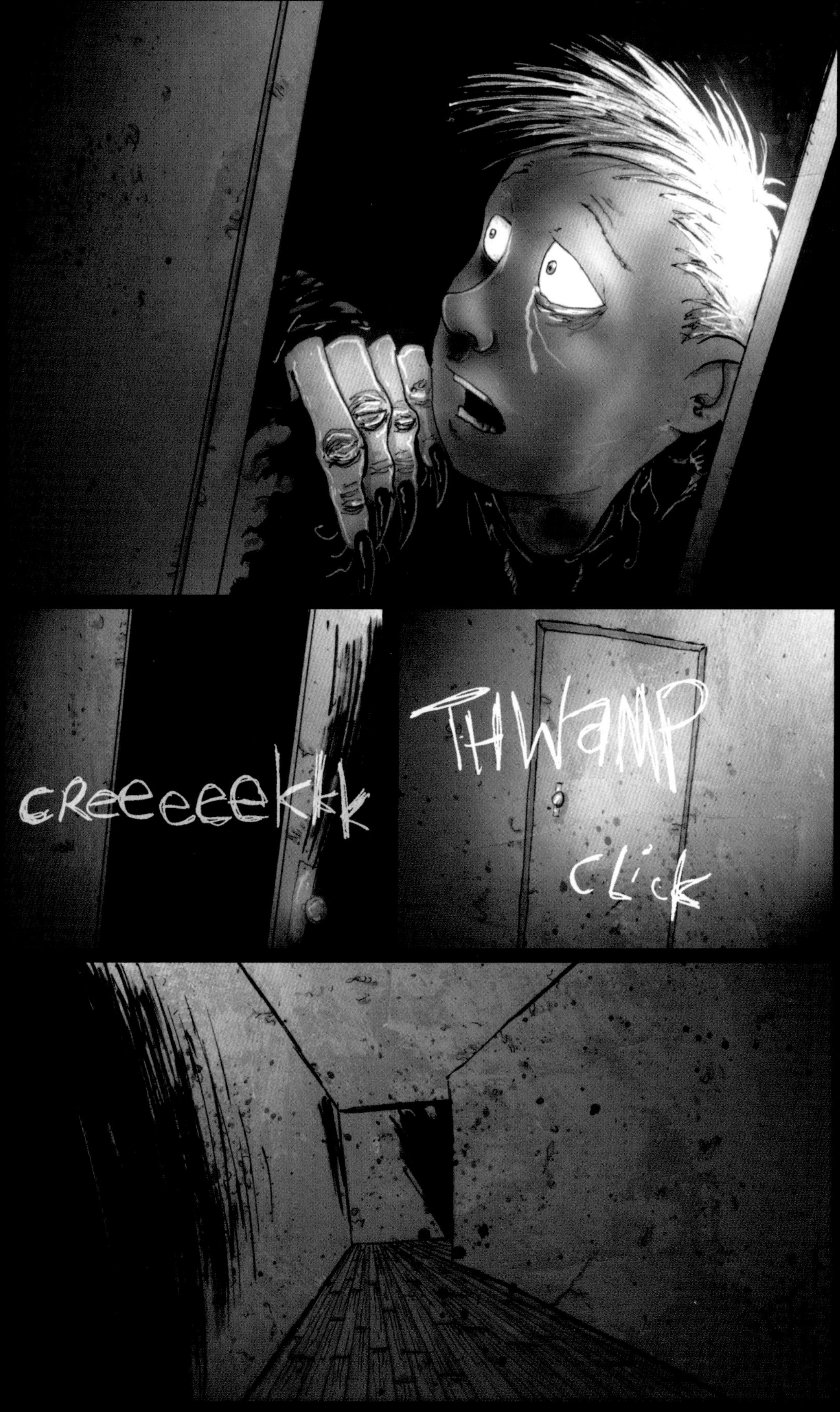
CREEEEEEKKK
THWAMP
CLICK

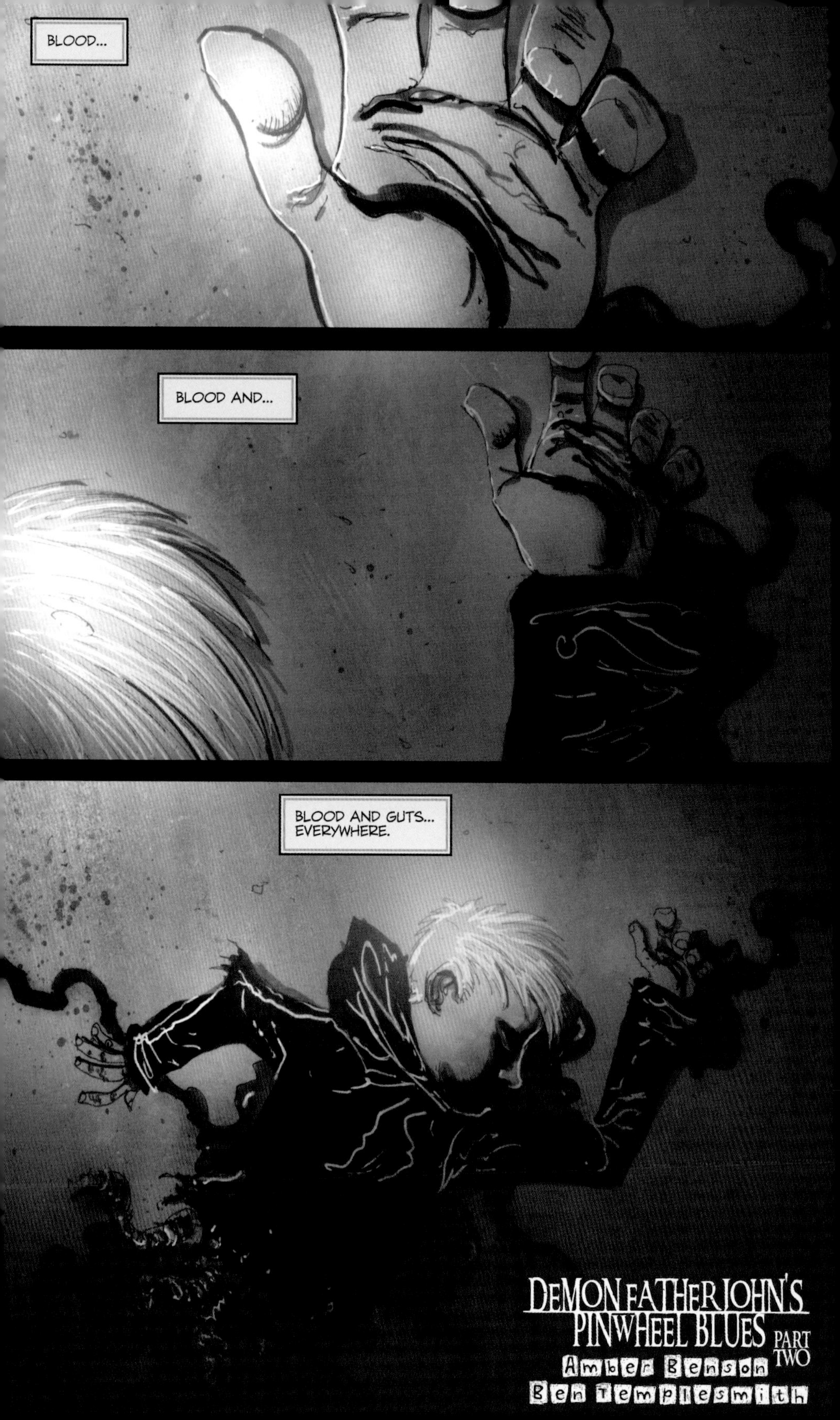
BLOOD...
BLOOD AND...
BLOOD AND GUTS... EVERYWHERE.
DEMON FATHER JOHN'S PINWHEEL BLUES PART TWO
Amber Benson
Ben Templesmith

I MISS MY MOMMY.

HELP ME.

I AM DEAD.

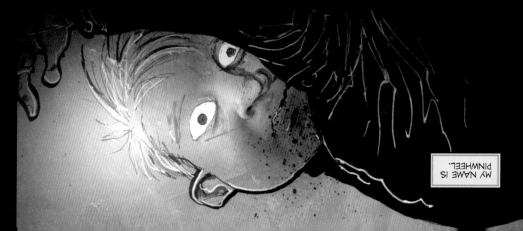

MY NAME IS PINWHEEL.

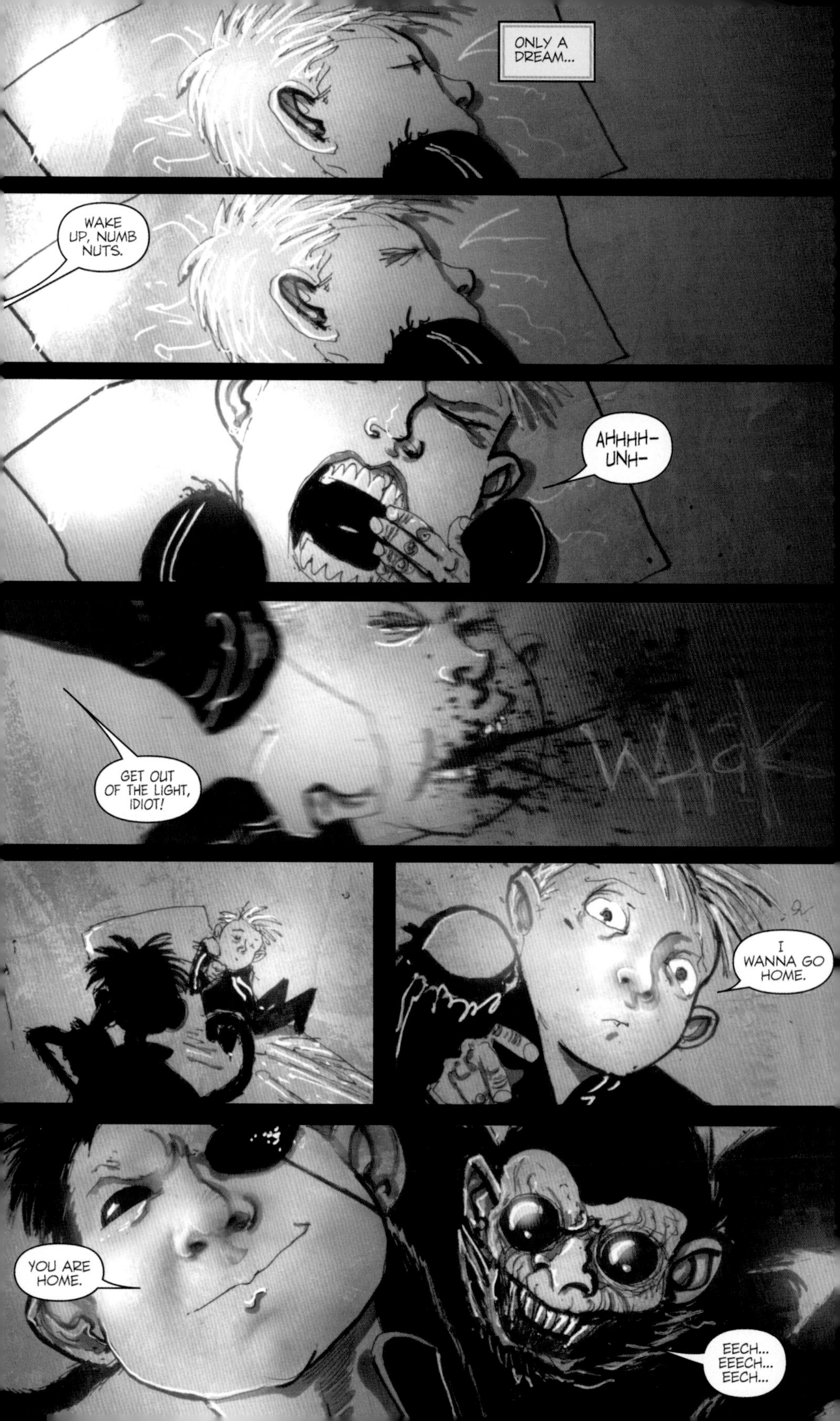
ONLY A DREAM...
WAKE UP, NUMB NUTS.
AHHHH- UNH-
GET OUT OF THE LIGHT, IDIOT!
WHGK
I WANNA GO HOME.
YOU ARE HOME.
EECH... EEECH... EECH...

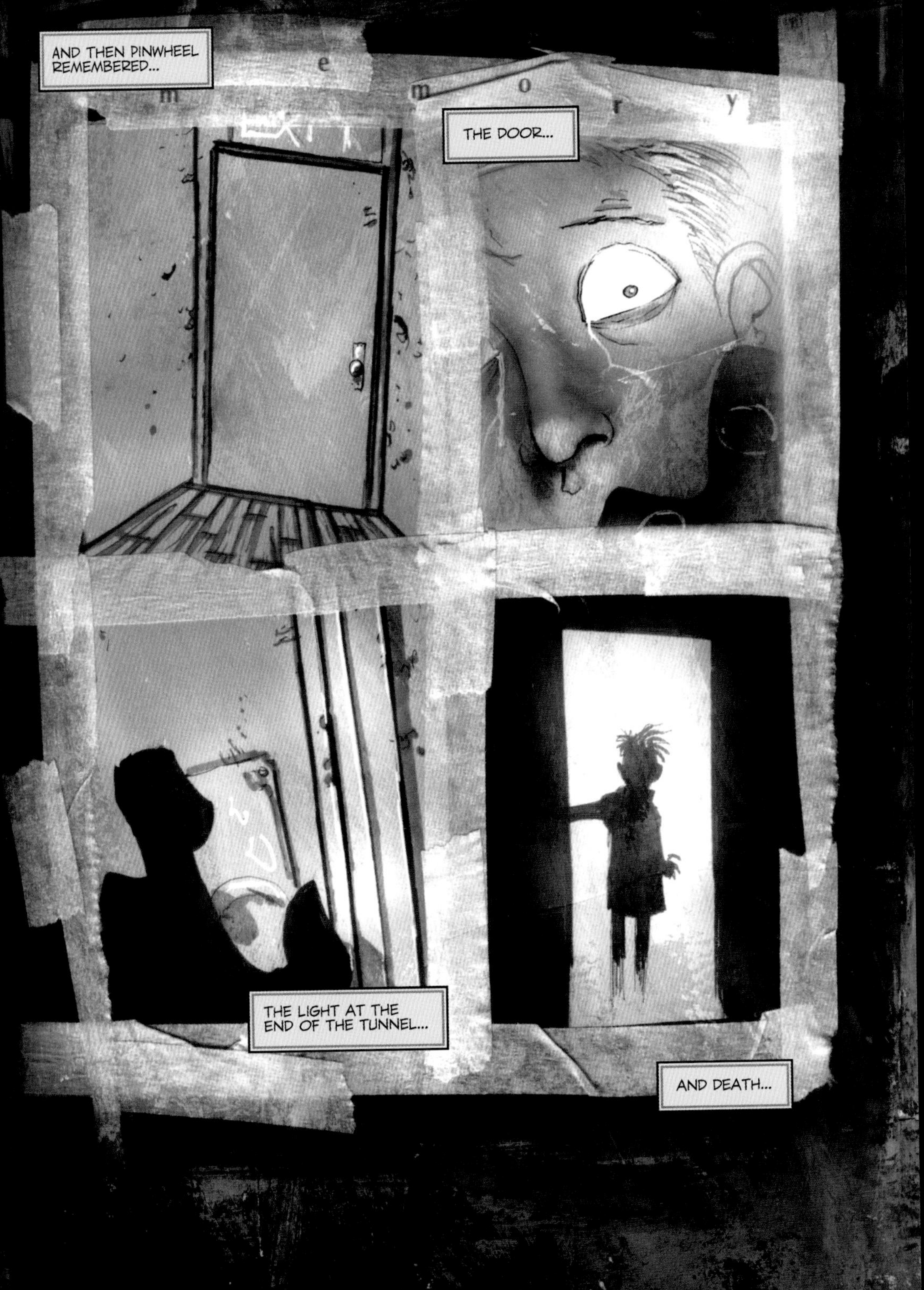
AND THEN PINWHEEL REMEMBERED...
m e m o r y
THE DOOR...
THE LIGHT AT THE END OF THE TUNNEL...
AND DEATH...

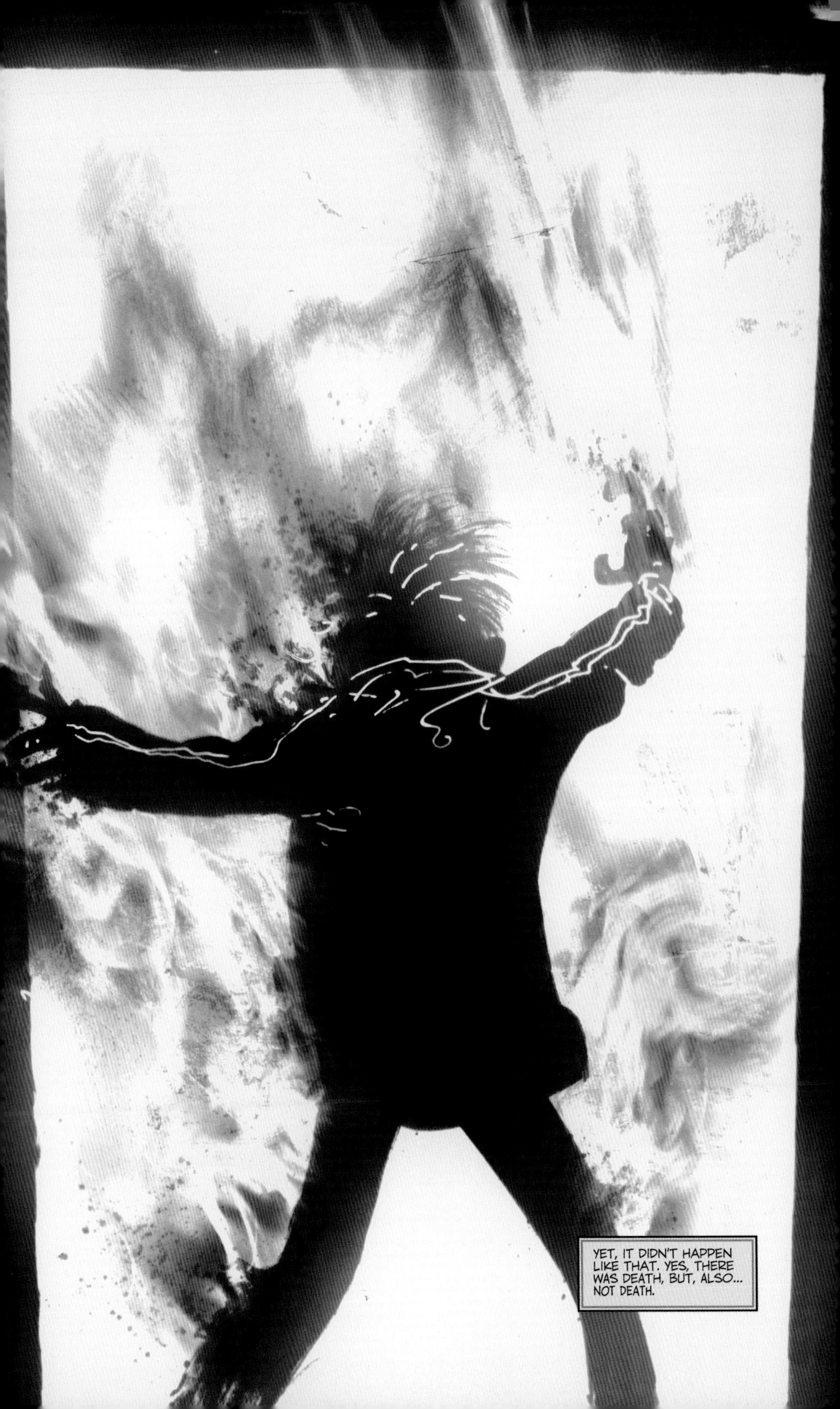
YET, IT DIDN'T HAPPEN LIKE THAT. YES, THERE WAS DEATH, BUT, ALSO... NOT DEATH.

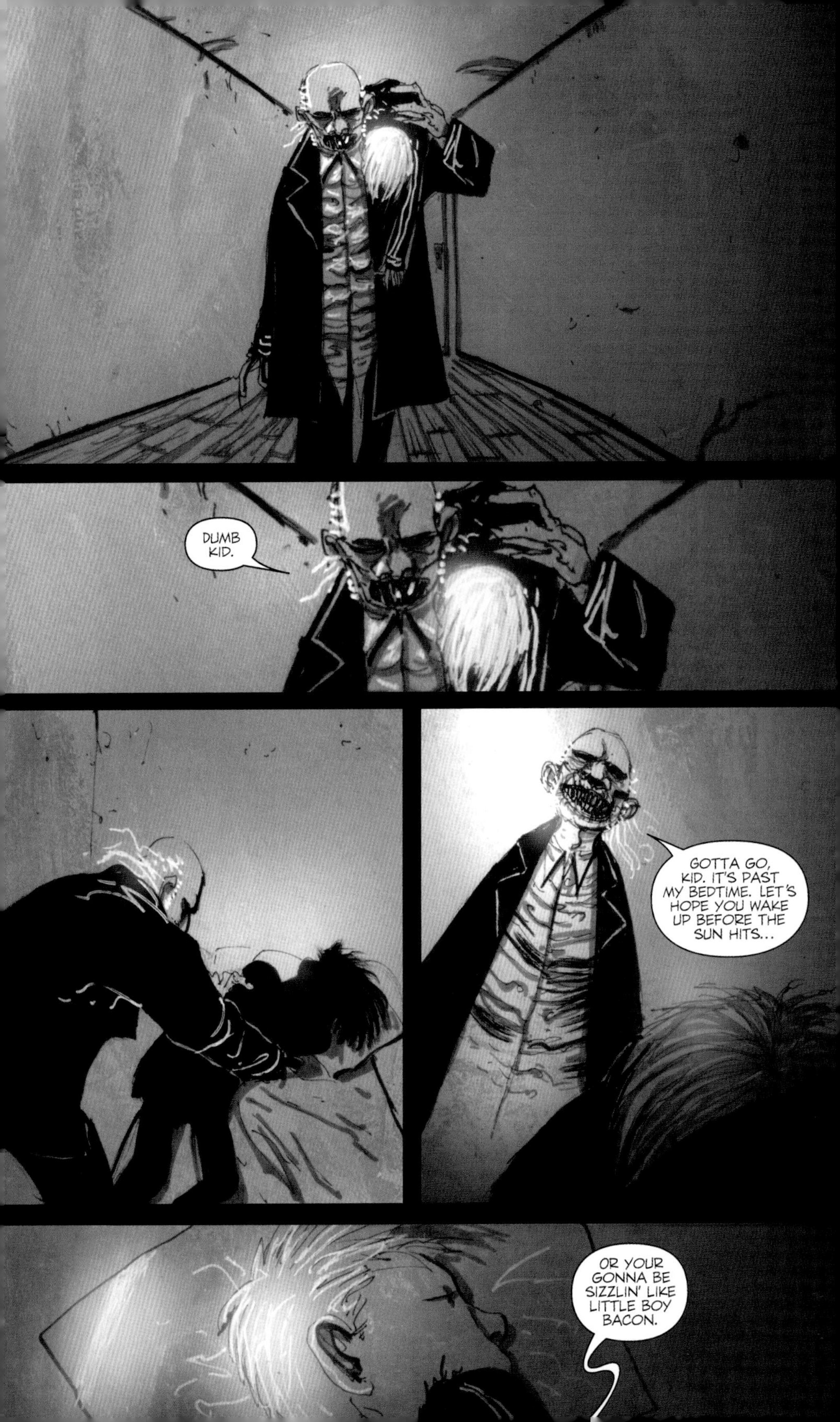
DUMB KID.
GOTTA GO, KID. IT'S PAST MY BEDTIME. LET'S HOPE YOU WAKE UP BEFORE THE SUN HITS...
OR YOUR GONNA BE SIZZLIN' LIKE LITTLE BOY BACON.

I WOULDN'T DO THAT IF I WERE YOU, NUMBSKULL. I ALREADY SAVED YOUR LIFE ONCE AND I AIN'T GONNA DO IT AGAIN.
YEAH? YOU REALLY THINK SO?
I KNOW SO. THERE'S STILL ONE MORE MINUTE OF SUNLIGHT LEFT OUT THERE FOR YOU TO CRISP UP THAT FAT HEAD OF YOURS WITH.
THAT'S RIGHT. YOU GOT THE IDEA...
YOU'RE ONE OF US NOW.

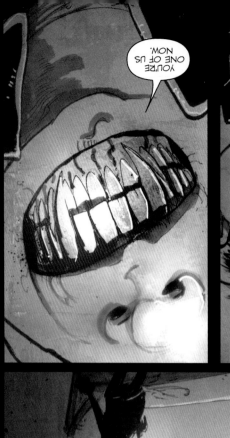

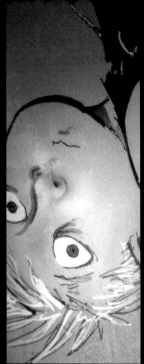

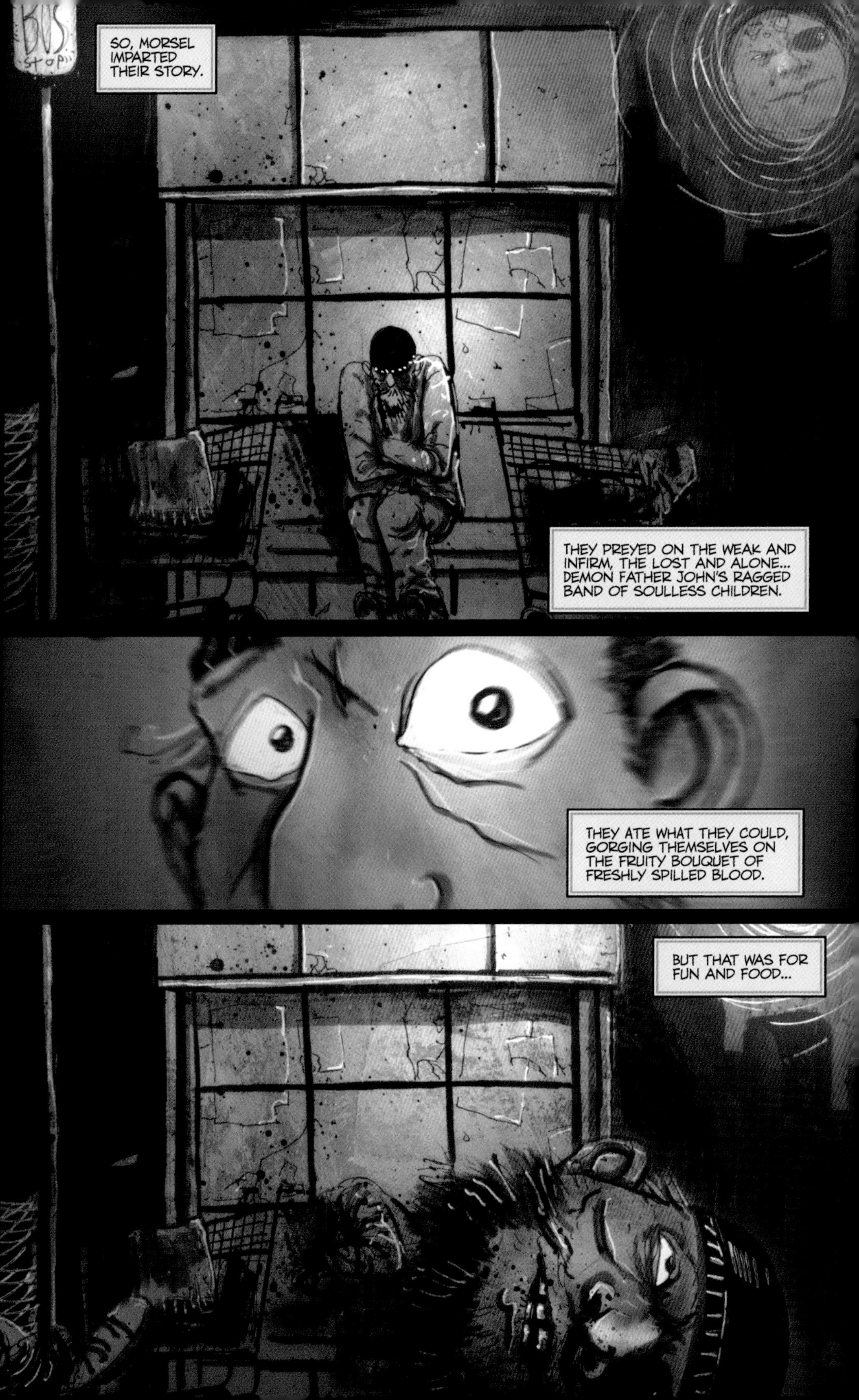
BUS STOP
SO, MORSEL IMPARTED THEIR STORY.
THEY PREYED ON THE WEAK AND INFIRM, THE LOST AND ALONE... DEMON FATHER JOHN'S RAGGED BAND OF SOULLESS CHILDREN.
THEY ATE WHAT THEY COULD, GORGING THEMSELVES ON THE FRUITY BOUQUET OF FRESHLY SPILLED BLOOD.
BUT THAT WAS FOR FUN AND FOOD...

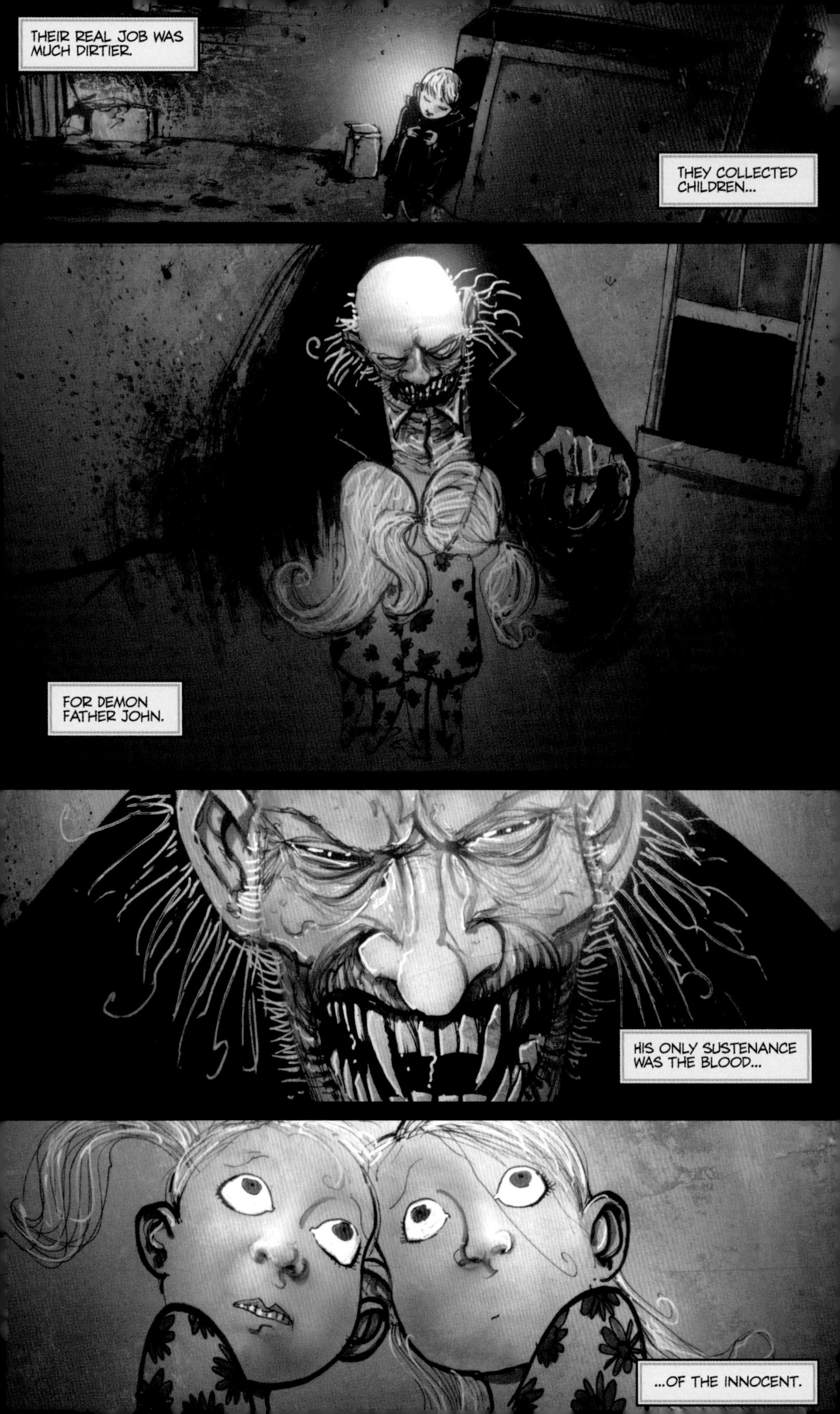
THEIR REAL JOB WAS MUCH DIRTIER.
THEY COLLECTED CHILDREN...
FOR DEMON FATHER JOHN.
HIS ONLY SUSTENANCE WAS THE BLOOD...
...OF THE INNOCENT.